Excel for Statistics

Excel for Statistics is a series of textbooks that explain how to use Excel to solve statistics problems in various fields of study. Professors, students, and practitioners will find these books teach how to make Excel work best in their respective field. Applications include any discipline that uses data and can benefit from the power and simplicity of Excel. Books cover all the steps for running statistical analyses in Excel 2016, Excel 2013, Excel 2010 and Excel 2007. The approach also teaches critical statistics skills, making the books particularly applicable for statistics courses taught outside of mathematics or statistics departments.

Series editor: Thomas J. Quirk

The following books are in this series:

T.J. Quirk, *Excel 2016 for Engineering Statistics: A Guide to Solving Practical Problems*, Excel for Statistics. Springer International Publishing Switzerland 2016.

T.J. Quirk, *Excel 2016 for Business Statistics: A Guide to Solving Practical Problems*, Excel for Statistics. Springer International Publishing Switzerland 2016.

T.J. Quirk, M. Quirk, H.F. Horton, *Excel 2016 for Biological and Life Sciences Statistics: A Guide to Solving Practical Problems*, Excel for Statistics. Springer International Publishing 2016.

T.J. Quirk, M. Quirk, H.F. Horton, *Excel 2016 for Physical Sciences Statistics: A Guide to Solving Practical Problems*, Excel for Statistics. Springer International Publishing 2016.

T.J. Quirk, E. Rhiney, *Excel 2016 for Marketing Statistics: A Guide to Solving Practical Problems*, Excel for Statistics. Springer International Publishing Switzerland 2016.

T.J. Quirk. *Excel 2016 for Educational and Psychological Statistics: A Guide to Solving Practical Problems*, Excel for Statistics. Springer International Publishing Switzerland 2016.

T.J. Quirk, *Excel 2016 for Social Science Statistics: A Guide to Solving Practical Problems*, Excel for Statistics. Springer International Publishing Switzerland 2016.

T.J. Quirk, S. Cummings, *Excel 2016 for Health Services Management Statistics: A Guide to Solving Practical Problems*. Excel for Statistics. Springer International Publishing Switzerland 2016.

T.J. Quirk, J. Palmer-Schuyler, *Excel 2016 for Human Resource Management Statistics: A Guide to Solving Practical Problems*, Excel for Statistics. Springer International Publishing Switzerland 2016.

T.J. Quirk, M. Quirk, H.F. Horton. *Excel 2016 for Environmental Sciences Statistics: A Guide to Solving Practical Problems*, Excel for Statistics. Springer International Publishing Switzerland 2016.

T.J. Quirk, J. Palmer-Schuyler, *Excel 2013 for Human Resource Management Statistics: A Guide to Solving Practical Problems*, Excel for Statistics. Springer International Publishing Switzerland 2016.

T.J. Quirk, S. Cummings, *Excel 2013 for Health Services Management Statistics: A Guide to Solving Practical Problems*. Excel for Statistics. Springer International Publishing Switzerland 2016.

T.J. Quirk, M. Quirk, H.F. Horton, *Excel 2013 for Physical Sciences Statistics: A Guide to Solving Practical Problems*. Excel for Statistics. Springer International Publishing Switzerland 2016.

T.J. Quirk. *Excel 2013 for Educational and Psychological Statistics: A Guide to Solving Practical Problems*, Excel for Statistics. Springer International Publishing Switzerland 2015.

T.J. Quirk, M. Quirk, H.F. Horton, *Excel 2013 for Biological and Life Sciences Statistics: A Guide to Solving Practical Problems*, Excel for Statistics. Springer International Publishing 2015.

T.J. Quirk, *Excel 2013 for Social Science Statistics: A Guide to Solving Practical Problems*, Excel for Statistics. Springer International Publishing Switzerland 2015.

Additional Statistics books by Dr. Tom Quirk that have been published by Springer

T.J. Quirk, *Excel 2010 for Engineering Statistics: A Guide to Solving Practical Problems*, Springer International Publishing Switzerland 2014.

T.J. Quirk, S. Cummings, *Excel 2010 for Health Services Management Statistics: A Guide to Solving Practical Problems*, Springer International Publishing Switzerland 2014.

T.J. Quirk, M. Quirk, H. Horton, *Excel 2010 for Physical Sciences Statistics: A Guide to Solving Practical Problems*, Springer International Publishing Switzerland 2013.

T.J. Quirk, M. Quirk, H.F. Horton, *Excel 2010 for Biological and Life Sciences Statistics: A Guide to Solving Practical Problems*, Springer Science+Business Media New York 2013.

T.J. Quirk, M. Quirk, H.F. Horton, *Excel 2007 for Biological and Life Sciences Statistics: A Guide to Solving Practical Problems*, Springer Science+Business Media New York 2013.

T.J. Quirk, *Excel 2010 for Social Science Statistics: A Guide to Solving Practical Problems*, Springer Science+Business Media New York 2012.

T.J. Quirk, *Excel 2010 for Educational and Psychological Statistics: A Guide to Solving Practical Problems*, Springer Science+Business Media New York 2012.

T.J. Quirk, *Excel 2007 for Business Statistics: A Guide to Solving Practical Problems*, Springer Science+Business Media New York 2012.

T.J. Quirk, *Excel 2007 for Social Science Statistics: A Guide to Solving Practical Problems*, Springer Science+Business Media New York 2012.

T.J. Quirk, *Excel 2007 for Educational and Psychological Statistics: A Guide to Solving Practical Problems*, Springer Science+Business Media New York 2012.

T.J. Quirk, *Excel 2010 for Business Statistics: A Guide to Solving Practical Problems*, Springer Science+Business Media 2011.

More information about this series at http://www.springer.com/series/13491

Thomas J. Quirk • Julie Palmer-Schuyler

Excel 2016 for Human Resource Management Statistics

A Guide to Solving Practical Problems

Springer

Thomas J. Quirk
Webster University
St. Louis, MO, USA

Julie Palmer-Schuyler
Webster University
St. Louis, MO, USA

Excel for Statistics
ISBN 978-3-319-40062-4   ISBN 978-3-319-40063-1 (eBook)
DOI 10.1007/978-3-319-40063-1

Library of Congress Control Number: 2016941690

Printed on acid-free paper

This Springer imprint is published by Springer Nature
The registered company is Springer International Publishing AG Switzerland

This book is dedicated to the more than 3,000 students I have taught at Webster University's campuses in St. Louis, London, and Vienna; the students at Principia College in Elsah, Illinois; and the students at the Cooperative State University of Baden-Wuerttemberg in Heidenheim, Germany. These students taught me a great deal about the art of teaching. I salute them all, and I thank them for helping me to become a better teacher.

Thomas J. Quirk

I am grateful to the hundreds of students at Webster University, Radford University, and the University of Missouri-Columbia who have challenged me to strive to become the best teacher, mentor, and faculty member possible. I am especially grateful to those who encouraged me to expand my horizons and become proficient at multiple modes of delivery. Every semester, many students leave their footprints on my heart.

Julie Palmer-Schuyler

Preface

Excel 2016 for Human Resource Management Statistics: A Guide to Solving Practical Problems is intended for anyone looking to learn the basics of applying Excel's powerful statistical tools to their human resource management courses or work activities. If understanding statistics isn't your strongest suit, you are not especially mathematically inclined, or if you are wary of computers, then this is the right book for you.

Here you'll learn how to use key statistical tests using Excel without being overpowered by the underlying statistical theory. This book clearly and methodically shows and explains how to create and use these statistical tests to solve practical problems in human resource management.

Excel is an easily available computer program for students, instructors, and managers. It is also an effective teaching and learning tool for quantitative analyses in human resource management courses. The powerful numerical computational ability and the graphical functions available in Excel make learning statistics much easier than in years past. However, this is the first book to show Excel's capabilities to more effectively teach human resource management statistics; it also focuses exclusively on this topic in an effort to render the subject matter not only applicable and practical, but also easy to comprehend and apply.

Unique features of this book:

- You will be told each step of the way, not only *how* to use Excel, but also *why* you are doing each step so that you can understand what you are doing and not merely learn how to use statistical tests by rote.
- Includes specific objectives embedded in the text for each concept, so you can know the purpose of the Excel steps.
- Includes 162 color screenshots so that you can be sure you are performing the Excel steps correctly.
- This book is a tool that can be used either by itself or along with *any* good statistics book.
- Practical examples and problems are taken from human resource management.

- Statistical theory and formulas are explained in clear language without bogging you down in mathematical fine points.
- You will learn both how to write statistical formulas using Excel and how to use Excel's drop-down menus that will create the formulas for you.
- This book does not come with a CD of Excel files which you can upload to your computer. Instead, you'll be shown how to create each Excel file yourself. In a work situation, your colleagues will not give you an Excel file; you will be expected to create your own. This book will give you ample practice in developing this important skill.
- Each chapter presents the steps needed to solve a practical human resource management problem using Excel. In addition, there are three practice problems at the end of each chapter so you can test your new knowledge of statistics. The answers to these problems appear in Appendix A.
- A "Practice Test" is given in Appendix B to test your knowledge at the end of the book. The answers to these practical human resource management problems appear in Appendix C.

This book is appropriate for use in any course in human resource management statistics (at both undergraduate and graduate levels) as well as for managers who want to improve the usefulness of their Excel skills.

Prof. Tom Quirk, a current Professor of Marketing at the George Herbert Walker School of Business and Technology at Webster University in St. Louis, Missouri (USA), teaches Marketing Statistics, Marketing Research, and Pricing Strategies. At the beginning of his academic career, Prof. Quirk spent 6 years in educational research at the American Institutes for Research and Educational Testing Service. He has published articles in *the Journal of Educational Psychology*, *Journal of Educational Research*, *Review of Educational Research*, *Journal of Educational Measurement*, *Educational Technology*, *The Elementary School Journal*, *Journal of Secondary Education*, *Educational Horizons*, *and Phi Delta Kappan*. In addition, Professor Quirk has published more than 20 articles in professional journals and presented more than 20 papers at professional meetings, including annual meetings of the American Educational Research Association, the American Psychological Association, and the National Council on Measurement in Education. He holds a B.S. in Mathematics from John Carroll University, both an M.A. in Education and a Ph.D. in Educational Psychology from Stanford University, and an M.B.A. from the University of Missouri-St. Louis.

Prof. "J.P." Palmer-Schuyler is currently an Associate Professor of Human Resource Management at the Walker School of Business and Technology at Webster University in St. Louis, Missouri, USA, where she teaches Human Resource Management as well as Organizational Behavior at the master's and doctoral level. She received her M.B.A. from the University of Nebraska-Lincoln and her Ph.D. from the University of Missouri-Columbia in Management. Her teaching awards include the Donald K. Anderson Graduate Student Teaching Award at the University of Missouri and the William T. Kemper Award at Webster

University. She is also a graduate of the Program for Excellence in Teaching at the University of Missouri. Her pedagogical research over the past 12 years includes articles in *Academy of Business Disciplines Journal* and *Regional Business Review*, and she has made conference presentations at the Organizational Behavior Teaching Conference, Academy of Management, Society for Industrial and Organizational Psychology, Southwest Academy of Management, Western Academy of Management, and Society for Advancement of Management.

St. Louis, MO, USA Thomas J. Quirk
St. Louis, MO, USA Julie Palmer-Schuyler

Acknowledgments

Excel 2016 for Human Resource Management Statistics: A Guide to Solving Practical Problems is the result of inspiration from three important people: my two daughters and my wife. Jennifer Quirk McLaughlin invited me to visit her M.B.A. classes several times at the University of the Witwatersrand in Johannesburg, South Africa. These visits to a first-rate M.B.A. program convinced me there was a need for a book to teach students how to solve practical problems using Excel. Meghan Quirk-Horton's dogged dedication to learning the many statistical techniques needed to complete her Ph.D. dissertation illustrated the need for a statistics book that would make this daunting task more user-friendly. And Lynne Buckley-Quirk was the number one cheerleader for this project from the beginning, always encouraging me and helping me remain dedicated to completing it.

Marc Strauss, our editor at Springer, caught the spirit of this idea in our first phone conversation and shepherded this book through the idea stages until it reached its final form. His encouragement and support were vital to this book seeing the light of day. We thank him for being such an outstanding product champion throughout this process. We also thank Christine Crigler at Springer who did her usual first-rate job in coordinating the editing and production of this book; she is always a pleasure to work with.

Thomas Quirk

Excel 2016 for Human Resource Management Statistics: A Guide to Solving Practical Problems began as an inquiry by my colleague, Prof. Tom Quirk, who challenged me to find a good textbook which was aimed at helping HR students to understand statistics. After much investigation, we both concluded that the field was in need of a practical guide to help prepare our undergraduate and graduate students learn the application of statistics specific to problems in the HR field. Through Tom's expertise and dedication to student learning, coupled with the encouragement of Webster University, we created what we hope will be a useful guide to HR students everywhere.

Julie Palmer-Schuyler

Contents

1 Sample Size, Mean, Standard Deviation, and Standard Error of the Mean 1
1.1 Mean 1
1.2 Standard Deviation 2
1.3 Standard Error of the Mean 3
1.4 Sample Size, Mean, Standard Deviation, and Standard Error of the Mean 4
1.4.1 Using the Fill/Series/Columns Commands 4
1.4.2 Changing the Width of a Column 6
1.4.3 Centering Information in a Range of Cells 6
1.4.4 Naming a Range of Cells 8
1.4.5 Finding the Sample Size Using the =COUNT Function 9
1.4.6 Finding the Mean Score Using the =AVERAGE Function 9
1.4.7 Finding the Standard Deviation Using the =STDEV Function 10
1.4.8 Finding the Standard Error of the Mean 10
1.5 Saving a Spreadsheet 12
1.6 Printing a Spreadsheet 13
1.7 Formatting Numbers in Currency Format (Two decimal places) 15
1.8 Formatting Numbers in Number Format (Three decimal places) 17
1.9 End-of-Chapter Practice Problems 18
References 21

2 Random Number Generator . . . 23
- 2.1 Creating Frame Numbers for Generating Random Numbers . . . 23
- 2.2 Creating Random Numbers in an Excel Worksheet . . . 27
- 2.3 Sorting Frame Numbers into a Random Sequence . . . 28
- 2.4 Printing an Excel File So That All of the Information Fits onto One Page . . . 32
- 2.5 End-of-Chapter Practice Problems . . . 35

3 Confidence Interval About the Mean Using the TINV Function and Hypothesis Testing . . . 37
- 3.1 Confidence Interval About the Mean . . . 37
  - 3.1.1 How to Estimate the Population Mean . . . 37
  - 3.1.2 Estimating the Lower Limit and the Upper Limit of the 95 % Confidence Interval About the Mean . . . 38
  - 3.1.3 Estimating the Confidence Interval for TIME TO FILL . . . 39
  - 3.1.4 Where Did the Number “1.96” Come From? . . . 40
  - 3.1.5 Finding the Value for t in the Confidence Interval Formula . . . 41
  - 3.1.6 Using Excel’s TINV Function to Find the Confidence Interval About the Mean . . . 42
  - 3.1.7 Using Excel to find the 95 % Confidence Interval for TIME TO FILL . . . 42
- 3.2 Hypothesis Testing . . . 50
  - 3.2.1 Hypotheses Always Refer to the Population That You Are Studying . . . 51
  - 3.2.2 The Null Hypothesis and the Research (Alternative) Hypothesis . . . 52
  - 3.2.3 The 7 Steps for Hypothesis-testing Using the Confidence Interval About the Mean . . . 55
- 3.3 Alternative Ways to Summarize the Result of a Hypothesis Test . . . 62
  - 3.3.1 Different Ways to Accept the Null Hypothesis . . . 63
  - 3.3.2 Different Ways to Reject the Null Hypothesis . . . 63
- 3.4 End-of-Chapter Practice Problems . . . 63
- References . . . 69

4 One-Group t-Test for the Mean . . . 71
- 4.1 The 7 STEPS for Hypothesis-Testing Using the One-Group t-Test . . . 71
  - 4.1.1 STEP 1: State the Null Hypothesis and the Research Hypothesis . . . 72
  - 4.1.2 STEP 2: Select the Appropriate Statistical Test . . . 72

4.1.3 STEP 3: Decide on a Decision Rule for the One-Group t-Test . . . 72
4.1.4 STEP 4: Calculate the Formula for the One-Group t-Test . . . 73
4.1.5 STEP 5: Find the Critical Value of t in the t-Table in Appendix E . . . 74
4.1.6 STEP 6: State the Result of Your Statistical Test . . . 75
4.1.7 STEP 7: State the Conclusion of Your Statistical Test in Plain English! . . . 76
4.2 One-Group t-Test for the Mean . . . 76
4.3 Can You Use Either the 95 % Confidence Interval About the Mean OR the One-Group t-Test When Testing Hypotheses? . . . 82
4.4 End-of–Chapter Practice Problems . . . 82
References . . . 86

5 Two-Group t-Test of the Difference of the Means for Independent Groups . . . 87
5.1 The 9 STEPS for Hypothesis-Testing Using the Two-Group t-Test . . . 88
5.1.1 STEP 1: Name One Group, Group 1, and the Other Group, Group 2 . . . 88
5.1.2 STEP 2: Create a Table That Summarizes the Sample Size, Mean Score, and Standard Deviation of Each Group . . . 88
5.1.3 STEP 3: State the Null Hypothesis and the Research Hypothesis for the Two-Group t-Test . . . 90
5.1.4 STEP 4: Select the Appropriate Statistical Test . . . 90
5.1.5 STEP 5: Decide on a Decision Rule for the Two-Group t-Test . . . 90
5.1.6 STEP 6: Calculate the Formula for the Two-Group t-Test . . . 91
5.1.7 STEP 7: Find the Critical Value of t in the t-Table in Appendix E . . . 91
5.1.8 STEP 8: State the Result of Your Statistical Test . . . 92
5.1.9 STEP 9: State the Conclusion of Your Statistical Test in Plain English! . . . 92
5.2 Formula #1: Both Groups Have A Sample Size Greater Than 30 . . . 97
5.2.1 An Example of Formula #1 for the Two-Group t-Test . . . 98
5.3 Formula #2: One or Both Groups Have a Sample Size Less Than 30 . . . 105
5.4 End-of–Chapter Practice Problems . . . 112
References . . . 115

6 Correlation and Simple Linear Regression 117
6.1 What Is a "Correlation?" 117
6.1.1 Understanding the Formula for Computing a Correlation 122
6.1.2 Understanding the Nine Steps for Computing a Correlation, r 122
6.2 Using Excel to Compute a Correlation Between Two Variables 124
6.3 Creating a Chart and Drawing the Regression Line onto the Chart 129
6.3.1 Using Excel to Create a Chart and the Regression Line Through the Data Points 131
6.4 Printing a Spreadsheet So That the Table and Chart Fit onto One Page 140
6.5 Finding the Regression Equation 142
6.5.1 Installing the Data Analysis ToolPak into Excel 142
6.5.2 Using Excel to Find the SUMMARY OUTPUT of Regression 145
6.5.3 Finding the Equation for the Regression Line 150
6.5.4 Using the Regression Line to Predict the y-Value for a Given x-Value 150
6.6 Adding the Regression Equation to the Chart 151
6.7 How to Recognize Negative Correlations in the SUMMARY OUTPUT Table 154
6.8 Printing Only Part of a Spreadsheet Instead of the Entire Spreadsheet 154
6.8.1 Printing Only the Table and the Chart on a Separate Page 155
6.8.2 Printing Only the Chart on a Separate Page 155
6.8.3 Printing Only the SUMMARY OUTPUT of the Regression Analysis on a Separate Page 156
6.9 End-of-Chapter Practice Problems 156
References 163

7 Multiple Correlation and Multiple Regression 165
7.1 Multiple Regression Equation 165
7.2 Finding the Multiple Correlation and the Multiple Regression Equation 168
7.3 Using the Regression Equation to Predict FIRST-YEAR GPA . . . 173
7.4 Using Excel to Create a Correlation Matrix in Multiple Regression 173
7.5 End-of-Chapter Practice Problems 177
References 182

8 One-Way Analysis of Variance (ANOVA) 183
8.1 Using Excel to Perform a One-Way Analysis of Variance (ANOVA) 185
8.2 How to Interpret the ANOVA Table Correctly 188
8.3 Using the Decision Rule for the ANOVA F-Test 189
8.4 Testing for the Difference Between Two Groups Using the ANOVA t-Test 190
8.4.1 Comparing Division B vs. Division C in Job Satisfaction Using the ANOVA t-Test 190
8.5 End-of-Chapter Practice Problems 195
References 200

Appendices 201
Appendix A: Answers to End-of-Chapter Practice Problems 201
Appendix B: Practice Test 233
Appendix C: Answers to Practice Test 244
Appendix D: Statistical Formulas 254
Appendix E: t-Table 256

Index 257

Chapter 1
Sample Size, Mean, Standard Deviation, and Standard Error of the Mean

This chapter deals with how you can use Excel to find the average (i.e., "mean") of a set of scores, the standard deviation of these scores (STDEV), and the standard error of the mean (s.e.) of these scores. All three of these statistics are used frequently and form the basis for additional statistical tests.

1.1 Mean

The *mean* is the "arithmetic average" of a set of scores. When my daughter was in the fifth grade, she came home from school with a sad face and said that she didn't get "averages." The book she was using described how to find the mean of a set of scores, and so I said to her:

> "Jennifer, you add up all the scores and divide by the number of numbers that you have."
> She gave me "that look," and said: "Dad, this is serious!" She thought I was teasing her. So I said:
> "See these numbers in your book; add them up. What is the answer?" (She did that.)
> "Now, how many numbers do you have?" (She answered that question.)
> "Then, take the number you got when you added up the numbers, and divide that number by the number of numbers that you have."

She did that, and found the correct answer. You will use that same reasoning now, but it will be much easier for you because Excel will do all of the steps for you.

We will call this average of the scores the "mean" which we will symbolize as: $\overline{X}$, and we will pronounce it as: "Xbar."

The formula for finding the mean with your calculator looks like this:

$$\overline{X} = \frac{\Sigma X}{n} \tag{1.1}$$

T.J. Quirk, J. Palmer-Schuyler, *Excel 2016 for Human Resource Management Statistics*, Excel for Statistics, DOI 10.1007/978-3-319-40063-1_1

The symbol Σ is the Greek letter sigma, which stands for "sum." It tells you to add up all the scores that are indicated by the letter X, and then to divide your answer by n (the number of numbers that you have).

Let's give a simple example:

A subordinate's rating of his or her supervisor's performance is an important statistic in human resources management. Let's suppose that you want to practice your Excel skills on just one item in a survey given to subordinates in which they were asked to rate their supervisor on a variety of important behaviors using a rating scale where 1 = Low and 7 = High. Suppose that you had these six ratings for a random sample of subordinates on an item dealing with the quality of the supervisor's supervision of the subordinates:

6
4
5
3
2
5

To find the mean of these scores, you add them up, and then divide by the number of scores. So, the mean is: 25/6 = 4.17.

To learn more about the mean of a set of scores, see Aamodt et al. (2007) and Whetzel and Wheaton (2007).

1.2 Standard Deviation

The *standard deviation* tells you "how close the scores are to the mean." If the standard deviation is a small number, this tells you that the scores are "bunched together" close to the mean. If the standard deviation is a large number, this tells you that the scores are "spread out" a greater distance from the mean. The formula for the standard deviation (which we will call STDEV) and use the letter, S, to symbolize is:

$$\text{STDEV} = S = \sqrt{\frac{\Sigma(X - \overline{X})^2}{n - 1}} \tag{1.2}$$

The formula look complicated, but what it asks you to do is this:

1. Subtract the mean from each score $(X - \overline{X})$.
2. Then, square the resulting numbers to make each a positive number.
3. Then, add up these squared numbers to get a total score.
4. Then, take this total score and divide it by n – 1 (where n stands for the number of numbers that you have).
5. The final step is to take the square root of the number you found in step 4.

You will not be asked to compute the standard deviation using your calculator in this book, but you could see examples of how it is computed in any basic statistics book (e.g. Weiers 2011 and Davis 2011). Instead, we will use Excel to find the standard deviation of a set of scores. When we use Excel on the six numbers we gave in the description of the mean above, you will find that the *STDEV* of these numbers, S, is 1.47.

1.3 Standard Error of the Mean

The formula for the *standard error of the mean* (*s.e.*, which we will use $S_{\overline{X}}$ to symbolize) is:

$$\text{s.e.} = S_{\overline{X}} = \frac{S}{\sqrt{n}} \tag{1.3}$$

To find ***s.e.***, all you need to do is to take the standard deviation, STDEV, and divide it by the square root of n, where n stands for the "number of numbers" that you have in your data set. In the example under the standard deviation description above, the *s.e.* = 0.60. (You can check this on your calculator).

If you want to learn more about the standard deviation and the standard error of the mean, see Black (2010) and Levine (2011).

Now, let's learn how to use Excel to find the sample size, the mean, the standard deviation, and the standard error or the mean using the monthly salaries of a sample of employees who have been classified as "Semi-professional" at your organization The hypothetical data appear in Fig. 1.1.

Fig. 1.1 Worksheet Data for Monthly Salary (Practical Example)

	A	B	C	D
1				
2				
3		Employee	Monthly salary ($)	
4		1	2125	
5		2	2340	
6		3	2680	
7		4	2935	
8		5	3040	
9		6	2260	
10		7	2590	
11		8	2160	
12				

1.4 Sample Size, Mean, Standard Deviation, and Standard Error of the Mean

Objective: To find the sample size (n), mean, standard deviation (STDEV), and standard error of the mean (s.e.) for these data

Start your computer, and click on the Excel 2016 icon to open a blank Excel spreadsheet.

Click on: Blank Workbook

Enter the data in this way:

B3: Employee
C3: Monthly salary ($)
B4: 1

1.4.1 Using the Fill/Series/Columns Commands

Objective: To add the numbers 2–8 in the Employee column underneath Employee #1

Put pointer in B4
Home (top left of screen)

Important note: The "Paste" command should be on the top of your screen on the far left of the screen.

Important note: Notice the Excel commands at the top of your computer screen: ***File Home Insert Page Layout Formulas etc.***

If these commands ever "disappear" when you are using Excel, you need to click on "Home" at the top left of your screen to make them reappear!

Fill (top right of screen: click on the Series down arrow; see Fig. 1.2)

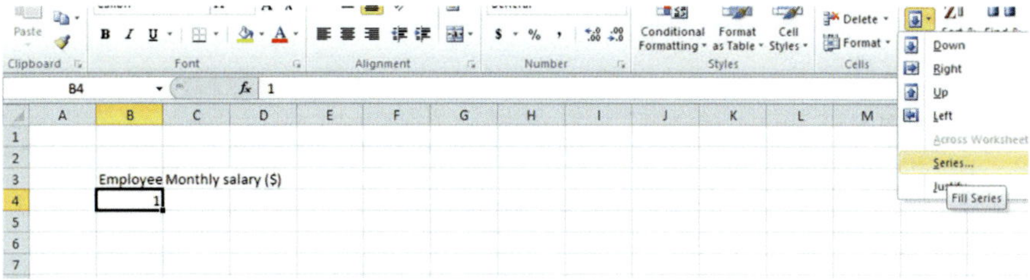

Fig. 1.2 Home/Fill/Series commands

Series
Columns
Step value: 1
Stop value: 8 (see Fig. 1.3)

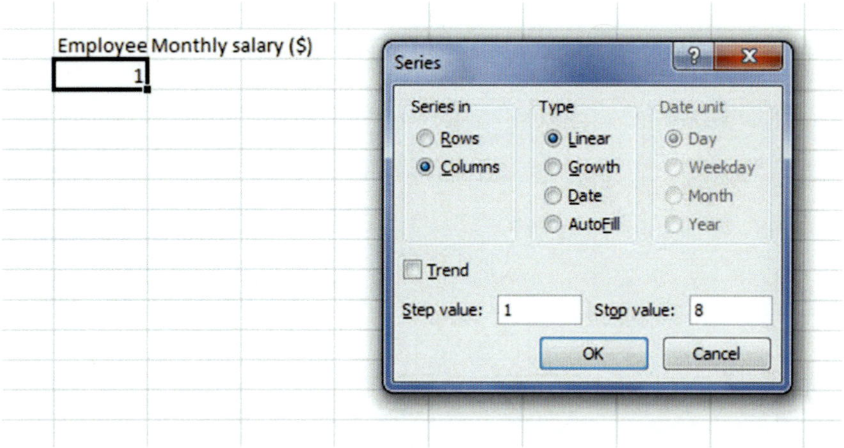

Fig. 1.3 Example of Dialogue Box for Fill/Series/Columns/Step Value/Stop Value commands

OK

The employee numbers should be identified as 1–8, with 8 in cell B11.

Now, enter the monthly salary figures in cells C4: C11. *(Note: Be sure to double-check your figures to make sure that they are correct or you will not get the correct answer!)*

Since your computer screen shows the information in a format that does not look professional, you need to learn how to "widen the column width" and how to "center the information" in a group of cells. Here is how you can do those two steps:

1.4.2 Changing the Width of a Column

Objective: To make a column width wider so that all of the information fits inside that column

If you look at your computer screen, you can see that Column C is not wide enough so that all of the information fits inside this column. To make Column C wider:

Click on the letter, C, at the top of your computer screen
Place your mouse pointer on your computer at the far right corner of C until you create a "cross sign" on that corner
Left-click on your mouse, hold it down, and move this corner to the right until it is "wide enough to fit all of the data"
Take your finger off your mouse to set the new column width (see Fig. 1.4)

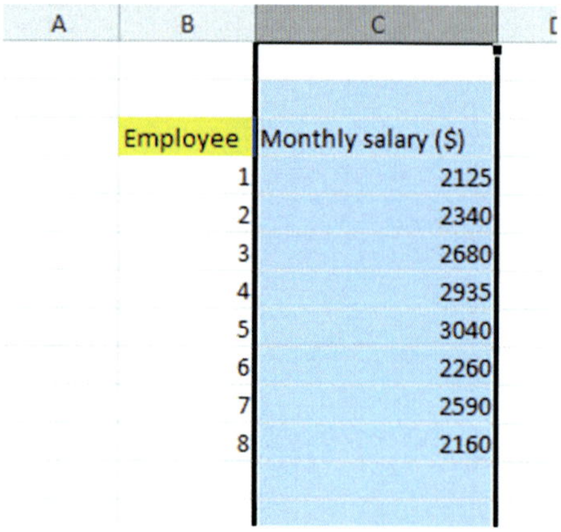

Fig. 1.4 Example of How to Widen the Column Width

Then, click on any empty cell (i.e., any blank cell) to "deselect" column C so that it is no longer a darker color on your screen.

When you widen a column, you will make all of the cells in all of the rows of this column that same width.

Now, let's go through the steps to center the information in both Column B and Column C.

1.4.3 Centering Information in a Range of Cells

Objective: To center the information in a group of cells

In order to make the information in the cells look "more professional," you can center the information using the following steps:

Left-click your mouse pointer on B3 and drag it to the right and down to highlight cells B3:C11 so that these cells appear in a darker color
Home

At the top of your computer screen, you will see a set of "lines" in which all of the lines are "centered" to the same width under "Alignment" (it is the second icon at the bottom left of the Alignment box; see Fig. 1.5)

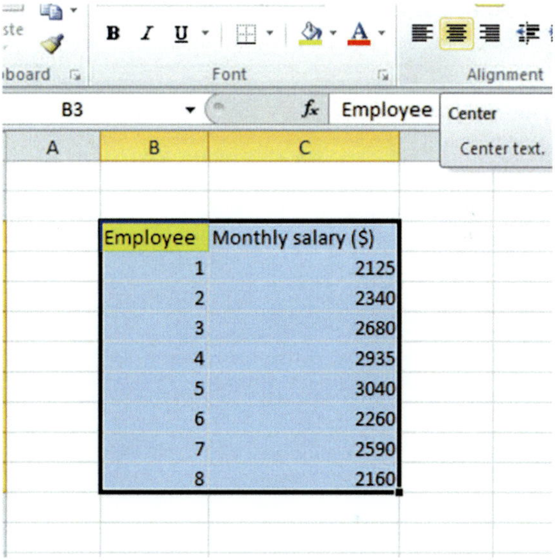

Fig. 1.5 Example of How to Center Information Within Cells

Click on this icon to center the information in the selected cells (see Fig. 1.6)

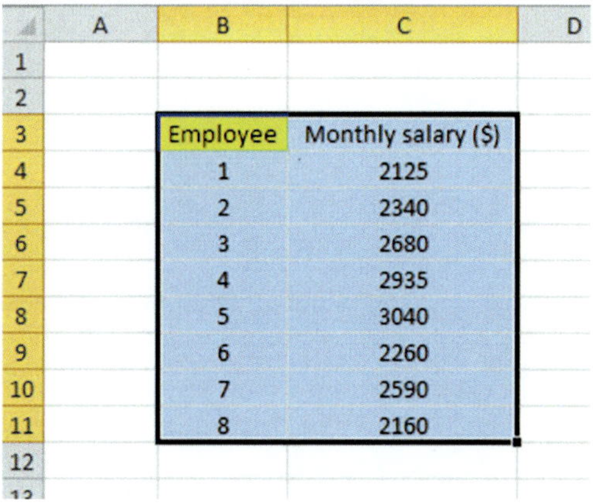

Fig. 1.6 Final Result of Centering Information in the Cells

Since you will need to refer to the monthly salaries of semi-professional employees in your formulas, it will be much easier to do this if you "name the range of data" with a name instead of having to remember the exact cells (C4: C11) in which these figures are located. Let's call that group of cells: salary, but we could give these cells any name that you want to use.

1.4.4 Naming a Range of Cells

Objective: To name the range of data for monthly salary with the name: salary

Highlight cells C4: C11 by left-clicking your mouse pointer on C4 and dragging it down to C11
Formulas (top left of your screen)
Define Name (top center of your screen)
salary (type this name in the top box; see Fig. 1.7)

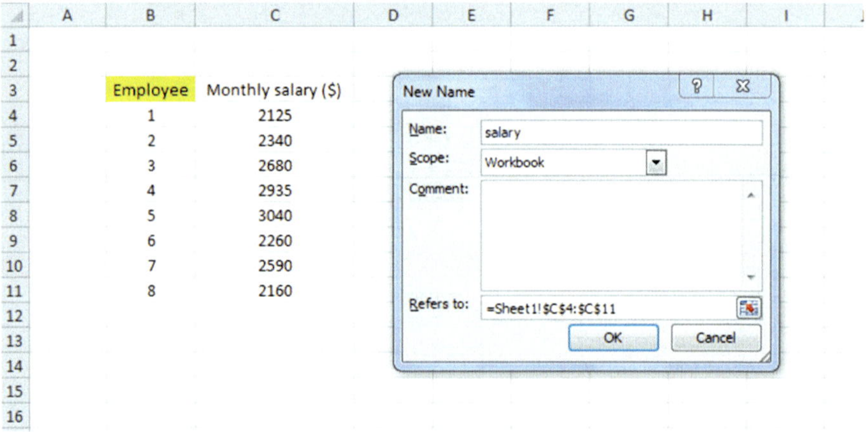

Fig. 1.7 Dialogue box for "naming a range of cells" with the name: salary

OK
Then, click on any cell of your spreadsheet that does not have any information in it (i.e., it is an "empty cell") to deselect cells C4:C11
Now, add the following terms to your spreadsheet:

E6: n
E9: Mean
E12: STDEV
E15: s.e. (see Fig. 1.8)

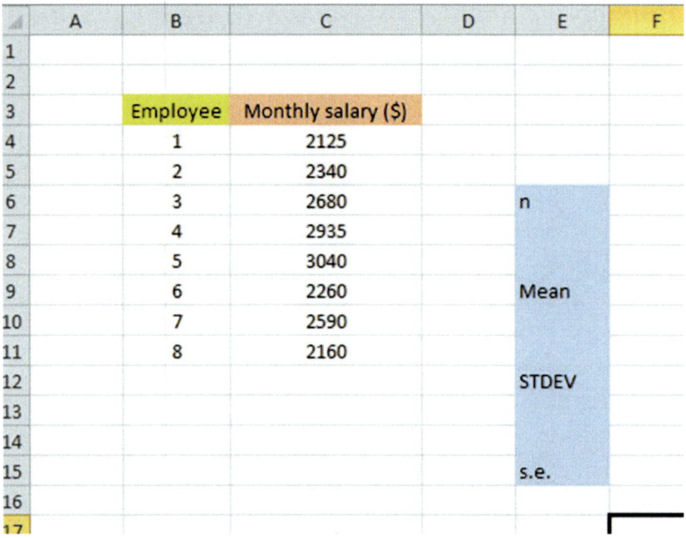

	A	B	C	D	E	F
1						
2						
3		Employee	Monthly salary ($)			
4		1	2125			
5		2	2340			
6		3	2680		n	
7		4	2935			
8		5	3040			
9		6	2260		Mean	
10		7	2590			
11		8	2160			
12					STDEV	
13						
14						
15					s.e.	
16						
17						

Fig. 1.8 Example of Entering the Sample Size, Mean, STDEV, and s.e. Labels

Note: Whenever you use a formula, you must add an equal sign (=) at the beginning of the name of the function so that Excel knows that you intend to use a formula.

1.4.5 Finding the Sample Size Using the =COUNT Function

Objective: To find the sample size (n) for these data using the =COUNT function

F6: =COUNT(salary)

This command should insert the number 8 into cell F6 since there are eight employees in your sample.

1.4.6 Finding the Mean Score Using the =AVERAGE Function

Objective: To find the mean salary figure using the =AVERAGE function

F9: =AVERAGE(salary)

This command should insert the number 2516.25 into cell F9.

1.4.7 Finding the Standard Deviation Using the =STDEV Function

Objective: To find the standard deviation (STDEV) using the =STDEV function

F12: =STDEV(salary)

This command should insert the number 350.2321 into cell F12.

1.4.8 Finding the Standard Error of the Mean

Objective: To find the standard error of the mean using a formula for these eight data points

F15: =F12/SQRT(8)

This command should insert the number 123.8257 into cell F15 (see Fig. 1.9).

	A	B	C	D	E	F	G
1							
2							
3		Employee	Monthly salary ($)				
4		1	2125				
5		2	2340				
6		3	2680		n	8	
7		4	2935				
8		5	3040				
9		6	2260		Mean	2516.25	
10		7	2590				
11		8	2160				
12					STDEV	350.2321	
13							
14							
15					s.e.	123.8257	
16							
17							

Fig. 1.9 Example of Using Excel Formulas for Sample Size, Mean, STDEV, and s.e.

Important note: Throughout this book, be sure to double-check all of the figures in your spreadsheet to make sure that they are in the correct cells, or the formulas will not work correctly!

1.4.8.1 Formatting Numbers in Number Format (Two decimal places)

Objective: To convert the mean, STDEV, and s.e. to one decimal place

Highlight cells F9: F15
Home (top left of screen)
Look under "Number" at the top center of your screen. In the bottom right corner, gently place your mouse pointer on you screen at the bottom of the .00.0 until it says: "Decrease Decimal" (see Fig. 1.10)

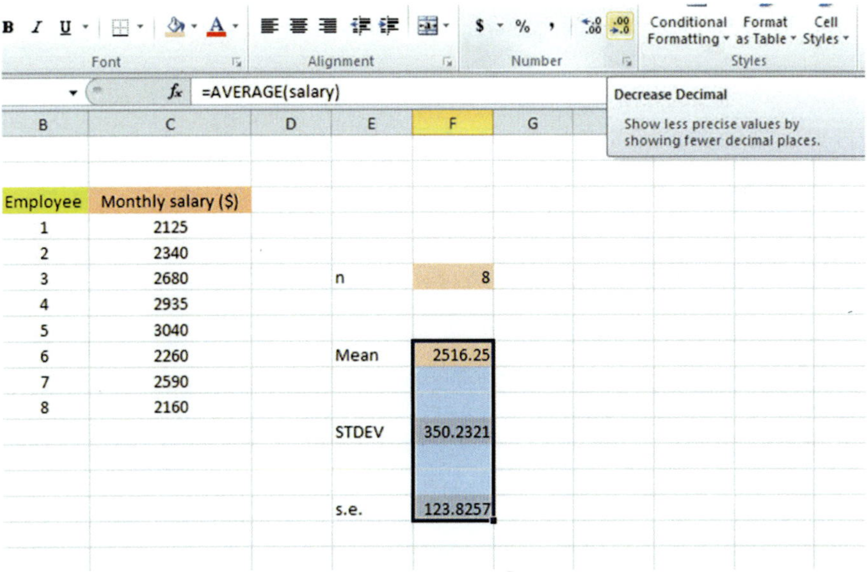

Fig. 1.10 Using the "Decrease Decimal Icon" to convert Numbers to Fewer Decimal Places

Click on this icon *once* and notice that the cells F9:F15 are now all in just one decimal place (see Fig. 1.11)

Fig. 1.11 Example of Converting Numbers to One Decimal Place

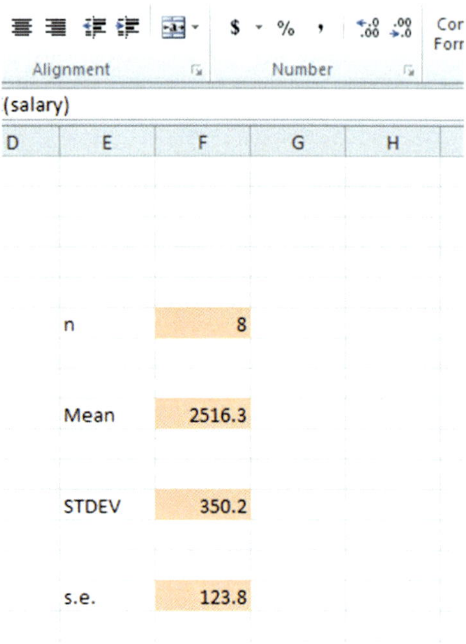

Now, click on any "empty cell" on your spreadsheet to deselect cells F9:F15.

But, since salary figures are typically in two decimal places, let's change the Mean, STDEV, and s.e. figures to two decimal places by:

Highlight cells: F9:F15
Number (top center of screen)
Click on the down arrow to the right of Number at top center of screen
Click on: Number (in the list of possible formats on the left)
Change to two decimal places (in the right center of the screen)
OK
Cells F9:F15 should now be in two decimal places.
Now, click on any "blank empty cell" with no information in it to "deselect": F9:F15.

1.5 Saving a Spreadsheet

Objective: To save this spreadsheet with the name: SALARY3

In order to save your spreadsheet so that you can retrieve it sometime in the future, your first decision is to decide "where" you want to save it. That is your decision and you have several choices. If it is your own computer, you can save it onto your hard drive (you need to ask someone how to do that on your computer).

Or, you can save it onto a "CD" or onto a "flash drive." To save a spreadsheet, you need to complete these steps:

File
Save as

(select the place where you want to save the file by scrolling either down or up the bar on the left, and click on the place where you want to save the file; for example: This PC: My Documents location)

File name: SALARY3 (enter this name to the right of File name; see Fig. 1.12)

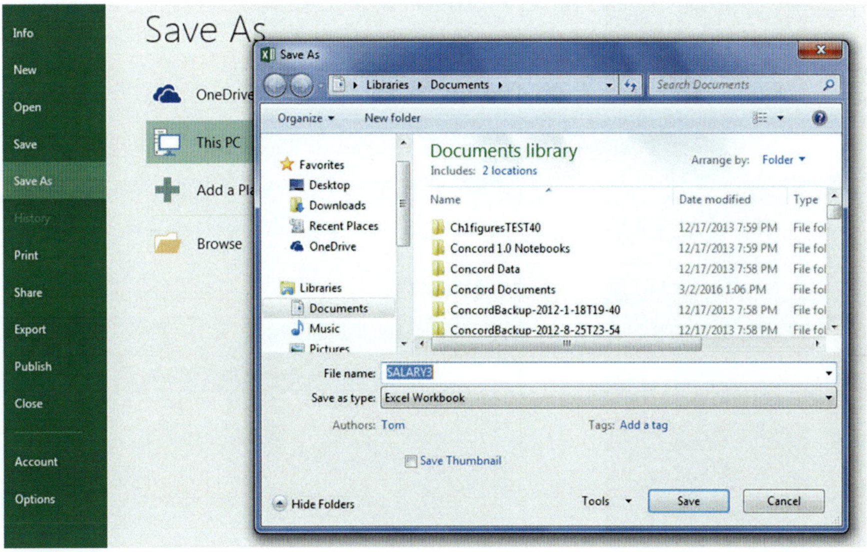

Fig. 1.12 Dialogue Box of Saving an Excel Workbook File as "SALARY3" in My Documents location

Save

Important note: Be very careful to save your Excel file spreadsheet every few minutes so that you do not lose your information!

1.6 Printing a Spreadsheet

Objective: To print the spreadsheet

Use the following procedure when printing any spreadsheet.
File
Print
Print Active Sheets (see Fig. 1.13)

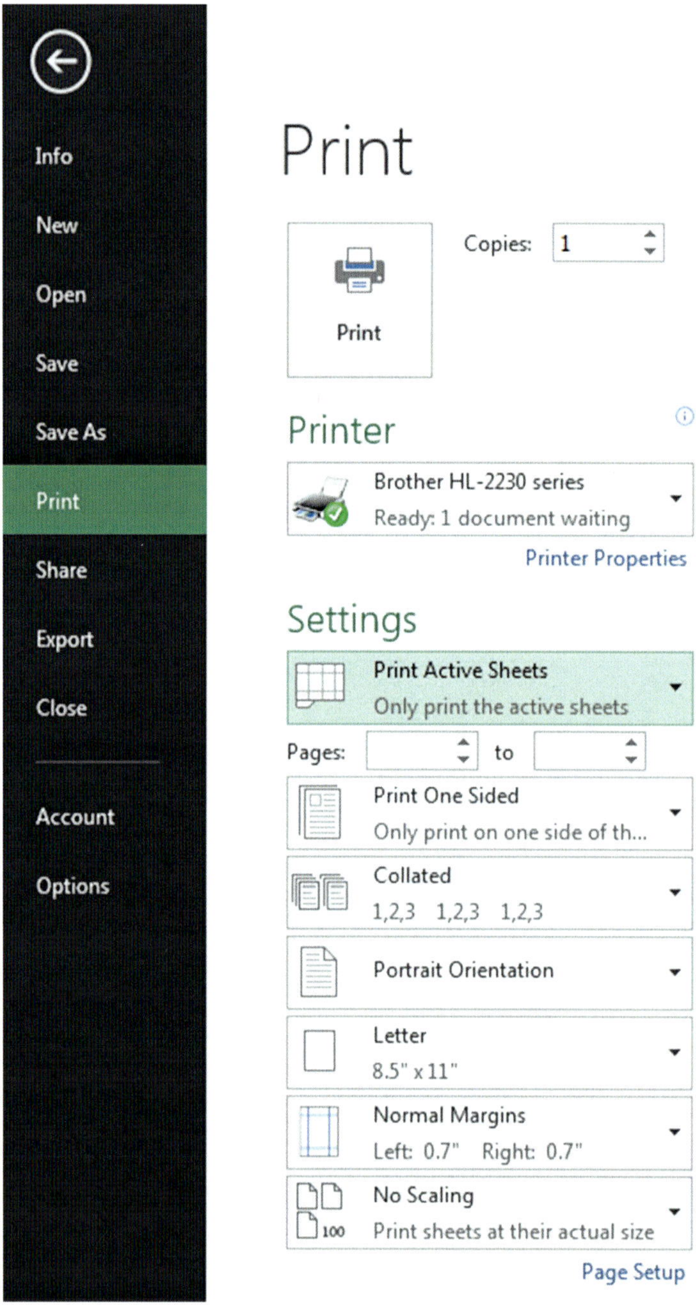

Fig. 1.13 Example of How to Print an Excel Worksheet Using the File/Print/Print Active Sheets Commands

Print (top of your screen)

The final spreadsheet is given in Fig 1.14

	A	B	C	D	E	F	G
1							
2							
3		Employee	Monthly salary ($)				
4		1	2125				
5		2	2340				
6		3	2680		n	8	
7		4	2935				
8		5	3040				
9		6	2260		Mean	2516.25	
10		7	2590				
11		8	2160				
12					STDEV	350.23	
13							
14							
15					s.e.	123.83	
16							
17							

Fig. 1.14 Final Result of Printing an Excel Spreadsheet

Before you leave this chapter, let's practice changing the format of the figures on a spreadsheet with two examples: (1) using two decimal places for figures that are dollar amounts, and (2) using three decimal places for figures.

Save the final spreadsheet by: File/Save, then close your spreadsheet by: File/Close, and open a blank Excel spreadsheet by using: File/New/Blank Workbook (on the top left of your screen).

1.7 Formatting Numbers in Currency Format (Two decimal places)

Objective: To change the format of figures to dollar format with two decimal places

A3: Price
A4: 1.25
A5: 3.45
A6: 12.95

Highlight cells A4:A6 by left-clicking your mouse on A4 and dragging it down so that these three cells are highlighted in a darker color
Home
Number (top center of screen: click on the down arrow on the right; see Fig. 1.15)

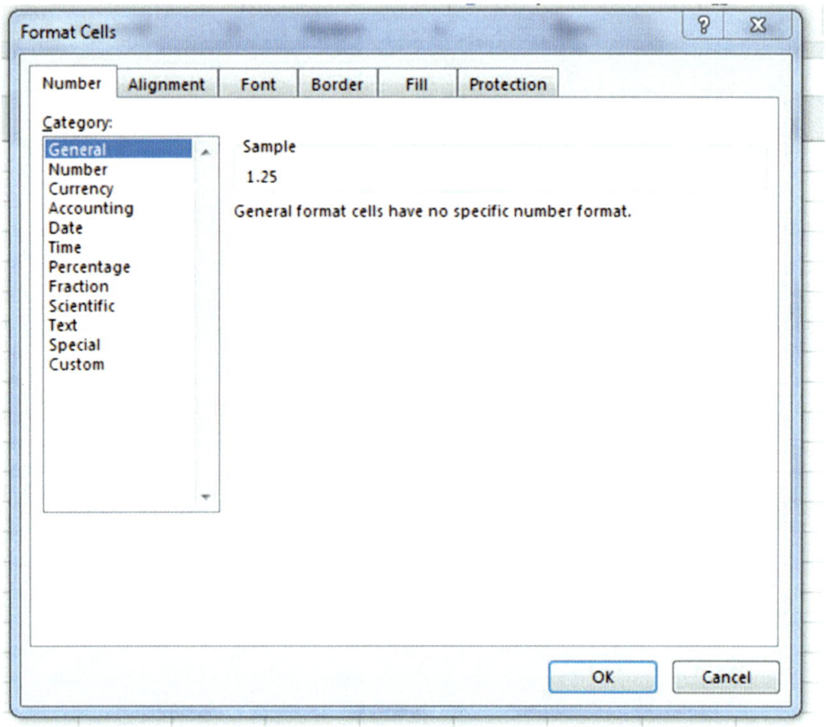

Fig. 1.15 Dialogue Box for Number Format Choices

Category: Currency
Decimal places: 2 (then see Fig. 1.16)

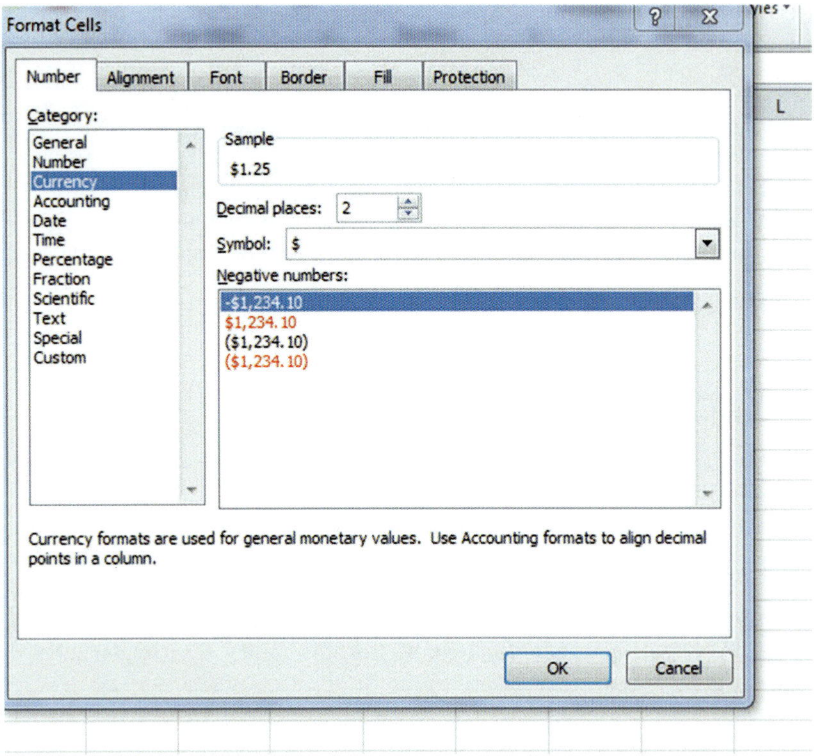

Fig. 1.16 Dialogue Box for Currency (two decimal places) Format for Numbers

OK

The three cells should have a dollar sign in them and be in two decimal places. Next, let's practice formatting figures in number format, three decimal places.

1.8 Formatting Numbers in Number Format (Three decimal places)

Objective: To format figures in number format, three decimal places

Home
Highlight cells A4:A6 on your computer screen
Number (click on the down arrow on the right)
Category: number

At the right of the box, change two decimal places to three decimal places by clicking on the "up arrow" once

OK

The three figures should now be in number format, each with three decimals.

Now, click on any blank cell to deselect cells A4:A6. Then, close this file by File/Close/Don't Save (since there is no need to save this practice problem).

You can use these same commands to format a range of cells in percentage format (and many other formats) to whatever number of decimal places you want to specify.

1.9 End-of-Chapter Practice Problems

1. Morale surveys of employees are an important aspect of the work of Human Resource (HR) departments in organizations so that top management can be made aware of employees' attitudes before major problems occur. Suppose that you have been asked to analyze the data from a recent HR survey of middle managers in your organization and that you want to test your Excel skills on a small sample of managers for Item #21 of this survey. The hypothetical data appear in Fig. 1.17.

HUMAN RESOURCES MORALE SURVEY						
Item #21:	"Management is doing a good job of keeping employee morale at a high level."					
1	2	3	4	5	6	7
Disagree						Agree
			Rating			
			3			
			6			
			5			
			7			
			2			
			3			
			6			
			5			
			4			
			7			
			6			
			1			
			3			
			2			
			4			
			5			
			6			
			4			
			5			
			3			
			6			
			4			
			7			

Fig. 1.17 Worksheet Data for Chap. 1: Practice Problem #1

(a) Use Excel to the right of the table to find the sample size, mean, standard deviation, and standard error of the mean for these data. Label your answers, and round off the mean, standard deviation, and standard error of the mean to two decimal places; use number format for these three figures.
(b) Print the result on a separate page.
(c) Save the file as: MGT21

2. On-time performance of workers arriving at their job in a department is an important statistic in any organization. Suppose that you wanted to find the average percent of on-time performance for workers in Department D of your organization during the past month. These data are given in Fig. 1.18.

Fig. 1.18 Worksheet Data for Chap. 1: Practice Problem #2

DEPARTMENT D (last month)
ON-TIME PERFORMANCE (%)
95
94
93
98
100
95
96
98
99
96
97
95
98
99
100
98

(a) Use Excel to create a table of these data, and at the right of the table use Excel to find the sample size, mean, standard deviation, and standard error of the mean for these data. Label your answers, and round off the mean, standard deviation, and standard error of the mean to one decimal place using number format.
(b) Print the result on a separate page.
(c) Save the file as: ONTIME3

3. Employee absence is a vexing problem in every organization and it can sometimes escalate to an alarming rate if it is not carefully monitored by the Human Resources department. There are many legitimate reasons for an employee to be absent from work, including sickness, family emergencies, personal business that must be conducted during working hours, vacation days, and holidays. But there are also other reasons for employees not coming to work such as low job satisfaction, dissatisfaction with pay, poor supervision, and excessive workload stress. Excessive absences can also be a forerunner of employee turnover. Tracking absences also requires accurate time records of employees and a company standard of an "acceptable" absence rate. A typical way to measure absence is given by the following formula:

$$\text{Monthly absence rate} = \text{WDL}/\ (\text{HC} \times \text{WD})$$

where WDL = total number of worker days lost through absence that month
HC = average number of employees that month
WD = total number of workdays in that month

Suppose that you wanted to determine the descriptive statistics summarizing your company's monthly absence rate during the past year. The hypothetical data are given in Fig. 1.19:

Fig. 1.19 Worksheet Data for Chap. 1: Practice Problem #3

ABSENCE RATE

MONTH	MONTHLY ABSENCE RATE (%)
JAN	2.5
FEB	2.8
MAR	2.6
APR	3.1
MAY	3.4
JUN	2.7
JUL	2.6
AUG	2.4
SEP	3.1
OCT	3.0
NOV	2.8
DEC	2.7

(a) Use Excel to create a table for these data, and at the right of the table, use Excel to find the sample size, mean, standard deviation, and standard error of the mean for these data. Label your answers, and round off the mean, standard deviation, and standard error of the mean to one decimal place using number format.
(b) Print the result on a separate page.
(c) Save the file as: ABSENCE3

References

Aamodt M, Surrette M, and Cohen D. Understanding statistics: a guide for I/O psychologists and human resource professionals. Belmont: Wadsworth Cengage Learning; 2007.

Black K. Business statistics: for contemporary decision making. 6th ed. Hoboken: John Wiley & Sons, Inc.; 2010.

Davis J H. Statistics for compensation: a practical guide to compensation analysis. Hoboken: John Wiley & Sons; 2011.

Levine D M. Statistics for managers using Microsoft Excel. 6th ed. Boston: Prentice Hall/Pearson; 2011.

Weiers R M. Introduction to business statistics. 7th ed. Mason: South-Western Cengage Learning; 2011.

Whetzel D L and Wheaton G R (Eds.). Applied measurement: industrial psychology in human resources management. Mahwah: Lawrence Erlbaum Associates; 2007.

Chapter 2
Random Number Generator

A Human Resources (HR) administrator wants to put together an in-house focus group of 5 of the 32 mid-level managers in her organization to discuss new ideas for benefits that could be developed and offered to employees at this organization. Suppose that she has asked you to take a random sample of 5 of these 32 managers so that she can contact them and attempt to arrange a time when this group could meet. In order for you to use your Excel skills to take this random sample, you will need to define a "sampling frame."

A sampling frame is a list of objects, events, or people from which you want to select a random sample. In this case, it is the group of 32 managers. In order to define the sampling frame, you will first need to assign a unique identifier to each person (or object) in the sampling frame. The frame starts with the identification code (ID) 1 that is assigned to the first manager in the group of 32 managers. The second manager has a code number of 2, the third a code number of 3, and so forth until the last manager has a code number of 32.

Since the group had 32 managers, your sampling frame would go from 1 to 32 with each manager having a unique ID number.

We will first create the frame numbers as follows in a new Excel worksheet:

2.1 Creating Frame Numbers for Generating Random Numbers

Objective: To create the frame numbers for generating random numbers

A3: FRAME NO.
A4: 1

T.J. Quirk, J. Palmer-Schuyler, *Excel 2016 for Human Resource Management Statistics*, Excel for Statistics, DOI 10.1007/978-3-319-40063-1_2

Now, create the frame numbers in column A with the Home/Fill commands that were explained in the first chapter of this book (see Sect. 1.4.1) so that the frame numbers go from 1 to 32, with the number 32 in cell A35. If you need to be reminded about how to do that, here are the steps:

Click on cell A4 to select this cell
Home
Fill (then click on the "down arrow" next to this command and select)
Series (see Fig. 2.1)

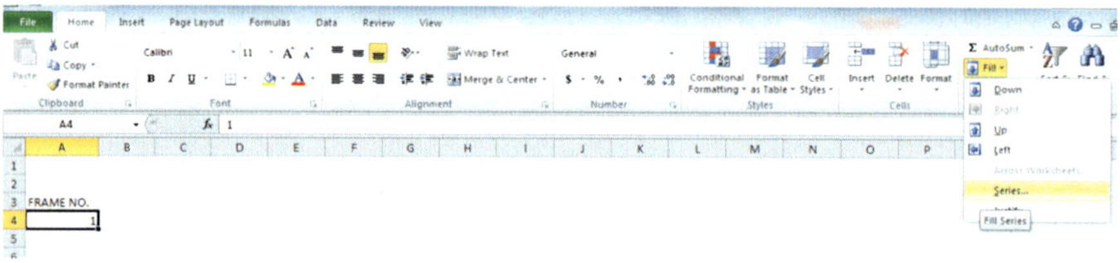

Fig. 2.1 Dialogue Box for Fill/Series Commands

Columns
Step value: 1
Stop value: 32 (see Fig. 2.2)

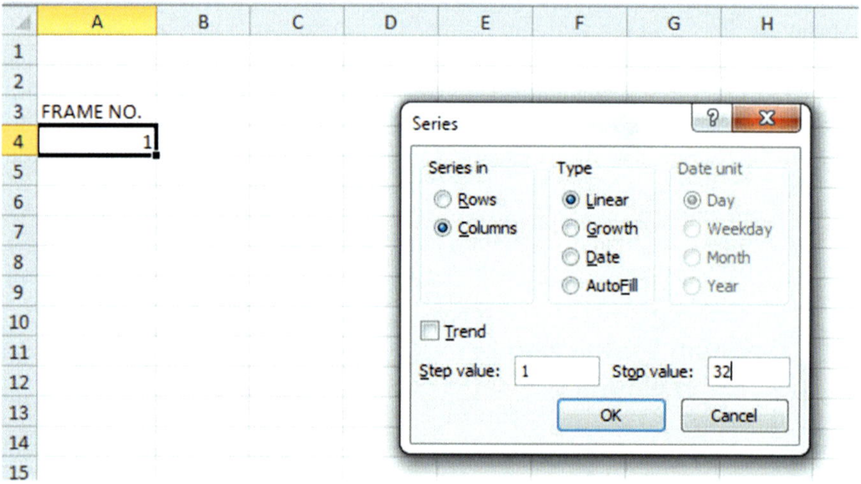

Fig. 2.2 Dialogue Box for Fill/Series/Columns/Step value/Stop value Commands

OK

Then, save this file as: Random29. You should obtain the result in Fig. 2.3.

Fig. 2.3 Frame Numbers from 1 to 32

FRAME NO.
1
2
3
4
5
6
7
8
9
10
11
12
13
14
15
16
17
18
19
20
21
22
23
24
25
26
27
28
29
30
31
32

Now, create a column next to these frame numbers in this manner:

B3: DUPLICATE FRAME NO.
B4: 1

Next, use the Home/Fill command again, so that the 32 frame numbers begin in cell B4 and end in cell B35. Be sure to widen the columns A and B so that all of the information in these columns fits inside the column width. Then, center the information inside both Column A and Column B on your spreadsheet. You should obtain the information given in Fig. 2.4.

Fig. 2.4 Duplicate Frame Numbers from 1 to 32

FRAME NO.	DUPLICATE FRAME NO.
1	1
2	2
3	3
4	4
5	5
6	6
7	7
8	8
9	9
10	10
11	11
12	12
13	13
14	14
15	15
16	16
17	17
18	18
19	19
20	20
21	21
22	22
23	23
24	24
25	25
26	26
27	27
28	28
29	29
30	30
31	31
32	32

Save this file as: Random30

You are probably wondering why you created the same information in both Column A and Column B of your spreadsheet. This is to make sure that before you sort the frame numbers that you have exactly 32 of them when you finish sorting them into a random sequence of 32 numbers.

Now, let's add a random number to each of the duplicate frame numbers as follows:

2.2 Creating Random Numbers in an Excel Worksheet

C3: RANDOM NO. (then widen columns A, B, C so that their labels fit inside the columns; then center the information in A3:C35)

C4: =RAND()

Next, hit the Enter key to add a random number to cell C4.

Note that you need *both* an open parenthesis *and* a closed parenthesis to create =*RAND*(). The =RAND() command "looks to the left of the cell with the =RAND() COMMAND in it" and assigns a random number to that cell.

Now, put the pointer using your mouse in cell C4 and then move the pointer to the bottom right corner of that cell until you see a "plus sign" in that cell. Then, click and drag the pointer down to cell C35 to add a random number to all 32 ID frame numbers (see Fig. 2.5).

Fig. 2.5 Example of Random Numbers Assigned to the Duplicate Frame Numbers

FRAME NO.	DUPLICATE FRAME NO.	RANDOM NO.
1	1	0.178997426
2	2	0.269196787
3	3	0.48649709
4	4	0.882904516
5	5	0.015953504
6	6	0.099651545
7	7	0.42850057
8	8	0.381659988
9	9	0.431296832
10	10	0.476642453
11	11	0.268603728
12	12	0.871330234
13	13	0.775421903
14	14	0.908450998
15	15	0.138749452
16	16	0.159535582
17	17	0.672417279
18	18	0.956231064
19	19	0.486746795
20	20	0.83596565
21	21	0.688574546
22	22	0.467838617
23	23	0.695493167
24	24	0.226521237
25	25	0.335451708
26	26	0.209245145
27	27	0.631291464
28	28	0.210229448
29	29	0.553196562
30	30	0.494647331
31	31	0.986702143
32	32	0.178067956

Then, click on any empty cell to deselect C4:C35 to remove the dark color highlighting these cells.

Save this file as: Random31

Now, let's sort these duplicate frame numbers into a random sequence:

2.3 Sorting Frame Numbers into a Random Sequence

Objective: To sort the duplicate frame numbers into a random sequence

Highlight cells B3: C35 (include the labels at the top of columns B and C)
Data (top of screen)
Sort (click on this word at the top center of your screen; see Fig. 2.6)

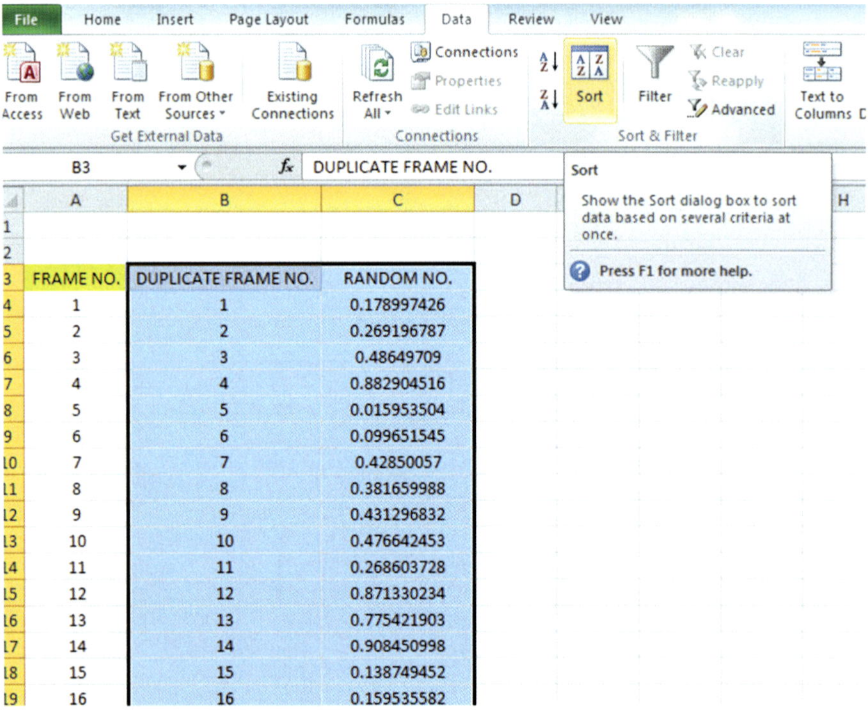

Fig. 2.6 Dialogue Box for Data/Sort Commands

Sort by: RANDOM NO. (click on the down arrow)
Smallest to Largest (see Fig. 2.7)

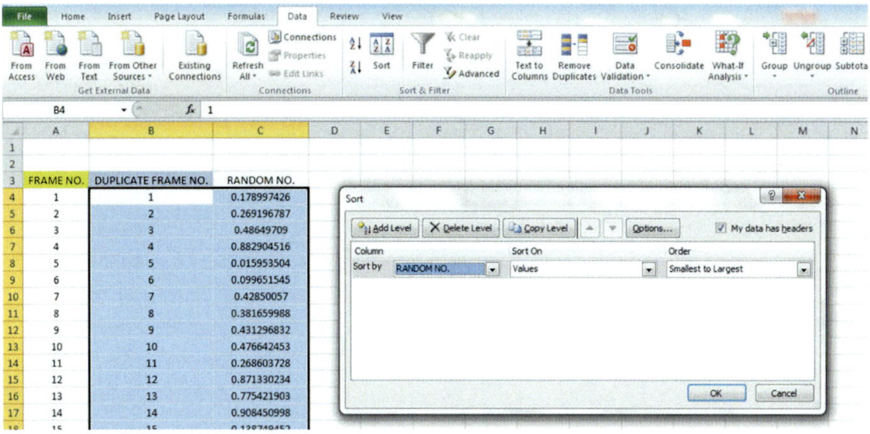

Fig. 2.7 Dialogue Box for Data/Sort/RANDOM NO./Smallest to Largest Commands

OK
Click on any empty cell to deselect B3:C35.
Save this file as: Random32
Print this file now.

These steps will produce Fig. 2.8 with the DUPLICATE FRAME NUMBERS sorted into a random order:

Important note: Because Excel randomly assigns these random numbers, your Excel commands will produce a different sequence of random numbers from everyone else who reads this book!

Fig. 2.8 Duplicate Frame Numbers Sorted by Random Number

FRAME NO.	DUPLICATE FRAME NO.	RANDOM NO.
1	5	0.063981403
2	6	0.977468743
3	15	0.225170263
4	16	0.765734052
5	32	0.274680922
6	1	0.594468001
7	26	0.511966171
8	28	0.625577233
9	24	0.906310053
10	11	0.488640116
11	2	0.020129977
12	25	0.723003676
13	8	0.975227547
14	7	0.469582962
15	9	0.14889954
16	22	0.955629903
17	10	0.897398234
18	3	0.314860892
19	19	0.442019486
20	30	0.078566335
21	29	0.172474705
22	27	0.104689528
23	17	0.406630369
24	21	0.961398315
25	23	0.094222677
26	13	0.323429051
27	20	0.470615753
28	12	0.978014724
29	4	0.618082813
30	14	0.727776384
31	18	0.919475329
32	31	0.324497007

Because your objective at the beginning of this chapter was to select randomly 5 of the 32 mid-level managers at your organization for a possible focus group session, you now can do that by selecting the *first five sorted ID numbers* in the DUPLICATE FRAME NO. column after the sort.

Although your first five random numbers will be different from those we have selected in the random sort that we did in this chapter, we would select these five IDs of managers using Fig. 2.9.

Fig. 2.9 First Five Managers Selected Randomly

FRAME NO.	DUPLICATE FRAME NO.	RANDOM NO.
1	5	0.063981403
2	6	0.977468743
3	15	0.225170263
4	16	0.765734052
5	32	0.274680922
6	1	0.594468001
7	26	0.511966171
8	28	0.625577233
9	24	0.906310053
10	11	0.488640116
11	2	0.020129977
12	25	0.723003676
13	8	0.975227547
14	7	0.469582962
15	9	0.14889954
16	22	0.955629903
17	10	0.897398234
18	3	0.314860892
19	19	0.442019486
20	30	0.078566335
21	29	0.172474705
22	27	0.104689528
23	17	0.406630369
24	21	0.961398315
25	23	0.094222677
26	13	0.323429051
27	20	0.470615753
28	12	0.978014724
29	4	0.618082813
30	14	0.727776384
31	18	0.919475329
32	31	0.324497007

5, 6, 15, 16, 32

Save this file as: Random33

Remember, your five ID numbers selected after your random sort will be different from the five ID numbers in Fig. 2.9 because Excel assigns a different random number *each time the =RAND() command is given.*

Before we leave this chapter, you need to learn how to print a file so that all of the information on that file fits onto a single page without "dribbling over" onto a second or third page.

2.4 Printing an Excel File So That All of the Information Fits onto One Page

Objective: To print a file so that all of the information fits onto one page

The three practice problems at the end of this chapter require you to sort random numbers when the files contain 63 students, 114 employees, and 75 new-hires, respectively. These files will be "too big" to fit onto one page when you print them unless you format these files so that they fit onto a single page.

Let's create a situation where the file does not fit onto one printed page unless you format it first to do that.

Go back to the file you just created, Random 33, and enter the name: *Jennifer* into cell: A50.

If you printed this file now, the name, *Jennifer*, would be printed onto a second page because it "dribbles over" outside of the page rage for this file in its current format.

So, you would need to change the page format so that all of the information, including the name, Jennifer, fits onto just one page when you print this file by using the following steps:

Click on any empty cell to change your location away from cell A50
Page Layout (top left of the computer screen)
(Notice the "Scale to Fit" section in the center of your screen; see Fig. 2.10)

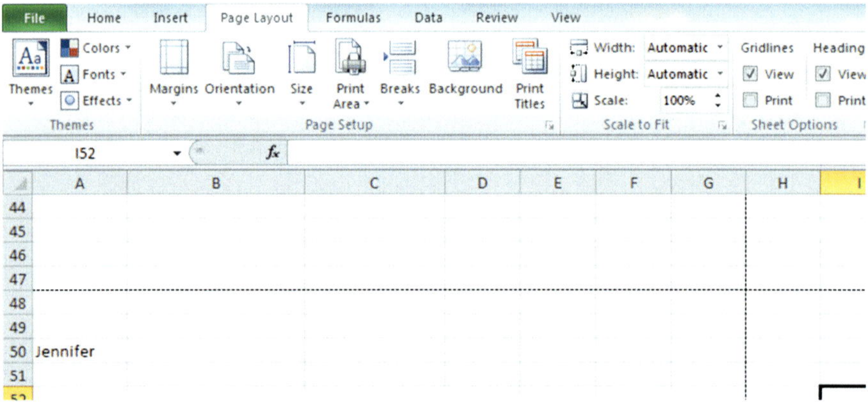

Fig. 2.10 Dialogue Box for Page Layout/Scale to Fit Commands

Hit the down arrow to the right of 100 % *once* to reduce the size of the page to 95 %

Now, note that the name, Jennifer, is still on a second page on your screen because her name is below the horizontal dotted line on your screen in Fig. 2.11 (the dotted lines tell you outline dimensions of the file if you printed it now).

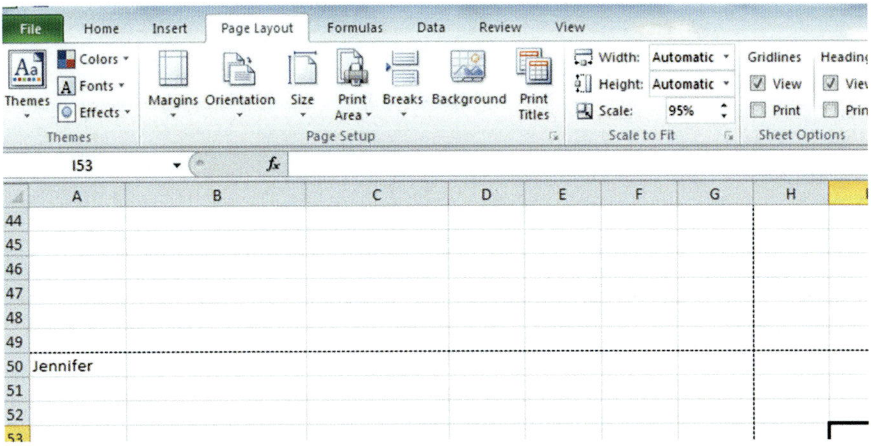

Fig. 2.11 Example of Scale Reduced to 95 % with "Jennifer" to be Printed on a Second Page

So, you need to repeat the "scale change steps" by hitting the down arrow on the right once more to reduce the size of the worksheet to 90 % of its normal size.

Notice that the "dotted lines" on your computer screen in Fig. 2.12 are now below Jennifer's name to indicate that all of the information, including her name, is now formatted to fit onto just one page when you print this file.

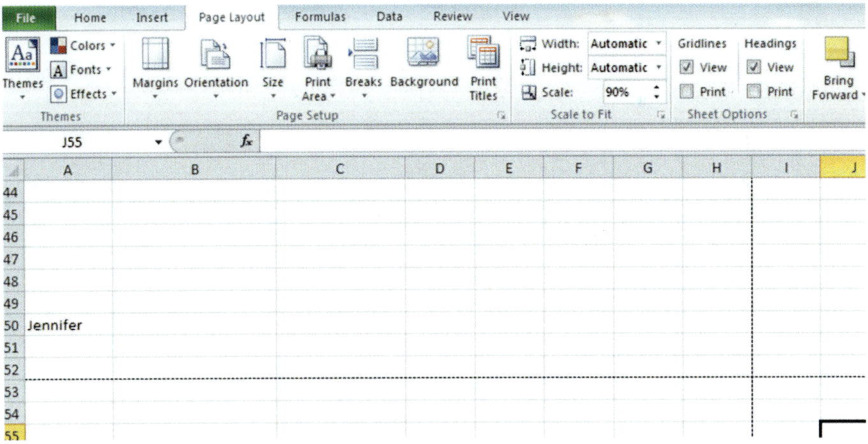

Fig. 2.12 Example of Scale Reduced to 90 % with "Jennifer" to be printed on the first page (note the dotted line below Jennifer on your screen)

Save the file as: Random34

Print the file. Does it all fit onto one page? It should (see Fig. 2.13).

Fig. 2.13 Final Spreadsheet of 90 % Scale to Fit

FRAME NO.	DUPLICATE FRAME NO.	RANDOM NO.
1	5	0.747176905
2	6	0.038774393
3	15	0.091368861
4	16	0.63147137
5	32	0.190734495
6	1	0.411943765
7	26	0.138033007
8	28	0.927874602
9	24	0.058336576
10	11	0.043243606
11	2	0.729011126
12	25	0.204119693
13	8	0.456656709
14	7	0.232589896
15	9	0.09096704
16	22	0.935399501
17	10	0.201267198
18	3	0.52638312
19	19	0.53734605
20	30	0.969840616
21	29	0.475657455
22	27	0.558049277
23	17	0.488444809
24	21	0.717097206
25	23	0.86192944
26	13	0.875595013
27	20	0.536748908
28	12	0.331784725
29	4	0.642847666
30	14	0.575767804
31	18	0.939789757
32	31	0.776050794

Jennifer

2.5 End-of-Chapter Practice Problems

1. Suppose that you are the Director of a Master's degree program in Human Resources at a university and that you want to interview a random sample of students who are scheduled to graduate from the program this next June so that you can obtain their suggestions about how the program can be improved. Suppose that you have 63 Master's students who are scheduled to graduate. You want to randomly select 15 of these 63 students for a personal interview.

   (a) Set up a spreadsheet of frame numbers for these students with the heading: FRAME NUMBERS using the Home/Fill commands.
   (b) Then, create a separate column to the right of these frame numbers which duplicates these frame numbers with the title: Duplicate frame numbers.
   (c) Then, create a separate column to the right of these duplicate frame numbers entitled RANDOM NO. and use the =RAND() function to assign random numbers to all of the frame numbers in the duplicate frame numbers column, and change this column format so that three decimal places appear for each random number.
   (d) Sort the duplicate frame numbers and random numbers into a random order.
   (e) Print the result so that the spreadsheet fits onto one page.
   (f) Circle on your printout the I.D. number of the first 15 students that you would use in your interviews.
   (g) Save the file as: RAND9

   Important note: Note that everyone who does this problem will generate a different random order of student ID numbers since Excel assigns a different random number each time the =RAND() command is used. For this reason, the answer to this problem given in this Excel Guide will have a completely different sequence of random numbers from the random sequence that you generate. This is normal and what is to be expected.

2. Suppose that you are the HR director at a large company and that you want to conduct a phone interview with 10 of the 114 employees who have elected to be included in the company's Vision Care Plan which was instituted a year ago to obtain their feedback about how well the plan has been working for them.

   (a) Set up a spreadsheet of frame numbers for these claims with the heading: FRAME NO.
   (b) Then, create a separate column to the right of these frame numbers which duplicates these frame numbers with the title: Duplicate frame no.
   (c) Then, create a separate column to the right of these duplicate frame numbers entitled "Random number" and use the =RAND() function to assign random numbers to all of the frame numbers in the duplicate frame numbers column. Then, change this column format so that three decimal places appear for each random number

(d) Sort the duplicate frame numbers and random numbers into a random order
(e) Print the result so that the spreadsheet fits onto one page
(f) Circle on your printout the I.D. number of the first ten employees that would be used in this research study.
(g) Save the file as: RANDOM6

3. Suppose, for the sake of argument, that you are the Director of HR for a large company and that you want to conduct a personal interview with 20 of the 75 new-hires in the company who recently completed a one-day orientation program about the various benefits programs available to employees at your company to see how the orientation program can be improved. You want to take a random sample of 20 of these 75 new-hires.

(a) Set up a spreadsheet of frame numbers for these new-hires with the heading: FRAME NUMBERS.
(b) Then, create a separate column to the right of these frame numbers which duplicates these frame numbers with the title: Duplicate frame numbers.
(c) Then, create a separate column to the right of these duplicate frame numbers entitled "Random number" and use the =RAND() function to assign random numbers to all of the frame numbers in the duplicate frame numbers column. Then, change this column format so that three decimal places appear for each random number.
(d) Sort the duplicate frame numbers and random numbers into a random order.
(e) Print the result so that the spreadsheet fits onto one page.
(f) Circle on your printout the I.D. number of the first 20 new-hires that you would select for your personal interview study.
(g) Save the file as: RAND5

Chapter 3
Confidence Interval About the Mean Using the TINV Function and Hypothesis Testing

This chapter focuses on two ideas: (1) finding the 95 % confidence interval about the mean, and (2) hypothesis testing.

Let's talk about the confidence interval and then about hypothesis testing.

3.1 Confidence Interval About the Mean

In statistics, we are often interested in *estimating the population mean*. How do we do that?

3.1.1 How to Estimate the Population Mean

Objective: To estimate the population mean, μ

The population mean is an average of all people in a target population. For example, if we were interested in how well adults ages 25–44 liked a new flavor of Ben & Jerry's ice cream, we could never ask this question of all of the people in the U.S. who were in that age group. Such a research study would take way too much time to complete and the cost of doing that study would be prohibitive.

So, instead of testing *everyone* in the population, we take a sample of people in the population and use the results of this sample to estimate the mean of the entire population. This saves both time and money. When we use the results of a sample to estimate the population mean, this is called "*inferential statistics*" because we are inferring the population mean from the sample mean.

T.J. Quirk, J. Palmer-Schuyler, *Excel 2016 for Human Resource Management Statistics*, Excel for Statistics, DOI 10.1007/978-3-319-40063-1_3

When we study a sample from a population, we know the size of our sample (n), the mean of our sample $(\overline{X})$, and the standard deviation of our sample (STDEV). We use these figures to estimate the accuracy of our estimated population mean with a test called the "confidence interval about the mean."

3.1.2 Estimating the Lower Limit and the Upper Limit of the 95 % Confidence Interval About the Mean

The theoretical background of this test is beyond the scope of this book, and you can learn more about this test from studying any good statistics textbook (e.g. McDaniel and Gates (2010) or Black (2010)), but the basic ideas are as follows.

We assume that the population mean is somewhere in an interval which has a "lower limit" and an "upper limit" to it. We also assume in this book that we want to be "95 % confident" that the population mean is inside this interval somewhere. So, we intend to make the following type of statement:

> "We are 95 % confident that the population mean of the TIME TO FILL an approved application for staffing during the past 12 months was between 33 days and 37 days."

If we want to claim that the TIME TO FILL during the past 12 months was 35 days, we can do this because 35 is *inside the 95 % confidence interval* in our research study in the above example. We do not know exactly what the population mean is, only that it is somewhere between 33 days and 37 days, and 35 days is inside this interval.

But we are only 95 % confident that the population mean is inside this interval, and 5 % of the time we will be wrong in assuming that the population mean is 35 days.

For our purposes in HR research, we are happy to be 95 % confident that our assumption is accurate. We should also point out that 95 % is an arbitrary level of confidence for our results. We could choose to be 80 % confident, or 90 % confident, or even 99 % confident in our results if we wanted to do that. In this book, *we will always assume that we want to be 95 % confident of our results.* That way, you will not have to guess on how confident you want to be in any of the problems in this book. We will always want to be 95 % confident of our results in this book.

So how do we find the 95 % confidence interval about the mean for our data? In words, we will find this interval this way:

> "Take the sample mean $(\overline{X})$, *and add to it* 1.96 times the standard error of the mean (s.e.) to get the upper limit of the confidence interval. Then, take the sample mean, *and subtract from it* 1.96 times the standard error of the mean to get the lower limit of the confidence interval."

You will remember (See Sect. 1.3) that the standard error of the mean (s.e.) is found by dividing the standard deviation of our sample (STDEV) by the square root of our sample size, n.

In mathematical terms, the formula for the 95 % confidence interval about the mean is:

$$\overline{X} \pm 1.96 \text{ s.e.} \tag{3.1}$$

Note that the "± *sign*" stands for "plus or minus," and this means that you first add 1.96 times the s.e. of the mean to get the upper limit of the confidence interval, and then subtract 1.96 times the s.e. of the mean to get the lower limit of the confidence interval. Also, the symbol 1.96 s.e. means that you multiply 1.96 times the standard error of the mean to get this part of the formula for the confidence interval.

Note: We will explain shortly where the number 1.96 came from.

Let's try a simple example to illustrate this formula.

3.1.3 Estimating the Confidence Interval for TIME TO FILL

Let's suppose that you have been asked to determine the average number of days last year between the delivery of an approved requisition for staffing and the date on which an applicant accepted the job offer (i.e., TIME TO FILL). Suppose that you took a random sample of 40 acceptances last year and that they required an average of 36 days for acceptance with a standard deviation of 4 days. The standard error (s.e.) would be 4 divided by the square root of 40 (i.e., 6.32) which gives a s.e. equal to 0.63 days.

The 95 % confidence interval for these data would be:

$$36 \pm 1.96(0.63)$$

The *upper limit of this confidence interval* uses the plus sign of the ± sign in the formula. Therefore, the upper limit would be:

$$36 + 1.96(0.63) = 36 + 1.23 = 37.23 \text{ days}$$

Similarly, *the lower limit of this confidence interval* uses the minus sign of the ± sign in the formula. Therefore, the lower limit would be:

$$36 - 1.96(0.63) = 36 - 1.23 = 34.77 \text{ days}$$

The result of our part of the ongoing research study would, therefore, be the following:

> "We are 95 % confident that the population mean for TIME TO FILL during the past 12 months was between 34.77 days and 37.23 days."

Based upon 35 days being inside the confidence interval, we could conclude that the average TIME TO FILL in the past 12 months was 35 days. Our data supports this claim because 35 days is inside of this 95 % confidence interval for the population mean.

You are probably asking yourself: "Where did that 1.96 in the formula come from?"

3.1.4 Where Did the Number "1.96" Come From?

A detailed mathematical answer to that question is beyond the scope of this book, but here is the basic idea.

We make an assumption that the data in the population are "normally distributed" in the sense that the population data would take the shape of a "normal curve" if we could test all of the people or properties in the population. The normal curve looks like the outline of the Liberty Bell that sits in front of Independence Hall in Philadelphia, Pennsylvania. The normal curve is "symmetric" in the sense that if we cut it down the middle, and folded it over to one side, the half that we folded over would fit perfectly onto the half on the other side. For a more detailed explanation of the normal curve, see Fitz-enz and Davison (2002).

A discussion of integral calculus is beyond the scope of this book, but essentially we want to find the lower limit and the upper limit of the population data in the normal curve so that 95 % of the area under this curve is between these two limits. *If we have more than 40 people in our research study*, the value of these limits is plus or minus 1.96 times the standard error of the mean (s.e.) of our sample. The number 1.96 times the s.e. of our sample is used to find the upper limit and the lower limit of our confidence interval. If you want to learn more about this idea, you can consult a good statistics book (e.g. Keller 2009).

The number 1.96 would change if we wanted to be confident of our results at a different level from 95 % as long as we have more than 40 people in our research study.

For example:

1. If we wanted to be 80 % confident of our results, this number would be 1.282.
2. If we wanted to be 90 % confident of our results, this number would be 1.645.
3. If we wanted to be 99 % confident of our results, this number would be 2.576.

But since we always want to be 95 % confident of our results in this book, we will always use 1.96 in this book whenever we have more than 40 people in our research study.

By now, you are probably asking yourself: "Is this number in the confidence interval about the mean always 1.96 ?" The answer is: "No!", and we will explain why this is true now.

3.1.5 Finding the Value for t in the Confidence Interval Formula

Objective: To find the value for t in the confidence interval formula

The correct formula for the confidence interval about the mean for different sample sizes is the following:

$$\overline{X} \pm \text{t s.e.} \tag{3.2}$$

To use this formula, you find the sample mean, $\overline{X}$, *and add to it the value of t times the s.e. to get the upper limit* of this 95 % confidence interval. Also, you take the sample mean, $\overline{X}$, and *subtract from it the value of t times the s.e. to get the lower limit* of this 95 % confidence interval. And, you find the value of t in the table given in Appendix E of this book in the following way:

Objective: To find the value of t in the t-table in Appendix E

Before we get into an explanation of what is meant by "the value of t," let's give you practice in finding the value of t by using the t-table in Appendix E.

Keep your finger on Appendix E as we explain how you need to "read" that table.

Since the test in this chapter is called the "confidence interval about the mean test," you will use the first column on the left in Appendix E to find the critical value of t for your research study (note that this column is headed: "sample size n").

To find the value of *t*, you go down this first column until you find the sample size in your research study, and then you go to the right and read the value of *t* for that sample size in the "critical t column" of the table (note that this column is the column that you would use for the 95 % confidence interval about the mean).

For example, if you have 14 people in your research study, the value of t is 2.160.

If you have 26 people in your research study, the value of t is 2.060.

If you have more than 40 people in your research study, the value of t is always 1.96.

Note that the "critical t column" in Appendix E represents the value of t that you need to use to be 95 % confident that your results are "significant" results.

Throughout this book, we are assuming that you want to be 95 % confident in the results of your statistical tests. Therefore, the value for t in the t-table in Appendix E tells you which value you should use for *t* when you use the formula for the 95 % confidence interval about the mean.

Now that you know how to find the value of t in the formula for the confidence interval about the mean, let's explore how you find this confidence interval using Excel.

3.1.6 Using Excel's TINV Function to Find the Confidence Interval About the Mean

Objective: To use the TINV function in Excel to find the confidence interval about the mean

When you use Excel, the formulas for finding the confidence interval are:

$$Lower\ \ limit := \overline{X} - TINV(1 - 0.95, n - 1)*s.e.(\text{no spaces between these symbols}) \tag{3.3}$$

$$Upper\ \ limit := \overline{X} + TINV(1 - 0.95, n - 1)*s.e.(\text{no spaces between these symbols}) \tag{3.4}$$

Note that the "* *symbol*" in this formula tells Excel to use multiplication in the formula, and it stands for "times" in the way we talk about multiplication.

You will recall from Chap. 1 that n stands for the sample size, and so $n - 1$ stands for the sample size minus one.

You will also recall from Chap. 1 that the standard error of the mean, s.e., equals the STDEV divided by the square root of the sample size, n (See Sect. 1.3).

Let's try a sample problem using Excel to find the 95 % confidence interval about the mean for a problem.

Let's suppose that you wanted to determine if the average number of days between the delivery of an approved application to staffing and the date on which the applicant accepted the job offer during the past 12 months (i.e., TIME TO FILL) was 35 days. Let's call 35 days the "reference value".

Suppose, further, that you have been asked to check this claim to see if it holds up based on some research evidence. You decide to collect some data and to use the confidence interval about the mean to test your results:

3.1.7 Using Excel to find the 95 % Confidence Interval for TIME TO FILL

Objective: To analyze the data using a 95 % confidence interval about the mean

You select a random sample of acceptances from the past 12 months and record the TIME TO FILL for these applicants during these 12 months. Your research study produces the hypothetical results given in Fig. 3.1:

TIME TO FILL	
Question:	"How many days does it take between the delivery of an approved
	job requisition for staffing and the date on which an applicant accepts
	the job offer?"
NO. OF DAYS	
34	
32	
31	
29	
36	
38	
37	
34	
35	
31	
30	
39	
42	
37	
36	
39	
38	
41	
38	
37	

Fig. 3.1 Worksheet Data for TIME TO FILL (Practical Example)

Create a spreadsheet with these data and use Excel to find the sample size (n), the mean, the standard deviation (STDEV), and the standard error of the mean (s.e.) for these data using the following cell references.

A3: TIME TO FILL
A5: Question:
B5: "How many days does it take between the delivery of an approved
B6: job requisition for staffing and the date on which an applicant accepts
B7: the job offer?"
A9: NO. OF DAYS
A10 34

Enter the other TIME TO FILL data in cells A11:A29

Now, highlight cells A10:A29 and format these numbers in number format (zero decimal places). Center these numbers in Column A.

C10: n
C13: Mean
C16: STDEV
C19: s.e.
C22: 95 % confidence interval
D24: Lower limit:
D26: Upper limit: (see Fig. 3.2)

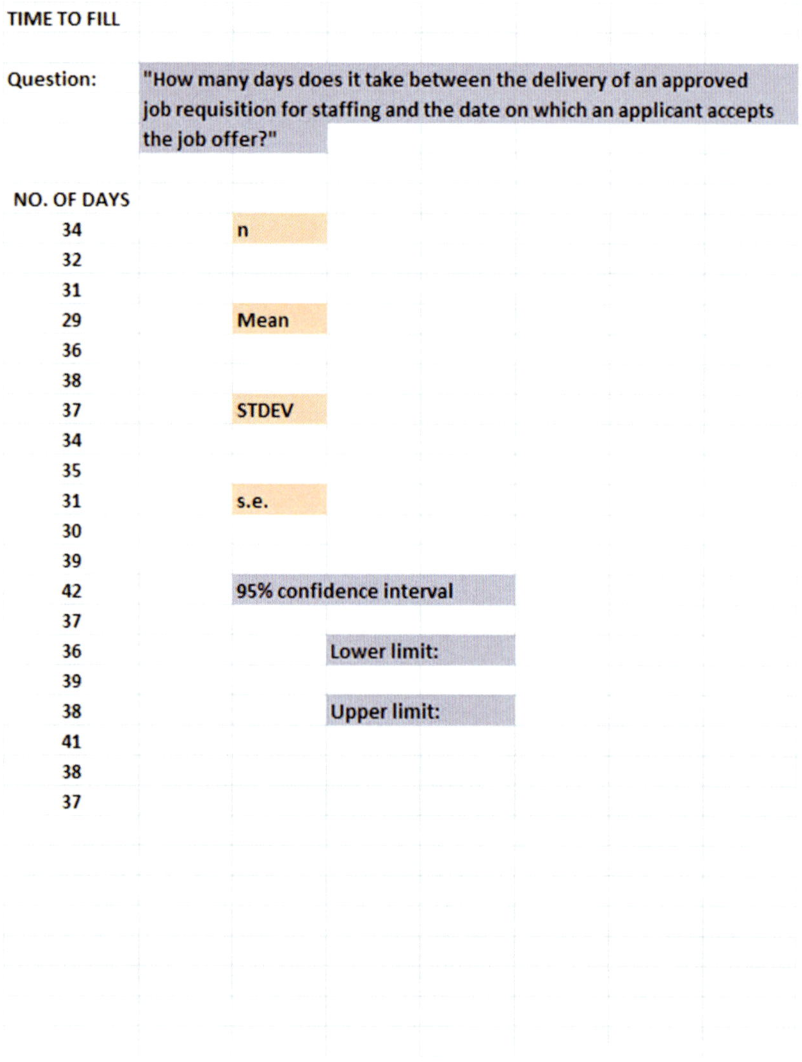

Fig. 3.2 Example of TIME TO FILL Format for the Confidence Interval About the Mean Labels

B29: Draw a picture below this confidence interval
B31: 33.99
B32: lower (right-align this word)
B33: limit (right-align this word)
C31: ‘----------- (note the single quotation mark at the beginning)
D31: ‘--------35 ---- (note that you need to begin cell D31 with a *single quotation mark* (‘) to tell Excel that this is a *label*, and not a number)
E31: ‘------- 35.70 ----
F31: ‘----------- (note the single quotation mark)
G31: 37.41 (left-align this number)
D32: ref. (right-align this word)
D33: value (right-align this word)
E32: Mean (right-align this word)
G32: upper
G33: limit
A35: Conclusion:

Now, align the labels underneath the picture of the confidence interval so that they look like Fig. 3.3.

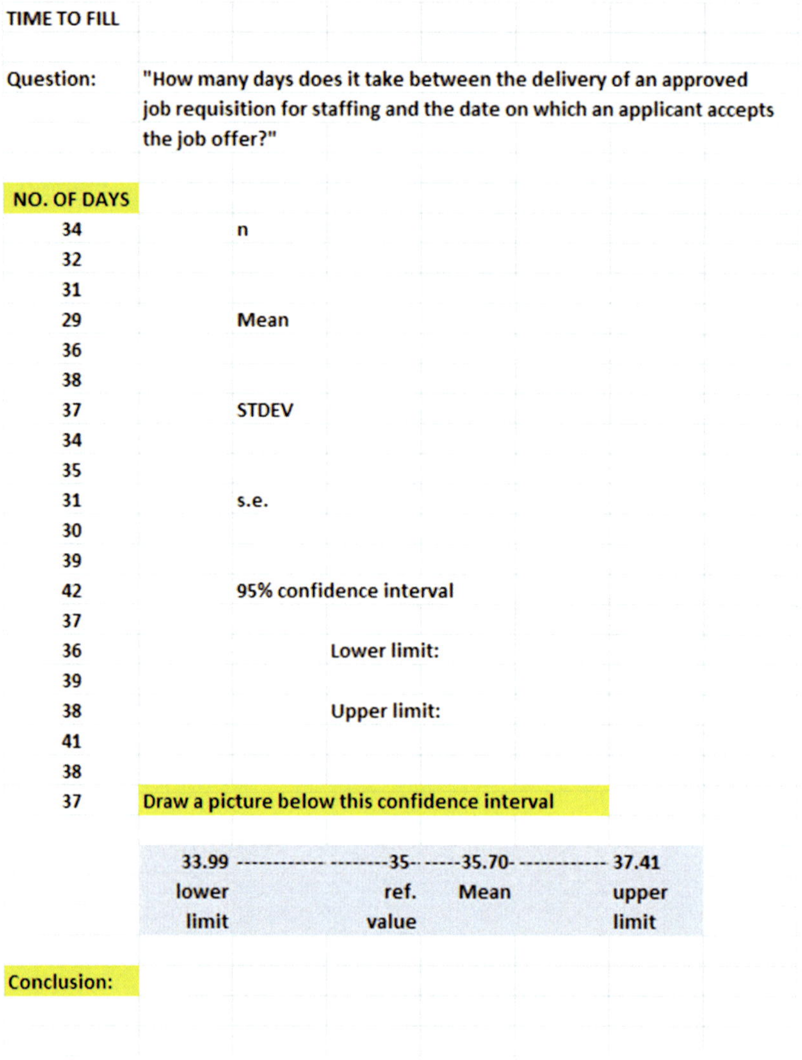

TIME TO FILL

Question: "How many days does it take between the delivery of an approved job requisition for staffing and the date on which an applicant accepts the job offer?"

NO. OF DAYS		
34	n	
32		
31		
29	Mean	
36		
38		
37	STDEV	
34		
35		
31	s.e.	
30		
39		
42	95% confidence interval	
37		
36		Lower limit:
39		
38		Upper limit:
41		
38		
37	Draw a picture below this confidence interval	

33.99 ----------- --------35-- -----35.70- ------------ 37.41
lower limit ref. value Mean upper limit

Conclusion:

Fig. 3.3 Example of Drawing a Picture of a Confidence Interval About the Mean Result

Next, name the range of data from A10:A29 as: TIME

D10: Use Excel to find the sample size
D13: Use Excel to find the mean
D16: Use Excel to find the STDEV
D19: Use Excel to find the s.e.

Now, you need to find the lower limit and the upper limit of the 95 % confidence interval for this study.

We will use Excel's TINV function to do this. We will assume that you want to be 95 % confident of your results. The confidence interval formula for the lower limit of the confidence interval is:

F24 := D13 − TINV(1 − .95, 19)*D19 (no spaces between symbols)

Note that this TINV formula uses 19 since 19 is one less than the sample size of 20 (i.e., 19 is n − 1). Note that D13 is the mean, while D19 is the standard error of the mean. The above formula gives the *lower limit of the confidence interval, 33.99.*

F26 := D13 + TINV(1 − .95, 19)*D19 (no spaces between symbols)

The above formula gives the *upper limit of the confidence interval, 37.41.*

Now, use number format (two decimal places) in your Excel spreadsheet for the mean, standard deviation, standard error of the mean, and for both the lower limit and the upper limit of your confidence interval. The resulting confidence interval appears in Fig. 3.4.

TIME TO FILL					
Question:	**"How many days does it take between the delivery of an approved job requisition for staffing and the date on which an applicant accepts the job offer?"**				
NO. OF DAYS					
34		**n**	**20**		
32					
31					
29		**Mean**	**35.70**		
36					
38					
37		**STDEV**	**3.64**		
34					
35					
31		**s.e.**	**0.81**		
30					
39					
42		**95% confidence interval**			
37					
36			**Lower limit:**	**33.99**	
39					
38			**Upper limit:**	**37.41**	
41					
38					
37	**Draw a picture below this confidence interval**				
	33.99 ------------ --------**35**-- -----**35.70**- ------------ **37.41**				
	lower limit		**ref. value**	**Mean**	**upper limit**
Conclusion:					

Fig. 3.4 Result of Using the TINV Function to Find the Confidence Interval About the Mean

Note that you have drawn a picture of the 95 % confidence interval beneath cell B29, including the lower limit, the upper limit, the mean, and the reference value of 35 days.

Now, let's write the conclusion to your research study on your spreadsheet:

B35: Since the reference value of 35 days is inside the confidence
B36: interval, we accept that the TIME TO FILL a job acceptance
B37: for an approved requisition for staffing was 35 days last year.

Important note: You are probably wondering why we wrote the conclusion on three separate lines of the spreadsheet instead of writing it on one long line. This is because if you wrote it on one line, two things would happen that you would not like: (1) If you printed the conclusion by reducing the size of the layout of the page so that the entire spreadsheet would fit onto one page, the print font size for the entire spreadsheet would be so small that you could not read it without a magnifying glass, and (2) If you printed the spreadsheet without reducing the page size layout, it would "dribble over" part of the conclusion to a separate page all by itself, and your spreadsheet would not look professional.

Your research study accepted the claim that the TIME TO FILL a job acceptance for an approved requisition for staffing during the past 12 months was 35 days. (See Fig. 3.5)

Save your resulting spreadsheet as: **FILL3**

TIME TO FILL				
Question:	"How many days does it take between the delivery of an approved job requisition for staffing and the date on which an applicant accepts the job offer?"			
NO. OF DAYS				
34	n	20		
32				
31				
29	Mean	35.70		
36				
38				
37	STDEV	3.64		
34				
35				
31	s.e.	0.81		
30				
39				
42	95% confidence interval			
37				
36			Lower limit:	33.99
39				
38			Upper limit:	37.41
41				
38				
37	Draw a picture below this confidence interval			

```
33.99 ----------- --------35-- -----35.70- ------------ 37.41
lower                      ref.      Mean                 upper
limit                      value                          limit
```

Conclusion: Since the reference value of 35 days is inside the confidence interval, we accept that the TIME TO FILL a job acceptance for an approved requisition for staffing was 35 days last year.

Fig. 3.5 Final Spreadsheet for TIME TO FILL Confidence Interval About the Mean

3.2 Hypothesis Testing

One of the important activities of research scientists is that they attempt to "check" their assumptions about the world by testing these assumptions in the form of hypotheses.

A typical hypothesis is in the form: *"If x, then y."*

Some examples would be:

1. "If we use this new method of conducting this type of procedure in the laboratory, the cost of completing this procedure will decrease by 3 percent."

2. "If we change the way we are teaching the online course in the course that deals with Staffing in our program, then we will obtain a five percent increase in enrollment in this course."
3. "If we change the format for teaching Advanced Research Methods to our graduate students in our Master's program in Human Resource Development, then their final exam scores will increase by 8 percent."

A hypothesis, then, to a research scientist is an "estimate" about what we think is true in the real world. We can test these estimates using statistical formulas to see if our predictions come true in the real world.

So, in order to perform these statistical tests, we must first state our hypotheses so that we can test our results against our hypotheses to see if our hypotheses match reality.

So, how do we generate hypotheses in our research?

3.2.1 Hypotheses Always Refer to the Population That You Are Studying

The first step is to understand that our hypotheses always refer to the *population* of people or events in a study.

For example, suppose we are interested in studying the overall evaluation of our Master's students in the Human Resource Management program by conducting an in-depth interview with students 2 months before they are scheduled to graduate from the program. If we select a random sample of students to be interviewed, the selected students would be our sample. This sample would then be used to generalize our findings to the population of all students scheduled to graduate in 2 months from this program.

All of the students scheduled to graduate from this program in 2 months would be the *population* that we are interested in studying, while the specific students interviewed in our study would be called the *sample* from this population.

Since our sample sizes typically contain only a portion of the population we are interested in studying, we are interested in the results of our sample *only insofar as the results of our sample can be "generalized" to the population in which we are really interested.*

That is why our hypotheses always refer to the population, and never to the sample of people or events in our study.

You will recall from Chap. 1 that we used the symbol: $\overline{X}$ to refer to the mean of the sample we use in our research study (See Sect. 1.1).

We will use the symbol: μ (the Greek letter "mu") to refer to the *population mean.*

In testing our hypotheses, we are trying to decide which one of two competing hypotheses *about the population mean* we should accept given our data set.

3.2.2 The Null Hypothesis and the Research (Alternative) Hypothesis

These two competing hypotheses are called the *null hypothesis* and the *research hypothesis*.

Statistics textbooks typically refer to the *null hypothesis* with the notation: H_0.

The *research hypothesis* is typically referred to with the notation: H_1, and it is sometimes called the *alternative hypothesis*.

Let's explain first what is meant by the null hypothesis and the research hypothesis:

(1) *The null hypothesis is what we accept as true unless we have compelling evidence that it is not true.*
(2) *The research hypothesis is what we accept as true whenever we reject the null hypothesis as true.*

This is similar to our legal system in America where we assume that a supposed criminal is innocent until he or she is proven guilty in the eyes of a jury. Our null hypothesis is that this defendant is innocent, while the research hypothesis is that he or she is guilty.

In the great state of Missouri, every license plate has the state slogan: "Show me." This means that people in Missouri think of themselves as not gullible enough to accept everything that someone says as true unless that person's actions indicate the truth of his or her claim. In other words, people in Missouri believe strongly that a person's actions speak much louder than that person's words.

Since both the null hypothesis and the research hypothesis cannot both be true, the task of hypothesis testing using statistical formulas is to decide which one you will accept as true.

Sometimes in human resource management research studies, rating scales are used in surveys to measure people's attitudes toward an organization's activities. These rating scales are typically 5-point, 7-point, or 10-point scales, although other scale values are often used as well.

3.2.2.1 Determining the Null Hypothesis and the Research Hypothesis When Rating Scales Are Used

The following examples are a way to test the null hypothesis and research hypothesis using rating scales. They illustrate how you would test these hypotheses if you encountered rating scales on your job.

The Society for Human Resource Management (SHRM) claims to be the largest association devoted to human resource management and has more than 250,000 members in more than 140 countries who work in the HR profession in a variety of HR settings. SHRM has more than 575 local chapters in the USA alone. SHRM holds an Annual Conference and Exposition every year.

Here is a typical example of a 7-point scale that could be used by the SHRM to obtain feedback from participants on the value of its annual international conference to participants through an email survey sent to attendees after the conference has ended (see Fig. 3.6):

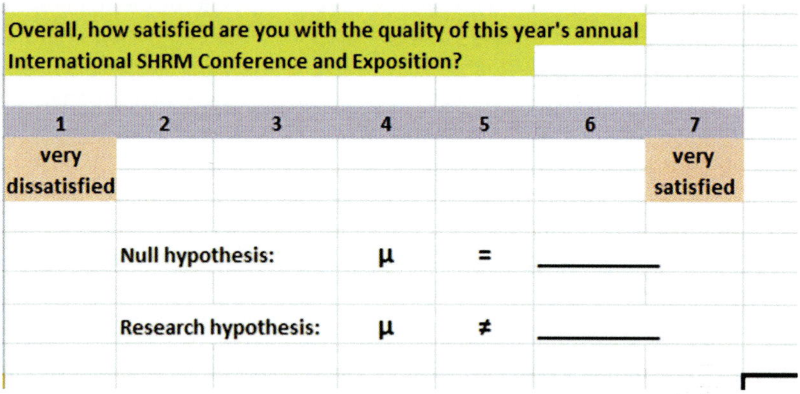

Fig. 3.6 Example of a Rating Scale Item for a SHRM Conference (Practical Example)

So, how do we decide what to use as the null hypothesis and the research hypothesis whenever rating scales are used?

Objective: To decide on the null hypothesis and the research hypothesis whenever rating scales are used.

In order to make this determination, we will use a simple rule:

Rule: Whenever rating scales are used, we will use the "middle" of the scale as the null hypothesis and the research hypothesis.

In the above example, since 4 is the number in the middle of the scale (i.e., three numbers are below it, and three numbers are above it), our hypotheses become:

Null hypothesis : $\mu = 4$

Research hypothesis : $\mu \neq 4$

In the above rating scale example, if the result of our statistical test for this one attitude scale item indicates that our population mean is "close to 4," we say that we accept the null hypothesis that the SHRM conference participants were neither satisfied nor dissatisfied with the overall quality of the conference.

In the above example, *if the result of our statistical test indicates that the population mean is significantly different from 4*, we reject the null hypothesis and accept the research hypothesis *by stating either that*:

"*SHRM conference participants were significantly satisfied with the overall quality of the conference*" (this is true whenever our sample mean is significantly greater than our expected population mean of 4).

or

"*SHRM conference participants were significantly dissatisfied with the overall quality of the conference*" (this is accepted as true whenever our sample mean is significantly less than our expected population mean of 4).

Both of these conclusions cannot be true. We accept one of the hypotheses as "true" based on the data set in our research study, and the other one as "not true" based on our data set.

The job of the researcher, then, is to decide which of these two hypotheses, the null hypothesis or the research hypothesis, he or she will accept as true given the data set in the research study.

Let's try some examples of rating scales so that you can practice figuring out what the null hypothesis and the research hypothesis are for each rating scale.

In the spaces in Fig. 3.7, write in the null hypothesis and the research hypothesis for the rating scales:

1. The M.A. program in Human Resources Management at Webster University is an excellent program.

1	2	3	4	5
Strongly Disagree				Strongly Agree

Null hypothesis: μ = _______

Research hypothesis: μ $\neq$ _______

2. How would you rate the quality of teaching in the M.A. in HRM core course in Compensation?

poor	1	2	3	4	5	6	7	excellent

Null hypothesis: μ = _______

Research hypothesis: μ $\neq$ _______

3. How would you rate the quality of the faculty in the M.A. in HRM program in terms of their teaching skill?

1	2	3	4	5	6	7	8	9	10
very poor									very good

Null hypothesis: μ = _______

Research hypothesis: μ $\neq$ _______

Fig. 3.7 Examples of Rating Scales for Determining the Null Hypothesis and the Research Hypothesis

How did you do?

Here are the answers to these three questions:

1. The null hypothesis is $\mu = 3$, and the research hypothesis is $\mu \neq 3$ on this 5-point scale (i.e. the "middle" of the scale is 3).
2. The null hypothesis is $\mu = 4$, and the research hypothesis is $\mu \neq 4$ on this 7-point scale (i.e., the "middle" of the scale is 4).
3. The null hypothesis is $\mu = 5.5$, and the research hypothesis is $\mu \neq 5.5$ on this 10-point scale (i.e., the "middle" of the scale is 5.5 since there are 5 numbers below 5.5 and 5 numbers above 5.5).

As another example, Webster University, whose main campus is in St. Louis, Missouri USA, uses a Course Feedback form for student evaluations at the end of all of its courses which are offered to more than 17,000 students in 60 cities and 11 countries. The Course Feedback form has 12 rating items referring to the course's planning and organization and the level of communication between the instructor and the students. The ratings are summarized and the results given to instructors after the course is completed. Each of the items is rated on the following 4-point scale:

1 = Very Effective
2 = Effective
3 = Ineffective
4 = Very Ineffective

On this scale, the null hypothesis is: $\mu = 2.5$ and the research hypothesis is: $\mu \neq 2.5$, because there are two numbers below 2.5, and two numbers above 2.5 on the rating scale. (Note that the scale is scored so that a low score, like a low score in golf, is a better score).

Now, let's discuss the 7 STEPS of hypothesis testing for using the confidence interval about the mean.

3.2.3 *The 7 Steps for Hypothesis-testing Using the Confidence Interval About the Mean*

Objective: To learn the 7 steps of hypothesis-testing using the confidence interval about the mean

There are seven basic steps of hypothesis-testing for this statistical test.

3.2.3.1 STEP 1: State the Null Hypothesis and the Research Hypothesis

If you are using numerical scales in your survey, you need to remember that the null and research hypotheses refer to the "middle" of the numerical scale. For example, if you are using 7-point scales with 1 = poor and 7 = excellent, these hypotheses would refer to the middle of these scales and would be:

Null hypothesis H_0 : $\mu = 4$

Research hypothesis H_1 : $\mu \neq 4$

3.2.3.2 STEP 2: Select the Appropriate Statistical Test

In this chapter we are studying the confidence interval about the mean, and so we will select that test.

3.2.3.3 STEP 3: Calculate the Formula for the Statistical Test

You will recall (see Sect. 3.1.5) that the formula for calculating the confidence interval about the mean is:

$$\overline{X} \pm t \text{ s.e.} \qquad (3.2)$$

We discussed the procedure for computing this formula for the confidence interval about the mean using Excel earlier in this chapter. The steps involved in using that formula are:

1. Use Excel's =COUNT function to find the sample size.
2. Use Excel's =AVERAGE function to find the sample mean, $\overline{X}$.
3. Use Excel's =STDEV function to find the standard deviation, STDEV.
4. Find the standard error of the mean (s.e.) by dividing the standard deviation (STDEV) by the square root of the sample size, n.
5. Use Excel's TINV function to find the lower limit of the confidence interval.
6. Use Excel's TINV function to find the upper limit of the confidence interval.

3.2.3.4 STEP 4: Draw a Picture of the Confidence Interval About the Mean, Including the Mean, the Lower Limit of the Interval, the Upper Limit of the Interval, and the Reference Value Given in the Null Hypothesis, H_0 (We Will Explain Step 4 Later in the Chapter.)

3.2.3.5 STEP 5: Decide on a Decision Rule

(a) *If the reference value is inside the confidence interval, accept the null hypothesis, H_0*
(b) *If the reference value is outside the confidence interval, reject the null hypothesis, H_0, and accept the research hypothesis, H_1*

3.2.3.6 STEP 6: State the Result of Your Statistical Test

There are two possible results when you use the confidence interval about the mean, and only one of them can be accepted as "true." So your result would be one of the following:

Either: Since the reference value is inside the confidence interval, *we accept the null hypothesis, H_0*

Or: Since the reference value is outside the confidence interval, *we reject the null hypothesis, H_0, and accept the research hypothesis, H_1*

3.2.3.7 STEP 7: State the Conclusion of Your Statistical Test in Plain English!

In practice, this is more difficult than it sounds because you are trying to summarize the result of your statistical test in simple English that is both concise and accurate so that someone who has never had a statistics course (such as your boss, perhaps) can understand the conclusion of your test. This is a difficult task, and we will give you lots of practice doing this last and most important step throughout this book.

Objective: To write the conclusion of the confidence interval about the mean test

Let's set some basic rules for stating the conclusion of a hypothesis test.

Rule #1: *Whenever you reject H_0 and accept H_1, you must use the word "significantly" in the conclusion to alert the reader that this test found an important result.*

Rule #2: *Create an outline in words of the "key terms" you want to include in your conclusion so that you do not forget to include some of them.*

Rule #3: *Write the conclusion in plain English so that the reader can understand it even if that reader has never taken a statistics course.*

Let's practice these rules using the TIME TO FILL Excel spreadsheet that you created earlier in this chapter (FILL3), but first we need to state the hypotheses.

If the organization wants to claim that the average TIME TO FILL for job applicants who accepted a job offer during the past 12 months with the organization was 35 days, the hypotheses would be:

$H_0: \quad \mu = 35 \text{ days}$

$H_1: \quad \mu \neq 35 \text{ days}$

You will remember that the reference value of 35 days was inside the 95 % confidence interval about the mean for your data, so we would accept H_0 that the average TIME TO FILL during the past 12 months was 35 days.

Objective: To state the result when you accept H_0

Result: Since the reference value of 35 days is inside the confidence interval, we accept the null hypothesis, H_0.

Let's try our three rules now:

Objective: To write the conclusion when you accept H_0

Rule #1: *Since the reference value was inside the confidence interval, we cannot use the word "significantly" in the conclusion. This is a basic rule we are using in this chapter for every problem.*

Rule #2: The key terms in the conclusion would be:

- TIME TO FILL
- a job acceptance for an approved requisition from staffing
- during the past 12 months
- average
- was 35 days

Rule #3: The average TIME TO FILL a job acceptance for an approved requisition from staffing during the past 12 months was 35 days.

The process of writing the conclusion when you accept H_0 is relatively straightforward since you put into words what you said when you wrote the null hypothesis.

However, the process of stating the conclusion when you reject H_0 and accept H_1 is more difficult, so let's practice writing that type of conclusion with three practice case examples:

Objective: To write the result and conclusion when you reject H_0

CASE #1: Suppose that your organization did a time and motion study several months ago of a specific laboratory procedure and determined that the average time required (to the nearest minute) to complete this procedure was 25 minutes. The hypotheses would be:

$H_0: \mu = 25$ minutes

$H_1: \mu \neq 25$ minutes

Suppose that your research yields the following confidence interval:

19	21	23	25
lower limit	Mean	upper limit	Ref. Value

Result: Since the reference value is outside the confidence interval, we reject the null hypothesis and accept the research hypothesis

The three rules for stating the conclusion would be:

Rule #1: We must include the word "significantly" since the reference value of 25 is outside the confidence interval.

Rule #2: The key terms would be:
- laboratory procedure
- average time needed to complete the procedure
- significantly
- either "more than" or "less than"
- and probably closer to

Rule #3: The average laboratory time needed to complete this procedure was significantly less than 25 minutes, and it was probably closer to 21 minutes (the sample mean).

Note that this conclusion says that the time needed to complete the procedure was less than 25 minutes because the sample mean was only 21 minutes. Note, also, that when you find a significant result by rejecting the null hypothesis, *it is not sufficient to say only: "significantly less than 25 minutes,"* because that does not tell the reader "how much less than 25 minutes" the sample mean was from 25 minutes. To make the conclusion clear, you need to add: "probably closer to 21 minutes" since the sample mean was only 21 minutes.

CASE #2: COST PER HIRE is an important budgeting statistic for organizations so that it can be managed before it becomes too high a cost for the organization to bear. If a financial officer wants to find out the cost per hire, the financial officer could select a random sample of new-hires during the past year and use it to estimate the true cost of hiring new workers. It is also important for the organization to determine the COST PER HIRE for both applicants hired from outside of the organization and applicants hired for a new job who were already working for the organization. For this example, let's focus on determining the INTERNAL COST PER HIRE that would include internal advertising costs, internal travel costs, internal referral bonuses paid, internal relocation costs, and the costs of an internal recruiter, as well as other costs specified by the organization. Let's suppose that the organization has budgeted that the average INTERNAL COST PER HIRE would be $4,000.00.

You want to practice your data interpretation skills on the hypothetical data which produces the confidence interval below:

The hypotheses for this test would be:

$$H_0: \mu = \$4,000$$

$$H_1: \mu \neq \$4,000$$

Essentially, the null hypothesis equal to $4,000 states that if the obtained average cost for this sample is not significantly different from $4,000, then it is reasonable to assume that the true cost of this hiring process is $4,000.

Suppose that your analysis produced the following confidence interval for this test:

$3,400	$3,600	$3,800	$4000
lower limit	Mean	upper limit	Ref. Value

Result: Since the reference value is outside the confidence interval, we reject the null hypothesis and accept the research hypothesis.

Rule #1: You must include the word "significantly" since the reference value is outside the confidence interval

Rule #2: The key terms would be:

- average INTERNAL COST PER HIRE
- applicants hired who were already working for the organization
- during the past year
- less than or greater than (depending on the confidence interval)
- significantly
- for a different job

– budgeted cost of $4,000 per hire
– and is probably closer to

Rule #3: The average INTERNAL COST PER HIRE during the past year for applicants hired for a different job who were already working for the organization was significantly less than the budgeted cost of $4,000, and was probably closer to $3,600.

Note that you need to use the word "less" since the sample mean of $3,600 was less than the reference value of $4,000.

CASE #3: The American Society for Training and Development (ASTD) is known for its extensive training and development programs through the year that are intended to help HR professionals improve their knowledge, skills, and credibility in the HR field. Let's suppose that ASTD wants to send a survey to a sample of its members, and one of the key questions on the survey asks members whether they agree or disagree that the professional relationships they have formed through ASTD have been important to their career paths. Members are asked to rate their opinion on a scale where Strongly Disagree is scored as 1, Disagree is scored as 2, Neutral is scored as 3, Agree is scored as 4, and Strongly Agree is scored as 5.

Suppose that you have been asked to use your Excel skills to determine the opinion of the sampled members.

The hypotheses would be:

$H_0: \quad \mu = 3$

$H_1: \quad \mu \neq 3$

Suppose that your research produced the following confidence interval for this survey item:

3	3.4	3.6	3.8
Ref. Value	lower limit	Mean	upper limit

Result: Since the reference value is outside the confidence interval, we reject the null hypothesis and accept the research hypothesis

The three rules for stating the conclusion would be:

Rule #1: You must include the word "significantly" since the reference value is outside the confidence interval

Rule #2: The key terms would be:

– members of ASTD sampled
– professional relationships

– through ASTD membership
– important to their career paths
– significantly
– agreed or disagreed

Rule #3: The sample of members of ASTD significantly agreed that the professional relationships they developed through ASTD membership have been important to their career paths

Important note: In this case, you should not use the phrase: "and was probably closer to 3.6" because words can be accurately used to summarize the conclusion without needing to refer to any numbers.

If you want a more detailed explanation of the confidence interval about the mean, see Zikmund and Babin (2010).

The three practice problems at the end of this chapter will give you additional practice in stating the conclusion of your result, and this book will include many more examples that will help you to write a clear and accurate conclusion to your research findings.

3.3 Alternative Ways to Summarize the Result of a Hypothesis Test

It is important for you to understand that in this book we are summarizing an hypothesis test in one of two ways: (1) We accept the null hypothesis, or (2) We reject the null hypothesis and accept the research hypothesis. We are consistent in the use of these words so that you can understand the concept underlying hypothesis testing.

However, there are many other ways to summarize the result of an hypothesis test, and all of them are correct theoretically, even though the terminology differs. If you are taking a course with a professor who wants you to summarize the results of a statistical test of hypotheses in language which is different from the language we are using in this book, do not panic! If you understand the concept of hypothesis testing as described in this book, you can then translate your understanding to use the terms that your professor wants you to use to reach the same conclusion.

Statisticians and professors of human resource management statistics all have their own language that they like to use to summarize the results of an hypothesis test. There is no one set of words that these statisticians and professors will ever agree on, and so we have chosen the one that we believe to be easier to understand in terms of the concept of hypothesis testing.

To convince you that there are many ways to summarize the results of a hypothesis test, we present the following quotes from prominent statistics and research books to give you an idea of the different ways that are possible.

3.3.1 Different Ways to Accept the Null Hypothesis

The following quotes are typical of the language used in statistics and research books *when the null hypothesis is accepted*:

"The null hypothesis is not rejected." (Black 2010, p. 310)
"The null hypothesis cannot be rejected." (McDaniel and Gates 2010, p. 545)
"The null hypothesis . . . claims that there is no difference between groups." (Salkind 2010, p. 193)
"The difference is not statistically significant." (McDaniel and Gates 2010, p. 545)
". . . the obtained value is not extreme enough for us to say that the difference between Groups 1 and 2 occurred by anything other than chance." (Salkind 2010, p. 225)
"If we do not reject the null hypothesis, we conclude that there is not enough statistical evidence to infer that the alternative (hypothesis) is true." (Keller 2009, p. 358)
"The research hypothesis is not supported." (Zikmund and Babin 2010, p. 552)

3.3.2 Different Ways to Reject the Null Hypothesis

The following quotes are typical of the quotes used in statistics and research books *when the null hypothesis is rejected*:

"The null hypothesis is rejected." (McDaniel and Gates 2010, p. 546)
"If we reject the null hypothesis, we conclude that there is enough statistical evidence to infer that the alternative hypothesis is true." (Keller 2009, p. 358)
"If the test statistic's value is inconsistent with the null hypothesis, we reject the null hypothesis and infer that the alternative hypothesis is true." (Keller 2009, p. 348)
"Because the observed value . . . is greater than the critical value . . ., the decision is to reject the null hypothesis." (Black 2010, p. 359)
"If the obtained value is more extreme than the critical value, the null hypothesis cannot be accepted." (Salkind 2010, p. 243)
"The critical t-value . . . must be surpassed by the observed t-value if the hypothesis test is to be statistically significant . . .." (Zikmund and Babin 2010, p. 567)
"The calculated test statistic . . . exceeds the upper boundary and falls into this rejection region. The null hypothesis is rejected." (Weiers 2011, p. 330)

You should note that all of the above quotes are used by statisticians and professors when discussing the results of a hypothesis test, and so you should not be surprised if someone asks you to summarize the results of a statistical test using different language than we are using in this book.

3.4 End-of-Chapter Practice Problems

1. Suppose that you work for an organization and that top management wants to know the average COST PER INTERVIEW for prospective job candidates that are invited to interview at the organization. You have been asked to take a

random sample of job candidates who came to the organization to be interviewed during the past quarter (i.e., 90 days). Suppose, further, that your organization has budgeted the COST PER INTERVIEW to be $120.00 per interview. You decide to test your Excel skills on a small number of applicants, and the hypothetical data appear in Fig. 3.8:

COST PER INTERVIEW

Question: "Does our COST PER INTERVIEW for prospective job candidates come close to the $120.00 per interview that we budgeted?

COST PER INTERVIEW ($)
127
128
135
118
110
129
127
134
142
135
129
128
117
128
135
131
134
132
119
125
126
134

Fig. 3.8 Worksheet Data for Chap. 3: Practice Problem #1

(a) To the right of this table, use Excel to find the sample size, mean, standard deviation, and standard error of the mean for the cost figures. Label your answers. Use currency format (two decimal places) for the mean, standard deviation, and standard error of the mean.
(b) Enter the null hypothesis and the research hypothesis onto your spreadsheet.
(c) Use Excel's TINV function to find the 95 % confidence interval about the mean for these figures. Label your answers. Use currency format (two decimal places).
(d) Enter your *result* onto your spreadsheet.
(e) Enter your *conclusion in plain English* onto your spreadsheet.
(f) Print the final spreadsheet to fit onto one page (if you need help remembering how to do this, see the objectives at the end of Chap. 2 in Sect. 2.4)
(g) On your printout, draw a diagram of this 95 % confidence interval by hand
(h) Save the file as: INTERVIEW3

2. COST PER HIRE is an important budgeting statistic for organizations so that it can be managed before it becomes too high a cost for the organization to bear. If a financial officer wants to find out the cost per hire, the financial officer could select a random sample of new-hires during the past year and use it to estimate the true cost of hiring new workers. It is also important for the organization to determine the COST PER HIRE for both applicants hired from outside of the organization, and applicants hired for a new job who were already working for the organization. For this example, let's focus on determining the COST PER EXTERNAL HIRE that would include external advertising costs, external travel costs, external referral bonuses paid, external relocation costs, external recruiter costs, as well as other costs specified by the organization. Let's suppose that the organization has budgeted that the average COST PER EXTERNAL HIRE would be \$6,500.00. Let's suppose that you have taken a small random sample of external hires to test your Excel skills, and that you want to analyze the hypothetical data in Fig. 3.9.

COST PER EXTERNAL HIRE

Question: "Does our COST PER EXTERNAL HIRE for prospective job candidates come close to the $6500.00 per external hire that we budgeted?

COST PER EXTERNAL HIRE ($)
6800
7100
7050
6855
6480
6610
6725
6250
6130
6050
6200
6350
6475
6250
6175
6325
6260
6410
6530
6675
6750
6450
6870
6420
6150
6275

Fig. 3.9 Worksheet Data for Chap. 3: Practice Problem #2

Create an Excel spreadsheet with these data.

(a) Use Excel to the right of the table to find the sample size, mean, standard deviation, and standard error of the mean for these data. Label your answers, and use currency format (zero decimal places) for the mean, standard deviation, and standard error of the mean

(b) Enter the null hypothesis and the research hypothesis for these data on your spreadsheet.

(c) Use Excel's TINV function to find the 95 % confidence interval about the mean for these data. Label your answers on your spreadsheet. Use currency format (zero decimal places) for the lower limit and the upper limit of the confidence interval.

(d) Enter the *result* of the test on your spreadsheet.
(e) Enter the *conclusion* of the test in plain English on your spreadsheet.
(f) Print your final spreadsheet so that it fits onto one page (if you need help remembering how to do this, see the objectives at the end of Chap. 2 in Sect. 2.4).
(g) Draw a picture of the confidence interval, including the reference value, onto your spreadsheet.
(h) Save the final spreadsheet as: EXTERNAL3

3. Webster University (headquartered in St. Louis, Missouri, USA) offers a Master's program in Human Resource Management. You have been asked to develop a mail survey that can be sent to students in this M.A. program one month before they are scheduled to graduate from the program to obtain feedback about the quality of the program from its graduate students. You are in the early stages of developing this survey, but a key item that you want to ask deals with the students' overall attitude toward the quality of this degree program. You want to test your Excel skills on this type of survey, and so you want to analyze the hypothetical data for Item #23 that are given in Fig. 3.10:

Webster University

End of M.A. Program in Human Resource Management Exit Survey

Item #23: "Overall, how would you rate the quality of the M.A. Program in Human Resource Management?"

1	2	3	4	5	6	7
Poor						Excellent

RATING
3
6
5
7
4
5
6
4
6
7
5
7
4
7
7
6
6
6
5
4
6
7

Fig. 3.10 Worksheet Data for Chap. 3: Practice Problem #3

Create an Excel spreadsheet with these data.

(a) Use Excel to the right of the table to find the sample size, mean, standard deviation, and standard error of the mean for these data. Label your answers, and use two decimal places for the mean, standard deviation, and standard error of the mean

(b) Enter the null hypothesis and the research hypothesis for this item onto your spreadsheet.

(c) Use Excel's TINV function to find the 95 % confidence interval about the mean for these data. Label your answers on your spreadsheet. Use two decimal places for the lower limit and the upper limit of the confidence interval.

(d) Enter the *result* of the test on your spreadsheet.

(e) Enter the *conclusion* of the test in plain English on your spreadsheet.

(f) Print your final spreadsheet so that it fits onto one page (if you need help remembering how to do this, see the objectives at the end of Chap. 2 in Sect. 2.4).

(g) Draw a picture of the confidence interval, including the reference value, onto your spreadsheet.

(h) Save the final spreadsheet as: HRM4

References

Black K. Business statistics: for contemporary decision making. 6th ed. Hoboken: John Wiley& Sons, Inc.; 2010.

Firz-enz J, Davison B. How to measure human resources management. 3rd ed. New York: McGraw-Hill; 2002.

Keller G. Statistics for management and economics. 8th ed. Mason: South-Western Cengage Learning; 2009.

McDaniel C, Gates R. Marketing research. 8th ed. Hoboken: John Wiley & Sons, Inc.; 2010.

Salkind N. Statistics for people who (think they) hate statistics. 2nd Excel 2007 ed. Los Angeles: Sage Publications; 2010.

Weiers R. Introduction to business statistics. 7th ed. Mason: South-Western Cengage Learning; 2011.

Zikmund W, Babin B. Exploring marketing research. 10th ed. Mason: South-Western Cengage Learning; 2010.

Chapter 4
One-Group t-Test for the Mean

In this chapter, you will learn how to use one of the most popular and most helpful statistical tests in human resource management research: the one-group t-test for the mean. One-group t-tests are used to determine whether there is a significant difference between a sample mean and a population mean.

The formula for the one-group t-test is as follows:

$$t = \frac{\overline{X} - \mu}{S_{\overline{X}}} \text{ where} \tag{4.1}$$

$$\text{s.e.} = S_{\overline{X}} = \frac{S}{\sqrt{n}} \tag{4.2}$$

This formula asks you to take the sample mean ($\overline{X}$) and subtract the population mean (μ) from it, and then divide the answer by the standard error of the sample mean (s.e.). The standard error of the sample mean equals the standard deviation divided by the square root of n (the sample size). If you want to learn more about this test, see Zikmund and Babin (2010).

Let's discuss the 7 STEPS of hypothesis testing using the one-group t-test so that you can understand how this test is used.

4.1 The 7 STEPS for Hypothesis-Testing Using the One-Group t-Test

Objective: To learn the 7 steps of hypothesis-testing using the one-group t-test

T.J. Quirk, J. Palmer-Schuyler, *Excel 2016 for Human Resource Management Statistics*, Excel for Statistics, DOI 10.1007/978-3-319-40063-1_4

Before you can try out your Excel skills on the one-group t-test, you need to learn the basic steps of hypothesis-testing for this statistical test. There are 7 steps in this process:

4.1.1 STEP 1: State the Null Hypothesis and the Research Hypothesis

Recall from Sect. 3.2.2 that the null hypothesis is what we accept as true unless we have compelling evidence that it is not true, which is generally a hypothesis of no difference between the sample mean and the population mean. The research hypothesis, on the other hand, is the alternative hypothesis, i.e., a hypothesized difference between the sample mean and the population mean.

If you are using numerical scales in your survey, you need to remember that these hypotheses refer to the "middle" of the numerical scale. For example, if you are using 7-point scales with 1 = poor and 7 = excellent, these hypotheses would refer to the middle of these scales and would be:

Null hypothesis H_0 : $\mu = 4$
Research hypothesis H_1 : $\mu \neq 4$

As a second example, suppose that you wanted to know if the current time expected to complete a specific laboratory procedure was still 45 minutes, the time determined by a time and motion study conducted 6 months ago. The hypotheses for testing this claim on actual data would be:

H_0 : $\mu = 45$ min.

H_1 : $\mu \neq 45$ min.

4.1.2 STEP 2: Select the Appropriate Statistical Test

In this chapter we will be studying the one-group t-test, and so we will select that test.

4.1.3 STEP 3: Decide on a Decision Rule for the One-Group t-Test

(a) If the absolute value of t is less than the critical value of t, accept the null hypothesis.

(b) If the absolute value of t is greater than the critical value of t, reject the null hypothesis and accept the research hypothesis.

You are probably saying to yourself: "That sounds fine, but how do I find the absolute value of t?"

4.1.3.1 Finding the Absolute Value of a Number

To do that, we need another objective:

Objective: To find the absolute value of a number

If you took a basic algebra course in high school, you may remember the concept of "absolute value." In mathematical terms, the absolute value of any number is *always* that number expressed as a positive number.

For example, the absolute value of 2.35 is +2.35.

And the absolute value of minus 2.35 (i.e. −2.35) is also +2.35.

This becomes important when you are using the t-table in Appendix E of this book. We will discuss this table later when we get to Step 5 of the one-group t-test where we explain how to find the critical value of t using Appendix E.

4.1.4 STEP 4: Calculate the Formula for the One-Group t-Test

Objective: To learn how to use the formula for the one-group t-test

The formula for the one-group t-test is as follows:

$$t = \frac{\overline{X} - \mu}{S_{\overline{X}}} \quad \text{where} \tag{4.1}$$

$$\text{s.e.} = S_{\overline{X}} = \frac{S}{\sqrt{n}} \tag{4.2}$$

This formula makes the following assumptions about the data (Foster et al. 1998): (1) The data are independent of each other (i.e., each person or event receives only one score), (2) the *population* of the data is normally distributed, and (3) the data have a constant variance (note that the standard deviation is the square root of the variance).

To use this formula, you need to follow these steps:

1. Take the sample mean in your research study and subtract the population mean μ from it (remember that the population mean for a study involving numerical rating scales is the "middle" number in the scale).
2. Then take your answer from the above step, and divide it by the standard error of the mean for your research study (remember that you learned how to find the standard error of the mean in Chap. 1; to find the standard error of the mean, just take the standard deviation of your research study and divide it by the square root of n, where n is the number of people or events in your research study).
3. The number you get after you complete the above step is the value for t that results when you use the formula stated above.

4.1.5 STEP 5: Find the Critical Value of t in the t-Table in Appendix E

Objective: To find the critical value of t in the t-table in Appendix E

Before we get into an explanation of what is meant by "the critical value of t," let's give you practice finding the critical value of t by using the t-table in Appendix E.

Keep your finger on Appendix E as we explain how you need to "read" that table.

Since the test in this chapter is called the "one-group t-test," you will use the first column on the left in Appendix E to find the critical value of t for your research study (note that this column is headed: "sample size n").

To find the critical value of t, you go down this first column until you find the sample size in your research study, and then you go to the right and read the critical value of t for that sample size in the critical t column in the table (note that *this is the column that you would use for both the one-group t-test and the 95 % confidence interval about the mean*).

For example, if you have 27 people in your research study, the critical value of t is 2.056.

If you have 38 people in your research study, the critical value of t is 2.026.

If you have more than 40 people in your research study, the critical value of t is always 1.96.

Note that the "critical t column" in Appendix E represents the value of t that you need to obtain to be 95 % confident that your results are "significant" results.

The critical value of t is the value that tells you whether or not you have found a "significant result" in your statistical test.

The t-table in Appendix E represents a series of "bell-shaped normal curves" (they are called bell-shaped because they look like the outline of the Liberty Bell that you can see in Philadelphia outside of Independence Hall).

The "middle" of these normal curves is treated as if it were zero point on the x-axis (the technical explanation of this fact is beyond the scope of this book, but any good statistics book (e.g. Zikmund and Babin 2010) will explain this concept to you if you are interested in learning more about it).

Thus, values of t that are to the right of this zero point are positive values that use a plus sign before them, and values of t that are to the left of this zero point are negative values that use a minus sign before them. Thus, some values of t are positive, and some are negative.

However, every statistics book that includes a t-table only reprints the *positive* side of the t-curves because the negative side is the mirror image of the positive side; this means that the negative side contains the exact same numbers as the positive side, but the negative numbers all have a minus sign in front of them.

Therefore, to use the t-table in Appendix E, you need to *take the absolute value of the t-value you found when you use the t-test formula* since the t-table in Appendix E only has the positive values for t.

Throughout this book, we assume that you want to be 95 % confident in the results of your statistical tests. Therefore, the value for t in the t-table in Appendix E tells you whether or not the t-value you obtained when you used the formula for the one-group t-test is within the 95 % interval of the t-curve range.

If the t-value you obtained when you used the formula for the one-group t-test is *inside* of the 95 % confidence range, we say that the result you found is *not significant* (note that this is equivalent to *accepting the null hypothesis!).*

If the t-value you found when you used the formula for the one-group t-test is *outside* of this 95 % confidence range, we say that you have found a *significant result* that would be expected to occur less than 5 % of the time (note that this is equivalent to *rejecting the null hypothesis and accepting the research hypothesis*).

4.1.6 STEP 6: State the Result of Your Statistical Test

There are two possible results when you use the one-group t-test, and only one of them can be accepted as "true."

Either: Since the absolute value of t that you found in the t-test formula is *less than the critical value of t* in Appendix E, you accept the null hypothesis.

Or: Since the absolute value of t that you found in the t-test formula is *greater than the critical value of t* in Appendix E, you reject the null hypothesis, and accept the research hypothesis.

4.1.7 STEP 7: State the Conclusion of Your Statistical Test in Plain English!

In practice, this is more difficult than it sounds because you are trying to summarize the result of your statistical test in simple English that is both concise and accurate so that someone who has never had a statistics course (such as your boss, perhaps) can understand the result of your test. This is a difficult task, and we will give you lots of practice doing this last and most important step throughout this book.

If you have read this far, you are ready to sit down at your computer and perform the one-group t-test using Excel on some hypothetical data.

Let's give this a try.

4.2 One-Group t-Test for the Mean

The Society for Human Resource Management (SHRM) is an international professional society of more than 250,000 HR professionals who work in a variety of organizations in more than 140 countries. SHRM is proud of its HR Jobs activities that are provided on its website. One of its most important career development activities is the posting of possible HR job-openings on its website so that its members can be made aware of job-openings in the HR profession. Both members and non-members can register and post their resumes on the website. Employers can post job openings at their organizations and search the HR Jobs website for potential candidates for their job openings. Job seekers can also find helpful articles on the job search process and watch videos on the website for HR job-related information. Suppose that SHRM has been asking its members who access its website to rate the helpfulness of its HR Jobs section in notifying members of job-openings in the HR profession, and that you have been asked to analyze the data from this survey. The data are based on members who visited the website and who used the HR Jobs section of the website as part of their website search process. Suppose that Item #7 on the survey asked visitors to rate the helpfulness of the job-openings feature on a 10-point scale where 1 = poor and 10 = excellent.

The survey contains a number of items, but suppose a hypothetical Item #7 is the one in Fig. 4.1:

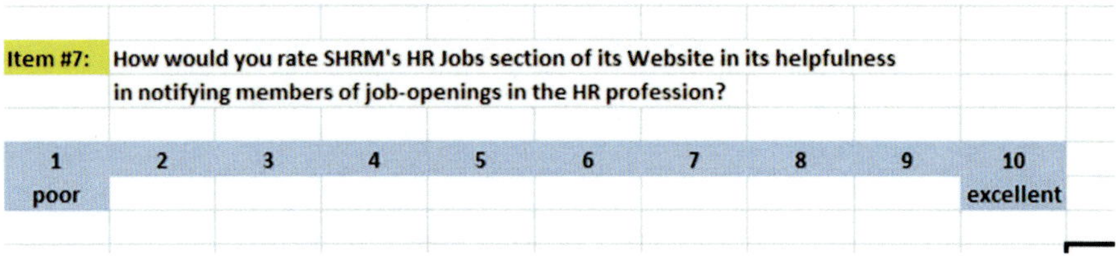

Fig. 4.1 Sample Survey Item for Item #7 of the SHRM Survey (Practical Example)

Suppose further, that you have decided to analyze the data from members using a one-group t-test.

Important note: You would need to use this test for each of the survey items separately.

Suppose that the hypothetical data for Item #7 of the SHRM Website survey were based on a sample size of 124 members who had a mean score on this item of 6.58 and a standard deviation on this item of 2.44.

Objective: To analyze the data for each question separately using a one-group t-test for each survey item.

Create an Excel spreadsheet with the following information:

B11: Null hypothesis:
B14: Research hypothesis:

Note: Remember that when you are using a rating scale item, both the null hypothesis and the research hypothesis refer to the "middle of the scale." For the 10-point scale in this example, the middle of the scale is 5.5 since five numbers are below 5.5 (i.e., 1–5) and five numbers are above 5.5 (i.e. 6–10). Therefore, the hypotheses for this rating scale item are:

$H_0: \mu = 5.5$
$H_1: \mu \neq 5.5$

B17: n
B20: mean
B23: STDEV

B26: s.e.
B29: critical t
B32: t-test
B36: Result:
B41: Conclusion:

Now, use Excel:

D17: enter the sample size
D20: enter the mean
D23: enter the STDEV (see Fig. 4.2)

Fig. 4.2 Basic Data Table for Item #7 of the SHRM Survey

Null hypothesis:	
Research hypothesis:	
n	**124**
mean	**6.58**
STDEV	**2.44**
s.e.	
critical t	
t-test	
Result:	
Conclusion:	

D26 compute the standard error using the formula in Chap. 1
D29: find the critical t value of t in the t-table in Appendix E

Now, enter the following formula in cell D32 to find the t-test result:

= (D20 – 5.5)/D26 (no spaces between symbols)

In Excel, this formula takes the sample mean (D20) and subtracts the population hypothesized mean of 5.5 from the sample mean, and THEN divides the answer by the standard error of the mean (D26). Note that you need to enter D20 – 5.5 with an open-parenthesis *before* D20 and a closed-parenthesis *after* 5.5 so that the *answer of 1.08 is THEN divided by the standard error of 0.22* to get the t-test result of 4.93 when you the Excel commands. (Remember: Excel computes all computations to 16 decimal places, so that when you use your calculator, your result will be 4.91 instead of 4.93; Excel is more accurate than your calculator).

Now, use two decimal places for both the s.e. and the t-test result (see Fig. 4.3).

Null hypothesis:		
Research hypothesis:		
n		124
mean		6.58
STDEV		2.44
s.e.		0.22
critical t		1.96
t-test		4.93
Result:		
Conclusion:		

Fig. 4.3 t-Test Formula Result for Item #7 of the SHRM Survey

Now, write the following sentence in D36:D39 to summarize the result of the t-test:

D36: Since the absolute value of t of 4.93 is
D37: greater than the critical t of 1.96, we
D38: reject the null hypothesis and accept
D39: the research hypothesis.

Lastly, write the following sentence in D41:D44 to summarize the conclusion of the result for Item #7 of the SHRM Survey:

D41: Members rated the HR Jobs section of the
D42: SHRM Website in its helpfulness in notifying
D43: members of job-openings in the HR profession
D44: as significantly positive.

Save your file as: SHRM5

Important note: We have used the term "significantly positive" because the mean rating of 6.58 is on the positive side of the rating scale. We purposely have not used the term "significantly excellent" because people who speak English do not use that term because something is either excellent or it is not excellent. Therefore, "significantly positive" is a more correct use of the English language in this type of rating scale item.

Important note: You are probably wondering why we entered both the result and the conclusion in separate cells instead of in just one cell. This is because if you enter them in one cell, you will be very disappointed when you print out your final spreadsheet, because one of two things will happen that you will not like: (1) if you print the spreadsheet to fit onto only one page, the result and the conclusion will force the entire spreadsheet to be printed in such small font size that you will be unable to read it, or (2) if you do not print the final spreadsheet to fit onto one page, both the result and the conclusion will "dribble over" onto a second page instead of fitting the entire spread-sheet onto one page. In either case, your spread-sheet will not have a "professional look."

Print the final spreadsheet so that it fits onto one page as given in Fig. 4.4. Enter the null hypothesis and the research hypothesis by hand on your spreadsheet

Null hypothesis:	μ	=	5.5
Research hypothesis:	μ	≠	5.5
n	124		
mean	6.58		
STDEV	2.44		
s.e.	0.22		
critical t	1.96		
t-test	4.93		
Result:	Since the absolute value of t of 4.93 is greater than the critical t of 1.96, we reject the null hypothesis and accept the research hypothesis.		
Conclusion:	Members rated the HR Jobs section of the SHRM Website in its helpfulness in notifying members of job-openings in the HR profession as significantly positive.		

Fig. 4.4 Final Spreadsheet for Item #7 of the SHRM Survey

Important note: It is important for you to understand that "technically" the above conclusion in statistical terms should state:

"Members rated the HR Jobs section of the SHRM Website in its helpfulness in notifying members of job-openings in the HR profession as positive, and this result was probably not obtained by chance."

However, throughout this book, we are using the term "significantly" in writing the conclusion of statistical tests to alert the reader that the result of the statistical test was probably not a chance finding, but instead of writing all of those words each time, we use the word "significantly" as a shorthand to the longer explanation. This makes it much easier for the reader to understand the conclusion when it is written "in plain English," instead of technical, statistical language.

4.3 Can You Use Either the 95 % Confidence Interval About the Mean OR the One-Group t-Test When Testing Hypotheses?

You are probably asking yourself:

"It sounds like you could use *either* the 95 % confidence interval about the mean *or* the one-group t-test to analyze the results of the types of problems described so far in this book? Is this a correct statement?"

The answer is a resounding: *"Yes!"*

Both the confidence interval about the mean and the one-group t-test are often used in human resource management research on the types of problems described so far in this book. *Both of these tests produce the same result and the same conclusion from the same data set!*

Both of these tests are explained in this book because some researchers prefer the confidence interval about the mean test, others prefer the one-group t-test, and still others prefer to use both tests on the same data to make their results and conclusions clearer to the reader of their research reports. Since we do not know which of these tests your researcher prefers, we have explained both of them so that you are competent in the use of both tests in the analysis of statistical data.

Now, let's try your Excel skills on the one-group t-test on the three problems at the end of this chapter.

4.4 End-of-Chapter Practice Problems

1. Employee "turnover" is a problem for every organization. Each time an employee leaves the employment of an organization, that employee's knowledge and experience are no longer available to the organization. Employees leave an organization for a variety of reasons: retirement, layoffs, termination for poor performance, failing to report to work for three days without calling in, resignations, death, disability, disciplinary reasons, to obtain a higher salary or find a more interesting and challenging job, to be closer to home, and so forth.
   The Bureau of National Affairs (BNA) defines turnover as the percent figure that results from dividing the number of permanent separations from the company for the time period by the average number of employees on the payroll for the time period in question. (For more information about BNA, especially for the difference between voluntary and involuntary turnover, see Phillips and Phillips 2005).

Suppose that you work for a large telemarketing company that has 23 Call Centers in different cities and that you want to determine the average turnover rate for these Call Centers during the past year. You decide to select randomly one city for each month, to compute the turnover rate for that city for that month, and to repeat this procedure for each of the past 12 months. Suppose, further, that the turnover rate for these Call Centers 2 years ago was 25 %, and that your company had set a turnover goal for these Call Centers for the year just ended to be 20 %. You complete this data gathering exercise, and you want to find the average turnover rate for these Call Centers for the year just ended using the hypothetical data given in Fig. 4.5.

Fig. 4.5 Worksheet Data for Chap. 4: Practice Problem #1

TURNOVER RATE FOR THE CALL CENTERS

MONTH	TURNOVER (%)
JAN	22
FEB	24
MAR	20
APR	19
MAY	18
JUN	24
JUL	23
AUG	25
SEP	21
OCT	20
NOV	19
DEC	18

(a) Write the null hypothesis and the research hypothesis on your spreadsheet
(b) Use Excel to find the sample size, mean, standard deviation, and standard error of the mean to the right of the data set. Use number format (two decimal places) for the mean, standard deviation, and standard error of the mean.
(c) Enter the critical t from the t-table in Appendix E onto your spreadsheet, and label it.
(d) Use Excel to compute the t-value for these data (use two decimal places) and label it on your spreadsheet
(e) Type the result on your spreadsheet, and then type the conclusion in plain English on your spreadsheet
(f) Save the file as: CALL3

2. Suppose your company has just completed a Webinar training program on Health and Safety issues for its managers, and that you have been asked to

develop a satisfaction survey and to analyze the data that would be collected by an email survey of participants after the Webinar has been completed. You are in the early stages of developing this survey, but you are sure that you want to include an item asking participants for their overall evaluation of the quality of the HR Webinar Training Program dealing with Health and Safety Issues, and that you want to practice your Excel skills on the hypothetical data are presented in Fig. 4.6:

HR WEBINAR TRAINING PROGRAM ON HEALTH AND SAFETY ISSUES

Item #10: ""Overall, how would you rate the quality of the HR Webinar Training Program dealing with Health and Saftey issues?"

1	2	3	4	5	6	7
very poor						very good

DATA
3
4
5
2
4
3
5
6
7
4
3
5
4
3
3
5
4
6
2
3

Fig. 4.6 Worksheet Data for Chap. 4: Practice Problem #2

(a) *On your Excel spreadsheet*, write the null hypothesis and the research hypothesis for these data.
(b) Use Excel to find the sample size, mean, standard deviation, and standard error of the mean for these data (two decimal places for the mean, standard deviation, and standard error of the mean).
(c) Use Excel to perform a one-group t-test on these data (two decimal places).
(d) On your printout, type the critical value of t given in your t-table in Appendix E.
(e) On your spreadsheet, type the result of the t-test.
(f) On your spreadsheet, type the conclusion of your study in plain English.
(g) save the file as: SAFETY3

3. Suppose that the HR department of your organization completed a training program a year ago that was intended to reduce the number of sexual harassment complaints received from employees. Suppose, further, that the HR department received an average of 25 complaints per month of sexual harassment from employees 2 years ago in the 12 months prior to this training program, and that you want to determine if the number of complaints has been reduced for the year just ended. You have collected data on each of the previous 12 months for this research question, and you want to practice your data interpretation skills on the hypothetical data which appear in Fig. 4.7.

Fig. 4.7 Worksheet Data for Chap. 4: Practice problem #3

SEXUAL HARASSMENT COMPLAINTS

MONTH	NO. OF COMPLAINTS
JAN	22
FEB	24
MAR	21
APR	18
MAY	16
JUN	26
JUL	27
AUG	22
SEP	24
OCT	19
NOV	21
DEC	24

(a) Write the null hypothesis and the research hypothesis on your spreadsheet
(b) Use Excel to find the sample size, mean, standard deviation, and standard error of the mean to the right of the data set. Use number format (two decimal places) for the mean, standard deviation, and standard error of the mean.

(c) (c) Enter the critical t from the t-table in Appendix E onto your spreadsheet, and label it.
(d) Use Excel to compute the t-value for these data (use two decimal places) and label it on your spreadsheet
(e) Type the result on your spreadsheet, and then type the conclusion in plain English on your spreadsheet
(f) Save the file as: COMPLAINTS3

References

Foster D, Stine R, Waterman R. Basic business statistics: a casebook. New York: Springer-Verlag; 1998.

Phillips J J, Phillips P P. Proving the value of HR: how and why to measure ROI. Alexandria: Society forHuman Resource Management; 2005.

Zikmund W, Babin B. Exploring marketing research. 10th ed. Mason: South-Western Cengage Learning; 2010.

Chapter 5
Two-Group t-Test of the Difference of the Means for Independent Groups

Up until now in this book, you have been dealing with the situation in which you have had only one group of people or events in your research study and only one measurement "number" on each of these people or events. We will now change gears and deal with the situation in which you are measuring two groups instead of only one group.

Whenever you have two completely different groups of people or events (i.e., no one person or event is in both groups, but every person or event is measured on only one variable to produce one "number" for each person or event), we say that the two groups are "independent of one another." This chapter deals with just that situation and that is why it is called the two-group t-test for independent groups.

Two assumptions underly the two-group t-test (Wheater and Cook 2000): (1) both groups are sampled from a normal population, and (2) the variances of the two populations are approximately equal. Note that the standard deviation is merely the square root of the variance. (There are different formulas to use when each person or event is measured twice to create two groups of data, and this situation is called "dependent," but those formulas are beyond the scope of this book.) This book only deals with two groups that are independent of one another so that no person or event is in both groups of data.

When you test for the difference between the means for two groups, it is important to remember that there are two different formulas that you need to use depending on the sample sizes of the two groups:

(1) Use Formula #1 in this chapter when both of the groups have a sample size greater than 30, and
(2) Use Formula #2 in this chapter when either one group, or both groups, have a sample size less than 30.

We will illustrate both of these situations in this chapter.

But, first, we need to understand the steps involved in hypothesis-testing when two groups are involved before we dive into the formulas for these tests.

T.J. Quirk, J. Palmer-Schuyler, *Excel 2016 for Human Resource Management Statistics*, Excel for Statistics, DOI 10.1007/978-3-319-40063-1_5

5.1 The 9 STEPS for Hypothesis-Testing Using the Two-Group t-Test

Objective: To learn the 9 steps of hypothesis-testing using two groups of people or events and the two-group t-test

You will see that these steps parallel the steps used in the previous chapter that dealt with the one-group t-test, but there are some important differences between the steps that you need to understand clearly before we dive into the formulas for the two-group t-test.

5.1.1 STEP 1: Name One Group, Group 1, and the Other Group, Group 2

The formulas used in this chapter will use the numbers 1 and 2 to distinguish between the two groups. If you define which group is Group 1 and which group is Group 2, you can use these numbers in your computations without having to write out the names of the groups.

For example, if you were testing entering college freshmen who said they wanted to major in human resources to see if there were gender differences in their SAT-Math scores as high school seniors, you could call the groups: "Freshmen Males" and "Freshmen Females," but this would require you to write out the words "Freshmen Males" and "Freshmen Females" whenever you wanted to refer to one of these groups. If you call the "Freshmen Males" group, Group 1, and the "Freshmen Females" group, Group 2, this makes it much easier to refer to the groups because it saves writing time.

Note, also, that it is completely arbitrary which group you name Group 1, and which Group you name Group 2. You will achieve the same result and the same conclusion from the formulas however you decide to define these two groups.

5.1.2 STEP 2: Create a Table That Summarizes the Sample Size, Mean Score, and Standard Deviation of Each Group

This step makes it easier for you to make sure that you are using the correct numbers in the formulas for the two-group t-test. If you get the numbers "mixed-up," your entire formula work will be incorrect and you will botch the problem terribly.

For example, suppose that you collected data on entering freshmen who said that they planned to major in human resources and found that the Freshmen Males group had 57 men in it and their SAT-Math scores averaged 610 with a standard deviation of 120, while the Freshmen Females group had 46 females in it and their SAT-Math scores averaged 640 with a standard deviation of 110.

The formulas for analyzing these data to determine if there was a significant different in the average SAT-Math score for Freshmen Males *versus* Freshmen Females require you to use six numbers correctly: the sample size, the mean, and the standard deviation of each of the two groups. All six of these numbers must be used correctly in the formulas if you are to analyze the data correctly.

If you create a table to summarize these data, a good example of the table, using both Step 1 and Step 2, would be the data presented in Fig. 5.1:

	A	B	C	D	E
1					
2					
3		Group	n	Mean	STDEV
4		1 (name it)			
5		2 (name it)			
6					

Fig. 5.1 Basic Table Format for the Two-group t-test

If you decide to name Group 1 the Freshmen Males group and Group 2 the Freshmen Females group, the following table would place the six numbers from your research study into the proper cells of the table as in Fig. 5.2:

	A	B	C	D	E
1					
2					
3		Group	n	Mean	STDEV
4		1 Freshmen Males SAT-Math scores	57	610	120
5		2 Freshmen Females SAT-Math scores	46	640	110
6					

Fig. 5.2 Results of Entering the Data Needed for the Two-Group t-test

You can now use the formulas for the two-group t-test with more confidence that the six numbers will be placed in the proper place in the formulas.

Note that you could just as easily name Group 1 the Freshmen Females group and Group 2 the Freshmen Males group; it makes no difference how you decide to name the two groups; this decision is up to you and you will get the same result from your statistical test no matter which decision you make.

5.1.3 STEP 3: State the Null Hypothesis and the Research Hypothesis for the Two-Group t-Test

If you have completed Step 1 above, this step is very easy because the null hypothesis and the research hypothesis will always be stated in the same way for the two-group t-test. The null hypothesis states that the population means of the two groups are equal, while the research hypothesis states that the population means of the two groups are not equal. In notation format, this becomes:

H_0: $\mu_1 = \mu_2$
H_1: $\mu_1 \neq \mu_2$

You can now see that this notation is much simpler than having to write out the names of the two groups in all of your formulas.

5.1.4 STEP 4: Select the Appropriate Statistical Test

Since this chapter deals with the situation in which you have two groups but only one measurement on each person or event in each group, we will use the two-group t-test throughout this chapter.

5.1.5 STEP 5: Decide on a Decision Rule for the Two-Group t-Test

The decision rule is exactly the same as what it was in the previous chapter (see Sect. 4.1.3) when we dealt with the one-group t-test.

(a) If the absolute value of t is less than the critical value of t, accept the null hypothesis.
(b) If the absolute value of t is greater than the critical value of t, reject the null hypothesis and accept the research hypothesis.

Since you learned how to find the absolute value of t in the previous chapter (see Sect. 4.1.3.1), you can use that knowledge in this chapter.

5.1.6 *STEP 6: Calculate the Formula for the Two-Group t-Test*

Since we are using two different formulas in this chapter for the two-group t-test depending on the sample size in the two groups, we will explain how to use those formulas later in this chapter.

5.1.7 *STEP 7: Find the Critical Value of t in the t-Table in Appendix E*

In the previous chapter where we were dealing with the one-group t-test, you found the critical value of t in the t-table in Appendix E by finding the sample size for the one group in the first column of the table, and then reading the critical value of t across from it on the right in the "critical t column" in the table (see Sect. 4.1.5). This process is fairly simple once you have had some practice in doing this step.

However, for the two-group t-test, the procedure for finding the critical value of t is more complicated because you have two different groups in your study, and they often have different sample sizes in each group.

To use Appendix E correctly in this chapter, you need to learn how to find the "degrees of freedom" for your study. We will discuss that process now.

5.1.7.1 Finding the Degrees of Freedom (df) for the Two-Group t-Test

Objective: To find the degrees of freedom for the two-group t-test and to use it to find the critical value of t in the t-table in Appendix E

The mathematical explanation of "degrees of freedom" is beyond the scope of this book, but you can find out more about this concept by reading any good statistics book (e.g. Keller 2009). For our purposes, you can easily understand how to find the degrees of freedom and to use it to find the critical value of t in Appendix E. The formula for the degrees of freedom (df) is:

$$\text{degrees of freedom} = \text{df} = n_1 + n_2 - 2 \tag{5.1}$$

In other words, you add the sample size for Group 1 to the sample size for Group 2 and then subtract 2 from this total to get the number of degrees of freedom to use in Appendix E.

Take a look at Appendix E.

Instead of using the first column as we did in the one-group t-test that is based on the "sample size n" of one group, we need to use the second-column of this table (df) to find the critical value of t for the two-group t-test.

For example, if you had 13 people in Group 1 and 17 people in Group 2, the degrees of freedom would be: $13 + 17 - 2 = 28$, and the critical value of t would be 2.048 *since you look down the second column which contains the degrees of freedom* until you come to the number 28, and then read 2.048 in the "critical t column" in the table to find the critical value of t when df = 28.

As a second example, if you had 52 people in Group 1 and 57 people in Group 2, the degrees of freedom would be: $52 + 57 - 2 = 107$. When you go down the second column in Appendix E for the degrees of freedom, you find that *once you go beyond the degrees of freedom equal to 39, the critical value of t is always 1.96*, and that is the value you would use for the critical t with this example.

5.1.8 STEP 8: State the Result of Your Statistical Test

The result follows the exact same result format that you found for the one-group t-test in the previous chapter (see Sect. 4.1.6):

Either: Since the absolute value of t that you found in the t-test formula is *less than the critical value of t* in Appendix E, you accept the null hypothesis.

Or: Since the absolute value of t that you found in the t-test formula is *greater than the critical value of t* in Appendix E, you reject the null hypothesis and accept the research hypothesis.

5.1.9 STEP 9: State the Conclusion of Your Statistical Test in Plain English!

Writing the conclusion for the two-group t-test is more difficult than writing the conclusion for the one-group t-test because you have to decide what the difference was between the two groups.

When you accept the null hypothesis, the conclusion is simple to write: "There is no difference between the two groups in the variable that was measured."

But when you reject the null hypothesis and accept the research hypothesis, you need to be careful about writing the conclusion so that it is both accurate and concise.

Let's give you some practice in writing the conclusion of a two-group t-test.

5.1.9.1 Writing the Conclusion of the Two-Group t-Test When You Accept the Null Hypothesis

Objective: To write the conclusion of the two-group t- test when you have accepted the null hypothesis.

The American Society of Training and Development (ASTD) is an international association for training and development professionals. ASTD's most important educational program is an annual ASTD International Conference and Exposition that typically hosts about 9,000 participants from over 80 countries and includes about 300 educational sessions that participants can attend. Suppose that you have been asked to design a survey that can be emailed to participants after the Conference has ended to determine the attitude of participants toward the many activities of the Conference. One key item that you are sure that you want to include is an item asking if the participants if they would recommend attending next year's Conference to their colleagues. Item #10 of this survey is given in Fig. 5.3.

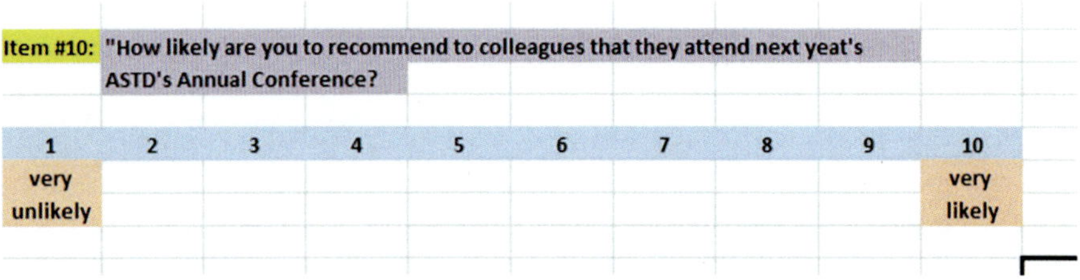

Fig. 5.3 ASTD Annual Conference Evaluation Survey Item #10

Suppose further, that you have decided to analyze the data from the Survey comparing the attitudes of men who attended the annual ASTD Conference to those of women who attended the annual ASTD Conference by using the two-group t-test.

Important note: You would need to use this test for each of the Survey items separately.

Suppose that the hypothetical data for Item #10 was based on a sample size of 124 Males who had a mean score on this item of 6.58 and a standard deviation on this item of 2.44. Suppose that you also had data from 86 Females who had a mean score of 6.45 with a standard deviation of 1.86.

We will explain later in this chapter how to produce the results of the two-group t-test using its formulas, but, for now, let's "cut to the chase" and tell you that those formulas would produce the following in Fig. 5.4:

Group	n	Mean	STDEV
1 Males	124	6.58	2.44
2 Females	86	6.45	1.86

Fig. 5.4 Worksheet Data for Item #10 for Accepting the Null Hypothesis

degrees of freedom:	208
critical t:	1.96 (in Appendix E)
t-test formula:	0.44 (when you use your calculator!)
Result:	Since the absolute value of 0.44 is less than the critical t of 1.96, we accept the null hypothesis.
Conclusion:	There was no difference between Males and Females in their likelihood of recommending to their colleagues that they attend next year's ASTD Annual Conference.

Now, let's see what happens when you reject the null hypothesis (H_0) and accept the research hypothesis (H_1).

5.1.9.2 Writing the Conclusion of the Two-Group t-Test When You Reject the Null Hypothesis and Accept the Research Hypothesis

Objective: To write the conclusion of the two-group t-test when you have rejected the null hypothesis and accepted the research hypothesis

Let's continue with this same example, but with the result that we reject the null hypothesis and accept the research hypothesis.

Let's assume that this time you have data on 85 Males and their mean score on Item #10 was 7.26 with a standard deviation of 2.35. Let's further suppose that you also have data on 48 Females and their mean score on this question was 4.37 with a standard deviation of 3.26. Let's call Males, Group 1, and Females, Group 2.

Without going into the details of the formulas for the two-group t-test, these data would produce the following result and conclusion based on Fig. 5.5:

Group	n	Mean	STDEV
1 Males	85	7.26	2.35
2 Females	48	4.37	3.26

Fig. 5.5 Worksheet Data for Item #10 for Obtaining a Significant Difference between Males and Females

Null Hypothesis:	$\mu_1 = \mu_2$
Research Hypothesis:	$\mu_1 \neq \mu_2$
degrees of freedom:	131
critical t:	1.96 (in Appendix E)
t-test formula:	5.40 (when you use your calculator!)
Result:	Since the absolute value of 5.40 is greater than the critical t of 1.96, we reject the null hypothesis and accept the research hypothesis.

Now, you need to write a conclusion comparing Males and Females on their likelihood of recommending to colleagues that they attend next year's ASTD Annual Conference using the following rule:

Rule: To summarize the conclusion of the two-group t-test, just compare the means of the two groups, and be sure to use the word "significantly" in your conclusion if you rejected the null hypothesis and accepted the research hypothesis.

A good way to prepare to write the conclusion of the two-group t-test when you are using a rating scale is to place the mean scores of the two groups on a drawing of the scale so that you can visualize the difference between the mean scores. For example, using our ASTD Annual Conference example from above, you would draw this "picture" of the scale in Fig. 5.6:

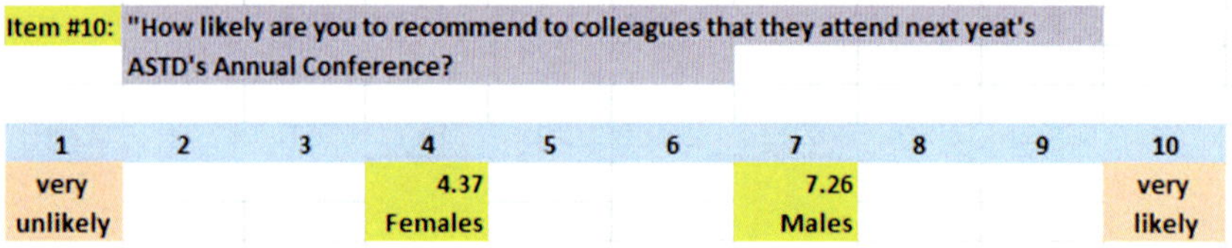

Fig. 5.6 Example of Drawing a "Picture" of the Means of the Two Groups on the Rating Scale

This drawing tells you visually that Males had a higher average rating than Females on Item #10 (7.26 vs. 4.37). *And, since you rejected the null hypothesis and accepted the research hypothesis, you know that you have found a significant difference between the two mean scores.*

So, our conclusion needs to contain the following key words:

- Males
- Females
- likelihood of recommending that colleagues attend next year's ASTD Annual Conference
- significantly
- more likely or less likely
- *either* (7.26 vs. 4.37) *or* (4.37 vs. 7.26)

We can use these key words to write either of two conclusions which are *logically identical*:

Either: Males were significantly more likely than Females to recommend that their colleagues attend next year's ASTD Annual Conference (7.26 vs. 4.37).

Or: Females were significantly less likely than Males to recommend that their colleagues attend next year's ASTD Annual Conference (4.37 vs. 7.26).

Both of these conclusions are accurate, so you can decide which one you want to write. It is your choice.

Also, note that the mean scores in parentheses at the end of these conclusions must match the sequence of the two groups in your conclusion. For example, if you say that: "Males were significantly more likely than Females," the end of this conclusion should be: (7.26 vs. 4.37) since you mentioned Males first, and Females second.

Alternately, if you wrote that: "Females were significantly less likely than Males," the end of this conclusion should be: (4.37 vs. 7.26) since you mentioned Females first, and Males second.

Putting the two mean scores at the end of your conclusion saves the reader from having to turn back to the table in your research report to find these mean scores to see how far apart the mean scores were.

Now, let's discuss FORMULA #1 that deals with the situation in which both groups have a sample size greater than 30.

Objective: To use FORMULA #1 for the two-group t-test when both groups have a sample size greater than 30

5.2 Formula #1: Both Groups Have A Sample Size Greater Than 30

The first formula we will discuss will be used when you have two groups with a sample size greater than 30 in each group and one measurement on each member in each group. This formula for the two-group t-test is:

$$t = \frac{\overline{X}_1 - \overline{X}_2}{S_{\overline{X}_1 - \overline{X}_2}} \tag{5.2}$$

$$\text{where } S_{\overline{X}_1 - \overline{X}_2} = \sqrt{\frac{{S_1}^2}{n_1} + \frac{{S_2}^2}{n_2}} \tag{5.3}$$

$$\text{and where degrees of freedom} = df = n_1 + n_2 - 2 \tag{5.1}$$

This formula looks daunting when you first see it, but let's explain some of the parts of this formula:

We have explained the concept of "degrees of freedom" earlier in this chapter, and so you should be able to find the degrees of freedom needed for this formula in order to find the critical value of t in Appendix E.

In the previous chapter, *the formula for the one-group t-test was the following*:

$$t = \frac{\overline{X} - \mu}{S_{\overline{X}}} \tag{4.1}$$

$$\text{where s.e.} = S_{\overline{X}} = \frac{S}{\sqrt{n}} \tag{4.2}$$

For the one-group t-test, you found the mean score and subtracted the population mean from it, and then divided the result by the standard error of the mean (s.e.) to get the result of the t-test. You then compared the t-test result to the critical value of t to see if you either accepted the null hypothesis, or rejected the null hypothesis and accepted the research hypothesis.

The two-group t-test requires a different formula because you have two groups, each with a mean score on some variable. You are trying to determine whether to accept the null hypothesis that the *population means of the two groups are equal* (in other words, there is no difference statistically between these two means), or whether the difference between the means of the two groups is "sufficiently large" that you would accept *that there is a significant difference* in the mean scores of the two groups.

The numerator of the two-group t-test asks you to find the difference between the means of the two groups:

$$\overline{X}_1 - \overline{X}_2 \tag{5.4}$$

The next step in the formula for the two-group t-test is to divide the answer you get when you subtract the two means by the standard error of the difference of the two means, and *this is a different standard error of the mean than that which you found for the one-group t-test because there are two means in the two-group t-test.*

The standard error of the mean when you have two groups is called the "standard error of the difference of the means." This formula looks less scary when you break it down into four steps:

1. Square the standard deviation of Group 1, and divide this result by the sample size for Group 1 (n_1).
2. Square the standard deviation of Group 2, and divide this result by the sample size for Group 2 (n_2).
3. Add the results of the above two steps to get a total score.
4. *Take the square root of this total score* to find the standard error of the difference of the means between the two groups, $S_{\overline{X}_1 - \overline{X}_2} = \sqrt{\frac{S_1{}^2}{n_1} + \frac{S_2{}^2}{n_2}}$

This last step is the one that gives students the most difficulty when they are finding this standard error using their calculator, because they are in such a hurry to get to the answer that they forget to carry the square root sign down to the last step, and thus get a larger number than they should for the standard error.

5.2.1 An Example of Formula #1 for the Two-Group t-Test

Now, let's use Formula #1 in a situation in which both groups have a sample size greater than 30.

Suppose that a university that offered a Master's degree in Human Resources Management (HRM) wanted to obtain feedback from students at the end of a course in Managing Human Resources from the previous semester to determine if there was a gender difference in the students' opinions of the course. Item #12 of the Course Evaluation Form asked the graduate students for their overall rating of the quality of the course using a 100-point scale. This rating item is given in Fig. 5.7.

Item #12: Overall, how would you rate the quality of the Managing Human Resources course?										
0	10	20	30	40	50	60	70	80	90	100
poor										Excellent

Fig. 5.7 Example of Item #12 of the Course Evaluation Form (Practical Example)

Suppose you collect these evaluation forms and take a random sample of students and determine (using your new Excel skills) that the 52 Males in Group 1 had a mean score of 55 with a standard deviation of 7, while the 57 Females in Group 2 had a mean score of 64 with a standard deviation of 13 on Item #12.

Note that the two-group t-test does not require that both groups have the same sample size. This is another way of saying that the two-group t-test is "robust" (a fancy term that statisticians like to use).

Your data then produce the following table in Fig. 5.8:

	A	B	C	D	E	F
1						
2						
3		Group	n	Mean	STDEV	
4		1 Males	52	55	7	
5		2 Females	57	64	13	
6						

Fig. 5.8 Worksheet Data for item #12 for Managing Human Resources

Create an Excel spreadsheet, and enter the following information:

B3: Group
B4: 1 Males
B5: 2 Females
C3: n
D3: Mean
E3: STDEV
C4: 52
D4: 55
E4: 7
C5: 57
D5: 64
E5: 13

Now, widen column B so that it is twice as wide as column A, and center the six numbers and their labels in your table (see Fig. 5.9)

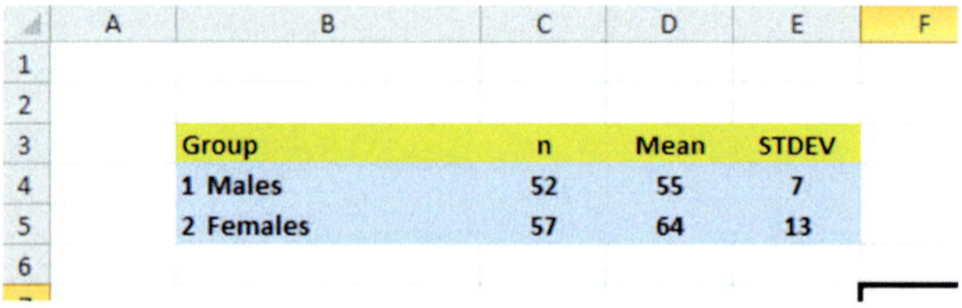

	A	B	C	D	E	F
1						
2						
3		Group	n	Mean	STDEV	
4		1 Males	52	55	7	
5		2 Females	57	64	13	
6						

Fig. 5.9 Results of Widening Column B and Centering the Numbers in the Cells

B8: Null hypothesis:
B10: Research hypothesis:

Since both groups have a sample size greater than 30, you need to use Formula #1 for the t-test for the difference of the means of the two groups.

Let's "break this formula down into pieces" to reduce the chance of making a mistake by entering the following into these cells:

B13: STDEV1 squared/n1 (note that you square the standard deviation of Group 1, and then divide the result by the sample size of Group 1)
B16: STDEV2 squared/n2
B19: D13 + D16
B22: s.e.
B25: critical t
B28: t-test
B31: Result:
B36: Conclusion: (see Fig. 5.10)

Fig. 5.10 Formula Labels for the Two-group t-test

You now need to compute the values of the above formulas in the following cells:

D13: the result of the formula needed to compute cell B13 (use two decimals)
D16: the result of the formula needed to compute cell B16 (use two decimals)
D19: the result of the formula needed to compute cell B19 (use two decimals)
D22: =SQRT(D19) (use two decimals)

This formula should give you a standard error (s.e.) of 1.98.

D25: 1.96 (Since $df = n1 + n2 - 2$, this gives $df = 109 - 2 = 107$, and the critical t is, therefore, 1.96 in Appendix E.)
D28: =(D4–D5)/D22 (use two decimals) (no spaces between symbols)

This formula should give you a value for the t-test of: −4.55.

Next, check to see if you have rounded off all figures in D13: D28 to two decimal places (see Fig. 5.11).

Group	n	Mean	STDEV
1 Males	52	55	7
2 Females	57	64	13
Null hypothesis:			
Research hypothesis:			
STDEV1 squared / n1		0.94	
STDEV2 squared / n2		2.96	
D13 + D16		3.91	
s.e.		1.98	
critical t		1.96	
t-test		-4.55	
Result:			
Conclusion:			

Fig. 5.11 Results of the t-test Formula for Comparisons of Males vs. Females

Now, write the following sentence in D31–D34 to summarize the result of the study:

D31: Since the absolute value of −4.55
D32: is greater than the critical t of
D33: 1.96 we reject the null hypothesis
D34: and accept the research hypothesis.

Finally, write the following sentence in D36–D39 to summarize the conclusion of the study in plain English:

D36: Overall, Females rated the quality of the
D37: Managing Human Resources course
D38: this past term as significantly higher
D39: quality than Males (64 vs. 55).

Save your file as: EVAL12

Important note: You are probably wondering why we entered both the result and the conclusion in separate cells instead of in just one cell. This is because if you enter them in one cell, you will be very disappointed when you print out your final spreadsheet, because one of two things will happen that you will not like: (1) if you print the spreadsheet to fit onto only one page, the result and the conclusion will force the entire spreadsheet to be printed in such small font size that you will be unable to read it, or (2) if you do not print the final spreadsheet to fit onto one page, both the result and the conclusion will "dribble over" onto a second page instead of fitting the entire spreadsheet onto one page. In either case, your spreadsheet will not have a "professional look."

Print this file so that it fits onto one page, and write by hand the null hypothesis and the research hypothesis on your printout.

The final spreadsheet appears in Fig. 5.12.

Group	n	Mean	STDEV
1 Males	52	55	7
2 Females	57	64	13

Null hypothesis:	μ_1	=	μ_2
Research hypothesis:	μ_1	≠	μ_2

STDEV1 squared / n1	0.94
STDEV2 squared / n2	2.96
D13 + D16	3.91
s.e.	1.98
critical t	1.96
t-test	-4.55
Result:	Since the absolute value of – 4.55 is greater than the critical t of 1.96 we reject the null hypothesis and accept the research hypothesis.
Conclusion:	Overall, Females rated the quality of the Managing Human Resources course this past term as significantly higher quality than Males (64 vs. 55).

Fig. 5.12 Final Worksheet for Item #12 Comparing Males vs. Females

Now, let's use the second formula for the two-group t-test which we use whenever either one group, or both groups, have a sample size less than 30.

> Objective: To use Formula #2 for the two-group t-test when one or both groups have a sample size less than 30

Now, let's look at the case when one or both groups have a sample size less than 30.

5.3 Formula #2: One or Both Groups Have a Sample Size Less Than 30

We would use this formula when the underlying population standard deviations are unknown, but are assumed to be equal. For more information about the two-group t-test, see Aamodt and others (2007).

Suppose that you have been asked to determine if there was a gender equity in salary among mid-level managers of your company. You have created one sampling frame of male managers and another sampling frame of female managers which contained managers of similar educational attainment and similar years of relevant work experience for both groups of managers. You decide to try out your new Excel skills on a small sample of managers in both groups and recorded their monthly salaries in US dollars. The hypothetical data given in Fig. 5.13:

Fig. 5.13 Worksheet Data for Salaries of Male and Female Managers (Practical Example)

MONTHLY SALARIES OF MANAGERS ($)

Males	Females
3750	3475
7250	7015
5650	5135
4583	4160
3900	3765
4783	4250
5192	4875
4954	4260
5741	5125
4866	
5500	

Let's call Males as Group 1, and Females as Group 2.

Null Hypothesis: $\mu_1 = \mu_2$
Research Hypothesis: $\mu_1 \neq \mu_2$

Note: Since both groups have a sample size less than 30, you need to use Formula #2 in the following steps:

Create an Excel spreadsheet, and enter the following information:

B2: MONTHLY SALARIES OF MANAGERS ($)
B4: Males
C4: Females
B5: 3750
B15: 5500
C5: 3475
C13: 5125

Now, enter the other figures into this table. Be sure to double-check all of your figures. If you have only one incorrect figure, you will not be able to obtain the correct answer to this problem.

Now, widen columns B and C so that all of the information fits inside the cells. To do this, click on both letters B and C at the top of these columns on your spreadsheet to highlight all of the cells in columns B and C. Then, move the mouse pointer to the right end of the B cell until you get a "cross" sign; then, click on this cross sign and drag the sign to the right until you can read all of the words on your screen. Then, stop clicking! Both Column B and Column C should now be the same width.

Then, center all information in the table except the top title by using the following steps:

Left-click your mouse and highlight cells B4:C15. Then, click on the bottom line, second from the left icon, under "Alignment" at the top-center of Home. All of the information in the table should now be in the center of each cell.

E5: Null hypothesis:
E7: Research hypothesis:
E9: Group
E10: 1 Males
E11: 2 Females
F9: n
G9: Mean
H9: STDEV

Now you need to use your Excel skills from Chap. 1 to fill in the sample sizes (n), the means, and the standard deviations (STDEV) in the Table in cells F10:H11. Be sure to double-check your work or you will not be able to obtain the correct answer to this problem if you have only one incorrect figure! Round off the means and standard deviations to zero decimal places and center these six figures within their cells.

Your spreadsheet should now look like Fig. 5.14.

MONTHLY SALARIES OF MANAGERS ($)

Males	Females
3750	3475
7250	7015
5650	5135
4583	4160
3900	3765
4783	4250
5192	4875
4954	4260
5741	5125
4866	
5500	

Null hypothesis:

Research hypothesis:

Group	n	Mean	STDEV
1 Males	11	5106	960
2 Females	9	4673	1050

Fig. 5.14 Worksheet Data for Hypothesis Testing

Since both groups have a sample size less than 30, you need to use Formula #2 for the t-test for the difference of the means of two independent samples.

Formula #2 for the two-group t-test is the following:

$$t = \frac{\overline{X}_1 - \overline{X}_2}{S_{\overline{X}_1 - \overline{X}_2}} \tag{5.1}$$

$$\text{where } S_{\overline{X}_1 - \overline{X}_2} = \sqrt{\frac{(n_1 - 1)S_1{}^2 + (n_2 - 1)S_2{}^2}{n_1 + n_2 - 2}\left(\frac{1}{n_1} + \frac{1}{n_2}\right)} \tag{5.5}$$

$$\text{and where degrees of freedom} = df = n_1 + n_2 - 2 \tag{5.6}$$

This formula is complicated, and so it will reduce your chance of making a mistake in writing it if you "break it down into pieces" instead of trying to write the formula as one cell entry.

Now, enter these words on your spreadsheet:

E14: (nl – 1) x STDEV1 squared
E16: (n2 – 1) x STDEV2 squared
E18: $n_1 + n_2 - 2$
E20: $1/n_1 + 1/n_2$
E23: s.e.
E26: critical t
E29: t-test
B32: Result:
B36: Conclusion: (see Fig. 5.15)

MONTHLY SALARIES OF MANAGERS ($)

Males	Females
3750	3475
7250	7015
5650	5135
4583	4160
3900	3765
4783	4250
5192	4875
4954	4260
5741	5125
4866	
5500	

SALARY11

Null hypothesis:

Research hypothesis:

Group	n	Mean	STDEV
1 Males	11	5106	960
2 Females	9	4673	1050

(n1-1) x STDEV1 squared

(n2-1) x STDEV2 squared

n1 + n2 - 2

1/n1 + 1/n2

s.e.

critical t

t-test

Result:

Conclusion:

Fig. 5.15 Formula Labels for the Two-group t-test

You now need to use your Excel skills to compute the values of the above formulas in the following cells:

H14: the result of the formula needed to compute cell E14 (use two decimals)
H16: the result of the formula needed to compute cell E16 (use two decimals)
H18: the result of the formula needed to compute cell E18
H20: the result of the formula needed to compute cell E20 (use two decimals)

H23 := SQRT(((H14 + H16)/H18)*H20) (no spaces between symbols)

Note the three open-parentheses after SQRT, and the three closed parentheses on the right side of this formula. You need three open parentheses and three closed parentheses in this formula or the formula will not work correctly.

The above formula gives a standard error of the difference of the means equal to 449.79 (two decimals) in cell H23.

H26: Enter the critical t value from the t-table in Appendix E in this cell using $df = n_1 + n_2 - 2$ to find the critical t value

H29: =(G10–G11)/H23 (no spaces between symbols)

Note that you need an open-parenthesis *before G10* and a closed-parenthesis *after G11* so that this answer of 433 is *THEN* divided by the standard error of the difference of the means of 449.79, to give a t-test value of 0.96. Use two decimal places for the t-test result (see Fig. 5.16).

MONTHLY SALARIES OF MANAGERS ($)

Males	Females
3750	3475
7250	7015
5650	5135
4583	4160
3900	3765
4783	4250
5192	4875
4954	4260
5741	5125
4866	
5500	

Null hypothesis:

Research hypothesis:

Group	n	Mean	STDEV
1 Males	11	5106	960
2 Females	9	4673	1050

(n1-1) x STDEV1 squared	9,210,262.18
(n2-1) x STDEV2 squared	8,815,850.00
n1 + n2 - 2	18
1/n1 + 1/n2	0.20
s.e.	449.79
critical t	2.101
t-test	0.96

Result:

Conclusion:

Fig. 5.16 Two-group t-test Formula Results

Now write the following sentence in C32–C33 to summarize the *result* of the study:

C32: Since the absolute value of 0.96 is less than the critical t of 2.101, we
C33: accept the null hypothesis.

Finally, write the following sentence in C36 to summarize the *conclusion* of the study:

C36: There was no difference in salary between male and female managers.

Save your file as: SALARY15

Print the final spreadsheet so that it fits onto one page.
Write the null hypothesis and the research hypothesis by hand on your printout.
The final spreadsheet appears in Fig. 5.17.

MONTHLY SALARIES OF MANAGERS ($)

Males	Females
3750	3475
7250	7015
5650	5135
4583	4160
3900	3765
4783	4250
5192	4875
4954	4260
5741	5125
4866	
5500	

Null hypothesis:	μ_1	=	μ_2
Research hypothesis:	μ_1	≠	μ_2

Group	n	Mean	STDEV
1 Males	11	5106	960
2 Females	9	4673	1050

(n1-1) x STDEV1 squared	9,210,262.18
(n2-1) x STDEV2 squared	8,815,850.00
n1 + n2 - 2	18
1/n1 + 1/n2	0.20
s.e.	449.79
critical t	2.101
t-test	0.96

Result: Since the absolute value of 0.96 is less than the critical t of 2.101, we accept the null hypothesis.

Conclusion: There was no difference in salary between male and female managers.

Fig. 5.17 Final Spreadsheet of Salaries of Male and Female Managers

5.4 End-of-Chapter Practice Problems

1. Suppose that the HR department in your organization has received an increased number of complaints from employees about possible sexual harassment incidents in the workplace and it has designed a training workshop to address this issue so that the number of future complaints could be reduced. Suppose, further, that all employees in one division of your company who were either Supervisors or Non-supervisors were required to complete this pilot training program. Participants in this workshop were asked to complete an email survey at the end of the workshop, and one of the key questions on the survey (Item #24) is given in Fig. 5.18, along with some hypothetical data, so that you can test your Excel skills on a small sample of participants to see if Supervisors and Non-supervisors rated the quality of this HR training program differently.

HR TRAINING PROGRAM

"REDUCING SEXUAL HARASSMENT IN THE WORKPLACE"

Item #24: "Overall, how would you rate the quality of the HR Training Program on the topic: Reducing Sexual Harassment in the Workplace.?"

1	2	3	4	5	6	7	8	9
very poor								very good

SUPERVISORS	NON-SUPERVISORS
6	7
5	6
7	5
8	6
4	4
5	8
6	5
7	9
6	8
9	6
8	7
6	4
7	6
5	5
6	6
5	5
7	7
4	8
8	4
6	9
9	3
	4
	5

Fig. 5.18 Worksheet Data for Chap. 5: Practice Problem #1

(a) State the null hypothesis and the research hypothesis on an Excel spreadsheet.
(b) Find the standard error of the difference between the means using Excel
(c) Find the critical t value using Appendix E, and enter it on your spreadsheet.
(d) Perform a t-test on these data using Excel. What is the value of t that you obtain?

Use two decimal places for all figures in the formula section of your spreadsheet.

(e) State your result on your spreadsheet.
(f) State your conclusion in plain English on your spreadsheet.
(g) Save the file as: HR20

2. Suppose that top management of a large national bank has asked your HR department to develop and test a training program for customer service reps who answer the bank's 1–800 phone number when it is called by the bank's VISA card customers. Top management wants to improve the quality of service provided by its customer service VISA reps, and you have been asked to design a training program and also an email Survey that could be completed by customers after they have talked to a Customer Service rep.
You decide to develop a training program for these reps and to randomly assign reps to one of two groups: (1) an Experimental Group that would complete the HR-designed training program intended to improve the quality of customer service, and (2) a Control Group of reps that did not experience this training program. This type of experimental design is called an "After-only with Control Group Design" (see, for example, McDaniel and Gates 2013, pp. 190–191).

You want to test the effectiveness of the HR training program for 3 weeks starting 2 weeks after the training program has been completed by collecting data from an email survey, and Item #10 of this survey is a key question on the survey that asks customers to rate the quality of service provided by the customer service representative that they talked to on a 7-point scale where 1 = Poor and 7 = Excellent. Let's suppose that the Experimental Group had 34 customers and that their mean score was 6.24 with a standard deviation of 1.12, while the Control Group had 37 customers with a mean of 4.37 and a standard deviation of 1.54.

(a) State the null hypothesis and the research hypothesis on an Excel spreadsheet.
(b) Find the standard error of the difference between the means using Excel
(c) Find the critical t value using Appendix E, and enter it on your spreadsheet.
(d) Perform a t-test on these data using Excel. What is the value of t that you obtain?
(e) State your result on your spreadsheet.
(f) State your conclusion in plain English on your spreadsheet.
(g) Save the file as: HR30

3. Suppose that the Chair of a Master's degree program in Human Resources Management wants to determine if there is a difference in GPAs between Male students and Female students who have completed all of the required core courses in the program. Suppose, further, that the Chair has obtained this data from the Registrar and has promised to keep the information confidential. You have been asked to analyze the data using your Excel skills. Suppose that you have been working on this analysis, and so far you have determined that the 47 Males in the program have an average GPA of 3.15 with a standard deviation of 0.42, while the 56 Females in the program have an average GPA of 3.45 with a standard deviation of 0.37. You now want to analyze these data.
   (a) State the null hypothesis and the research hypothesis on an Excel spreadsheet.
   (b) Find the standard error of the difference between the means using ExceL
   (c) Find the critical t value using Appendix E, and enter it on your spreadsheet.
   (d) Perform a t-test on these data using Excel. What is the value of t that you obtain?
   (e) Use three decimals for all figures that require a formula.
   (f) State your result on your spreadsheet.
   (g) State your conclusion in plain English on your spreadsheet.
   (h) Save the file as: HRM23

References

Aamodt M, Surrette M, and Cohen D. Understanding statistics: a guide for I/O psychologists and human resource professionals. Belmont: Wadsworth Cengage Learning; 2007.

Keller G. Statistics for management and economics. 8th ed. Mason: South-Western Cengage Learning; 2009.

McDaniel C, Gates R. Marketing research essentials. 8th ed. New York: John Wiley & Sons; 2013.

Wheater C, Cook P. Using statistics to understand the environment. New York: Routledge; 2000.

Chapter 6
Correlation and Simple Linear Regression

There are many different types of "correlation coefficients," but the one we will use in this book is the Pearson product–moment correlation which we will call: *r*.

6.1 What Is a "Correlation?"

Basically, a correlation is a number between −1 and +1 that summarizes the relationship between two variables, which we will call X and Y.

A correlation can be either positive or negative. *A positive correlation means that as X increases, Y increases. A negative correlation means that as X increases, Y decreases.* In statistics books, this part of the relationship is called the *direction* of the relationship (i.e., it is either positive or negative).

The correlation also tells us the *magnitude* of the relationship between X and Y. As the correlation approaches closer to +1, we say that the relationship is *strong and positive*.

As the correlation approaches closer to −1, we say that the relationship is *strong and negative*.

A zero correlation means that there is no relationship between X and Y. This means that neither X nor Y can be used as a predictor of the other.

A good way to understand what a correlation means is to see a "picture" of the scatterplot of data points produced in a chart. Let's suppose that you want to know if variable X can be used to predict variable Y. We will place *the predictor variable X on the x-axis* (the horizontal axis of a chart) and *the dependent (criterion) variable Y on the y-axis* (the vertical axis of a chart). Suppose, further, that you have collected data given in the scatterplots below (see Fig. 6.1 through Fig. 6.6).

Figure 6.1 shows the scatterplot for a perfect positive correlation of $r = +1.0$. This means that you can perfectly predict each y-value from each x-value because the data points move "upward-and-to-the-right" along a perfectly-fitting straight line (see Fig. 6.1).

T.J. Quirk, J. Palmer-Schuyler, *Excel 2016 for Human Resource Management Statistics*, Excel for Statistics, DOI 10.1007/978-3-319-40063-1_6

X	Y
1	1
2	2
3	3
4	4
5	5
6	6

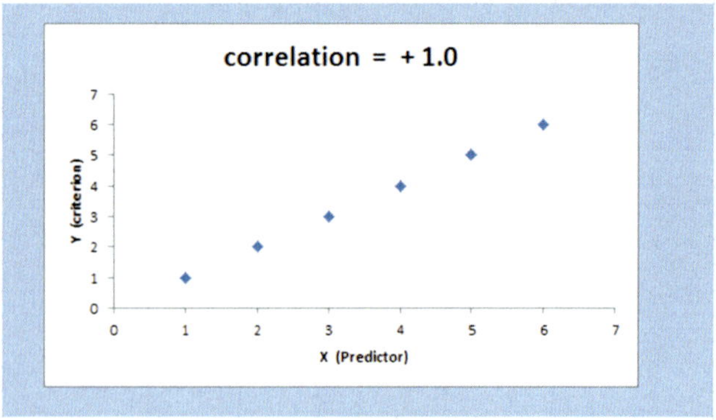

Fig. 6.1 Example of a Scatterplot for a Perfect, Positive Correlation (r = +1.0)

Figure 6.2 shows the scatterplot for a moderately positive correlation of $r = +.54$. This means that each x-value can predict each y-value moderately well because you can draw a picture of a "football" around the outside of the data points that move upward-and-to-the-right, but not along a straight line (see Fig. 6.2).

X	Y
1	2
2	4
3	3
4	1
5	6
6	5

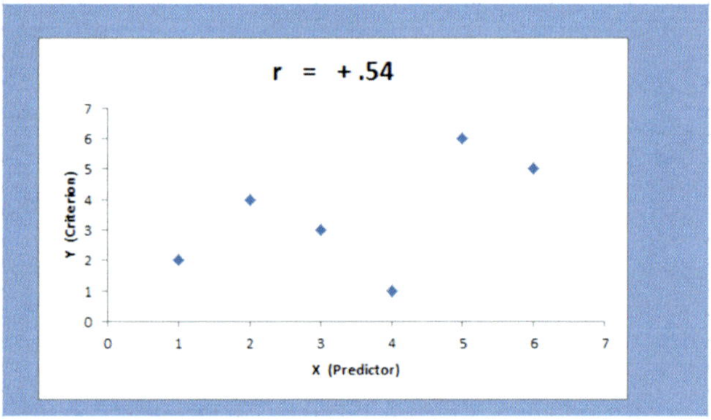

Fig. 6.2 Example of a Scatterplot for a Moderate, Positive Correlation (r = +.54)

Figure 6.3 shows the scatterplot for a low, positive correlation of $r = +.09$. This means that each x-value is a poor predictor of each y-value because the "picture" you could draw around the outside of the data points approaches a circle in shape (see Fig. 6.3)

X	Y
1	2
2	4
3	6
4	1
5	5
6	3

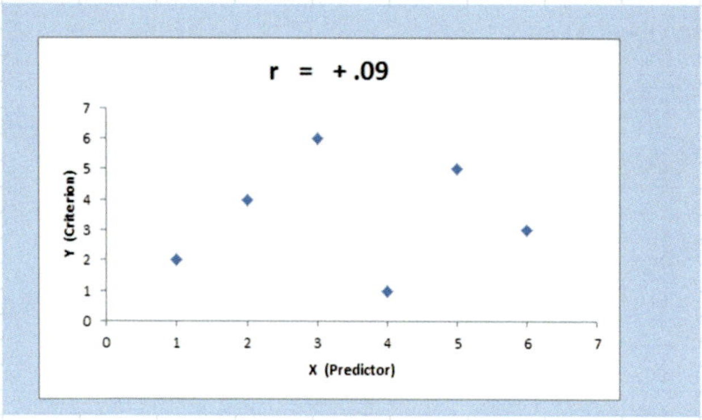

Fig. 6.3 Example of a Scatterplot for a Low, Positive Correlation (r = +.09)

We have not shown a Figure of a zero correlation because it is easy to imagine what it looks like as a scatterplot. A zero correlation of $r = .00$ means that there is no relationship between X and Y and the "picture" drawn around the data points would be a perfect circle in shape, indicating that you cannot use X to predict Y because these two variables are not correlated with one another.

Figure 6.4 shows the scatterplot for a low, negative correlation of $r = -.09$ which means that each X is a poor predictor of Y in an inverse relationship, meaning that as X increases, Y decreases (see Fig. 6.4). In this case, it is a negative correlation because the "football" you could draw around the data points slopes down and to the right.

X	Y
1	3
2	5
3	1
4	6
5	4
6	2

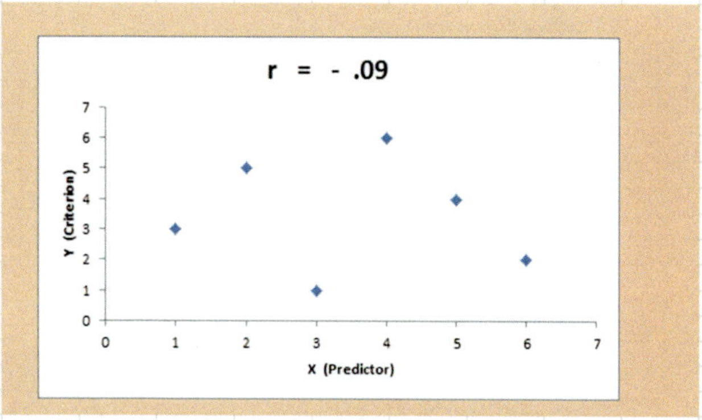

Fig. 6.4 Example of a Scatterplot for a Low, Negative Correlation (r = −.09)

Figure 6.5 shows the scatterplot for a moderate, negative correlation of $r = -.54$ which means that X is a moderately good predictor of Y, although there is an inverse relationship between X and Y (i.e., as X increases, Y decreases; see Fig. 6.5).

In this case, it is a negative correlation because the "football" you could draw around the data points slopes down and to the right.

X	Y
1	5
2	6
3	1
4	3
5	4
6	2

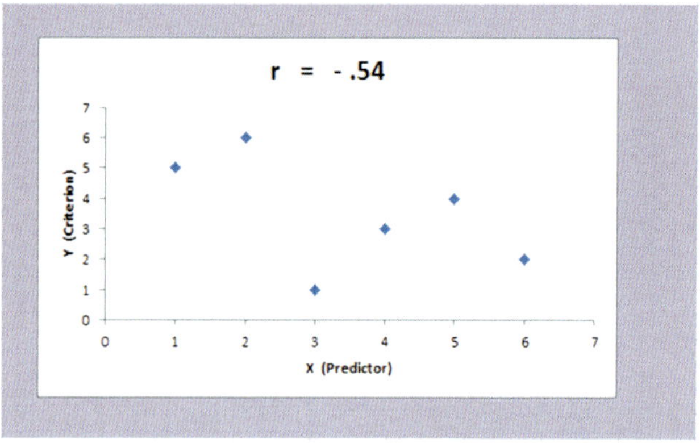

Fig. 6.5 Example of a Scatterplot for a Moderate, Negative Correlation (r = −.54)

Figure 6.6 shows a perfect negative correlation of $r = -1.0$ which means that X is a perfect predictor of Y, although in an inverse relationship such that as X increases, Y decreases. The data points fit perfectly along a downward-sloping straight line (see Fig. 6.6)

X	Y
1	6
2	5
3	4
4	3
5	2
6	1

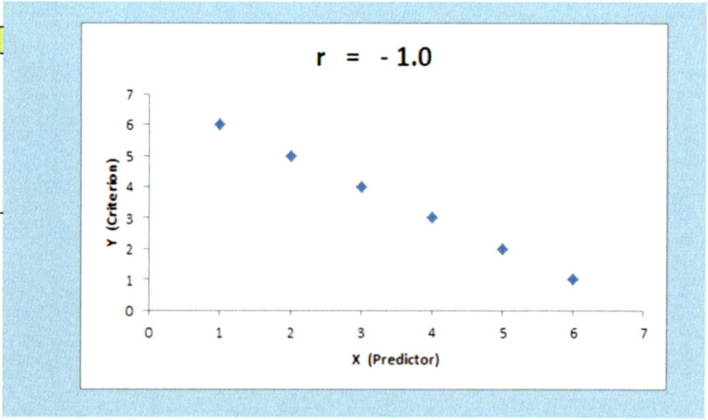

Fig. 6.6 Example of a Scatterplot for a Perfect, Negative Correlation (r = −1.0)

Let's explain the formula for computing the correlation *r* so that you can understand where the number summarizing the correlation came from.

In order to help you to understand *where* the correlation number that ranges from −1.0 to +1.0 comes from, we will walk you through the steps involved in using the formula as if you were using a calculator. This is the one time in this book that we will ask you to use your calculator to find a correlation. Knowing how a correlation is computed step-by-step will give you the opportunity to understand *how* the formula works in practice.

To do that, let's create a situation in which you need to find the correlation between two variables.

Suppose you wanted to find out if there was a relationship between high school grade-point average (HSGPA) and freshman GPA (FROSHGPA) for Human Resource Management majors at a major university. You have decided to call HSGPA the X-variable (i.e., the predictor variable) and FROSHGPA as the Y-variable (i.e., the criterion variable) in your analysis. To test your Excel skills, you take a random sample of freshmen Human Resource Management majors at the end of their freshman year and record their GPA. The hypothetical data for eight students appear in Fig. 6.7. (*Note: We are using only one decimal place for the GPAs in this example to simplify the mathematical computations*).

Fig. 6.7 Worksheet Data for High School GPA and Frosh GPA (Practical Example)

	A	B	C
1			
2		X	Y
3	Student	High School GPA	FROSH GPA
4	1	2.8	2.9
5	2	2.5	2.8
6	3	3.1	2.8
7	4	3.5	3.2
8	5	2.4	2.6
9	6	2.6	2.3
10	7	2.4	2.1
11	8	3.6	3.2
12			
13	n	8	8
14	MEAN	2.86	2.74
15	STDEV	0.48	0.39

Notice also that we have used Excel to find the sample size for both variables, X and Y, and the MEAN and STDEV of both variables. (You can practice your Excel skills by seeing if you get the same results when you create an Excel spreadsheet for these data).

Now, let's use the above table to compute the correlation *r* between HSGPA and FROSHGPA using your calculator.

6.1.1 Understanding the Formula for Computing a Correlation

Objective: To understand the formula for computing the correlation r

The formula for computing the correlation r is as follows:

$$r = \frac{\frac{1}{n-1}\Sigma\left(X - \overline{X}\right)\left(Y - \overline{Y}\right)}{S_x S_y} \tag{6.1}$$

This formula looks daunting at first glance, but let's "break it down into its steps" to understand how to compute the correlation r.

6.1.2 Understanding the Nine Steps for Computing a Correlation, r

Objective: To understand the nine steps of computing a correlation r

The nine steps are as follows:

Step	Computation	Result
1	Find the sample size n by noting the number of students	8
2	Divide the number 1 by the sample size minus 1 (i.e., 1/7)	0.14286
3	*For each student*, take the HSGPA and subtract the mean HSGPA for the 8 students and call this $X - \overline{X}$ (For example, for student # 6, this would be: 2.6 – 2.86) *Note: With your calculator, this difference is –0.26, but when Excel uses 16 decimal places for every computation, this result could be slightly different for each student*	–0.26
4	*For each student*, take the FROSHGPA and subtract the mean FROSHGPA for the 8 students and call this $Y - \overline{Y}$ (For example, for student # 6, this would be: 2.3 – 2.74)	–0.44
5	Then, *for each student*, multiply $(X - \overline{X})$ times $(Y - \overline{Y})$ (For example, for student # 6 this would be: (–0.26) × (–0.44))	+0.1144
6	Add the results of $(X - \overline{X})$ times $(Y - \overline{Y})$ for the 8 students	+1.09

Steps 1–6 would produce the Excel table given in Fig. 6.8.

	A	B	C	D	E	F	G
1							
2		X	Y				
3	Student	High School GPA	FROSH GPA	$X-\bar{X}$	$Y-\bar{Y}$	$(X-\bar{X})(Y-\bar{Y})$	
4	1	2.8	2.9	-0.06	0.16	-0.01	
5	2	2.5	2.8	-0.36	0.06	-0.02	
6	3	3.1	2.8	0.24	0.06	0.01	
7	4	3.5	3.2	0.64	0.46	0.29	
8	5	2.4	2.6	-0.46	-0.14	0.06	
9	6	2.6	2.3	-0.26	-0.44	0.11	
10	7	2.4	2.1	-0.46	-0.64	0.29	
11	8	3.6	3.2	0.74	0.46	0.34	
12						-------	
13	n	8	8		Total	1.09	
14	MEAN	2.86	2.74				
15	STDEV	0.48	0.39				

Fig. 6.8 Worksheet for Computing the Correlation, r

Notice that when Excel multiplies a negative number by a negative number, the result is a positive number (for example for student #7: $(-0.46) \times (-0.64) = +0.29$). And when Excel multiplies a negative number by a positive number, the result is a negative number (for example for student #1: $(-0.06) \times (+0.16) = -0.01$).

Note: Excel computes all calculations to 16 decimal places. So, when you check your work with a calculator, you may get a slightly different answer than Excel's answer.

For example, when you compute the answer for Student #2:

$$\begin{aligned} &\left(X-\overline{X}\right) \times \left(Y-\overline{Y}\right) \text{for student \#2, if you use two decimal places,} \\ &\text{your calculator gives: } (-0.36) \times (+0.06) = -0.02 \end{aligned} \tag{6.2}$$

As you can see from the table, Excel's answer is −0.02 which is really *more accurate* because Excel uses 16 decimal places for every number, even though only two decimal places are shown in Fig. 6.8.

You should also note that when you do Step 6, you have to be careful to add all of the positive numbers first to get *+1.10* and then add all of the negative numbers second to get *−0.03*, so that when you subtract these two numbers you get *+1.07* as your answer to Step 6. When you do these computations using Excel, this total figure will be *+1.09* because Excel carries every number and computation out to 16 decimal places which is more accurate than your calculator.

Step		
7	Multiply the answer for step 2 above by the answer for step 6 (0.14286 × 1.09)	0.1557
8	Multiply the STDEV of X times the STDEV of Y (0.48 × 0.39)	0.1872
9	Finally, divide the answer from step 7 by the answer from step 8 (0.1557 divided by 0.1872)	+ 0.83

This number of *0.83* is the correlation between HSGPA (X) and FROSHGPA (Y) for these 8 students. The number *+0.83* means that there is a strong, positive correlation between these two variables. That is, as HSGPA increases, FROSHGPA increases. For a more detailed discussion of correlation, see Zikmund and Babin (2010).

You could also use the results presented in Fig. 6.8 in the formula for computing the correlation r in the following way:

$$\text{correlation r} = \left[\,(1/(\text{n}-1)) \times \sum \left(X-\overline{X}\right)\left(Y-\overline{Y}\right)\right] / \left(\text{STDEV}_{\text{x}} \times \text{STDEV}_{\text{y}}\right)$$

$$\text{correlation r} = [(1/7) \times 1.09]/[(.48) \times (.39)]$$

$$\text{correlation} = \text{r} = 0.83$$

When you use Excel for these computations, you obtain a slightly different correlation of +0.82 because Excel uses 16 decimal places for all numbers and computations and is, therefore, more accurate than your calculator.

For more information about correlation, see Aamodt et al. (2007) and Davis (2011).

Now, let's discuss how you can use Excel to find the correlation between two variables in a much simpler, and much faster, fashion than using your calculator.

6.2 Using Excel to Compute a Correlation Between Two Variables

Objective: To use Excel to find the correlation between two variables

Suppose that you work in an HR department of a manufacturing company and that you have been asked to determine the relationship between the gross pay of the company's electrical engineers and their years of relevant work experience in business.

To test your Excel skills, you have organized the resulting data into a table in which you have recorded the years of relevant business experience of these electrical engineers along with their salary ($000). Note that salary has been recorded in thousands of dollars ($000), so that a salary of $65,000 would be recorded as 65 when it is converted to thousands of dollars. The hypothetical data appear in Fig. 6.9.

PAY AND EXPERIENCE FOR ELECTRICAL ENGINEERS

Is there a relationship between the gross pay of electrical engineers and their years of relevant business experience?

EXPERIENCE (yrs)	SALARY ($000)
3	65
5	72
9	84
4	61
7	80
9	135
12	101
14	115
15	105
18	121
13	135
17	146

Fig. 6.9 Worksheet Data for Experience and Salary (Practical Example)

You want to determine if there is a *relationship* between the years of relevant business experience of these engineers and their salaries, and you decide to use a correlation to determine this relationship. Let's call EXPERIENCE the predictor variable, X, and SALARY as the criterion variable, Y.

Create an Excel spreadsheet with the following information:

A3: PAY AND EXPERIENCE FOR ELECTRICAL ENGINEERS
B5: Is there a relationship between the gross pay of electrical engineers
B6: and their years of relevant business experience?
B8: EXPERIENCE (yrs)
C8: SALARY ($000)
B9: 3
C9: 65

Next, change the width of Columns B and C so that the information fits inside the cells.

Now, complete the remaining figures in the table given above so that B20 is 17 and C20 is 146. (Be sure to double-check your figures to make sure that they are correct!) Then, center the information in all of these cells.

A22: n
A23: mean
A24: stdev

Next, define the "name" to the range of data from B9:B20 as: YEARS

We discussed earlier in this book (see Sect. 1.4.4) how to "name a range of data," but here is a reminder of how to do that:

To give a "name" to a range of data:

Click on the top number in the range of data and drag the mouse down to the bottom number of the range.

For example, to give the name: "YEARS" to the cells: B9:B20, click on B9, and drag the pointer down to B20 so that the cells B9:B20 are highlighted on your computer screen. Then, click on:

Formulas
Define name (top center of your screen)
YEARS (enter this in the Name box; see Fig. 6.10)

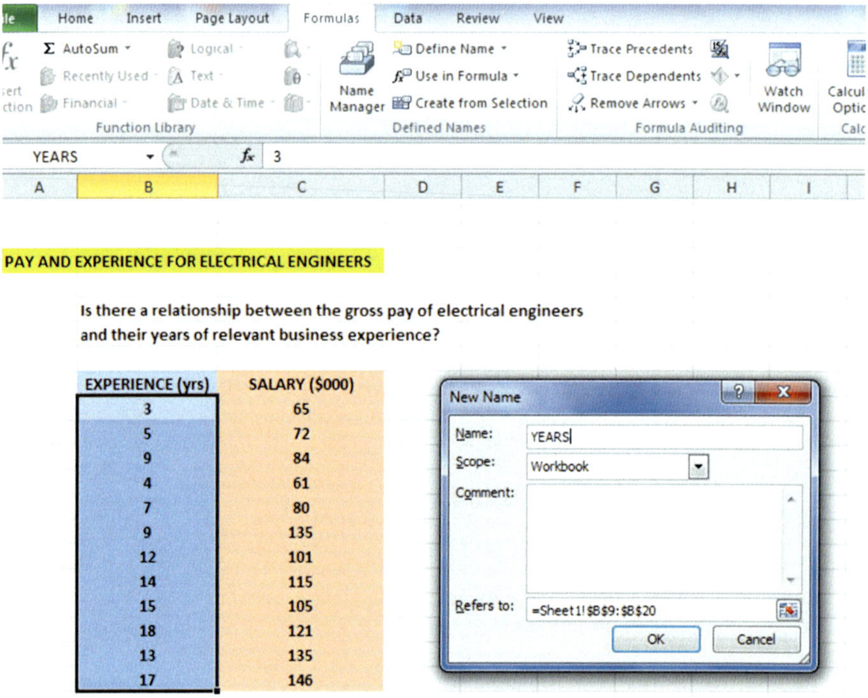

Fig. 6.10 Dialogue Box for Naming a Range of Data as: "YEARS"

OK

Now, repeat these steps to give the name: PAY to C9:C20

Finally, click on any blank cell on your spreadsheet to "deselect" cells C9:C20 on your computer screen.

Now, complete the data for these sample sizes, means, and standard deviations in columns B and C so that B23 is 10.50, and C24 is 29.25 (use two decimals for the means and standard deviations; see Fig. 6.11). Then, center these data in their cells.

PAY AND EXPERIENCE FOR ELECTRICAL ENGINEERS

Is there a relationship between the gross pay of electrical engineers and their years of relevant business experience?

	EXPERIENCE (yrs)	SALARY ($000)
	3	65
	5	72
	9	84
	4	61
	7	80
	9	135
	12	101
	14	115
	15	105
	18	121
	13	135
	17	146
n	12	12
mean	10.50	101.67
stdev	5.09	29.25

Fig. 6.11 Example of Using Excel to Find the Sample Size, Mean, and STDEV

Objective: Find the correlation between YEARS and PAY

B26: correlation

C26: =correl(YEARS,PAY); see Fig. 6.12

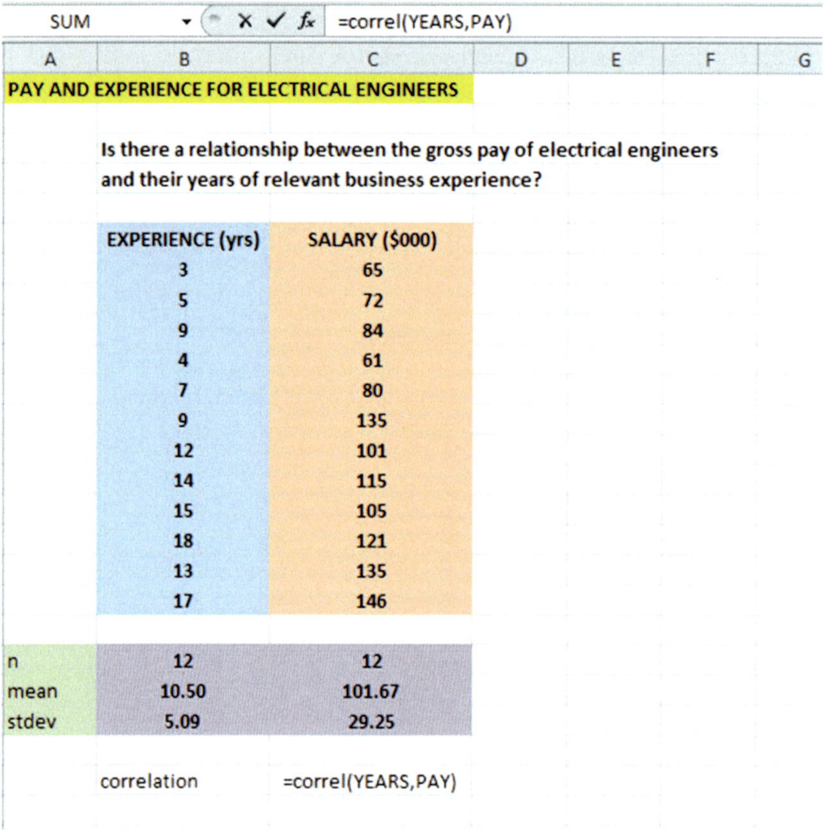

SUM =correl(YEARS,PAY)

PAY AND EXPERIENCE FOR ELECTRICAL ENGINEERS

Is there a relationship between the gross pay of electrical engineers and their years of relevant business experience?

	EXPERIENCE (yrs)	SALARY ($000)
	3	65
	5	72
	9	84
	4	61
	7	80
	9	135
	12	101
	14	115
	15	105
	18	121
	13	135
	17	146
n	12	12
mean	10.50	101.67
stdev	5.09	29.25
	correlation	=correl(YEARS,PAY)

Fig. 6.12 Example of Using Excel's =correl Function to Compute the Correlation Coefficient

Hit the Enter key to compute the correlation

C26: format this cell to two decimals, and center this figure.

Note that the equal sign in =correl(YEARS,PAY) in C26 tells Excel that you are going to use a formula in this cell.

The correlation between YEARS (X) and PAY (Y) is +*.81*, a very strong positive correlation. This means that you have evidence that there is a strong relationship between these two variables. In effect, the more years of relevant business experience, the higher the pay for these electrical engineers.

Save this file as: PAY10

The final spreadsheet appears in Fig. 6.13.

PAY AND EXPERIENCE FOR ELECTRICAL ENGINEERS			
	Is there a relationship between the gross pay of electrical engineers and their years of relevant business experience?		
	EXPERIENCE (yrs)	SALARY ($000)	
	3	65	
	5	72	
	9	84	
	4	61	
	7	80	
	9	135	
	12	101	
	14	115	
	15	105	
	18	121	
	13	135	
	17	146	
n	12	12	
mean	10.50	101.67	
stdev	5.09	29.25	
	correlation	0.81	

Fig. 6.13 Final Result of Using the =correl Function to Compute the Correlation Coefficient

6.3 Creating a Chart and Drawing the Regression Line onto the Chart

This section deals with the concept of "linear regression." Technically, the use of a simple linear regression model (i.e., the word "simple" means that only one predictor, X, is used to predict the criterion, Y), requires that the data meet the following four assumptions:

1. The underlying relationship between the two variables under study (X and Y) is *linear* in the sense that a straight line, and not a curved line, can fit among the data points on the chart.
2. The errors of measurement are independent of each other (e.g. the errors from a specific time period are sometimes correlated with the errors in a previous time period).
3. The errors fit a normal distribution of Y-values at each of the X-values.
4. The variance of the errors is the same for all X-values (i.e., the variability of the Y-values is the same for both low and high values of X).

A detailed explanation of these assumptions is beyond the scope of this book, but the interested reader can find a detailed discussion of these assumptions in Levine et al. (2011, pp. 529–530).

Now, let's create a chart summarizing these data.

Important note: *Whenever you draw a chart, it is ESSENTIAL that you put the predictor variable (X) on the left, and the criterion variable (Y) on the right in your Excel spreadsheet, so that you know which variable is the predictor variable and which variable is the criterion variable. If you do this, you will save yourself a lot of grief whenever you do a problem involving correlation and simple linear regression using Excel!*

Important note: *You need to understand that in any chart that has one predictor and a criterion that there are really TWO LINES that can be drawn between the data points:*

(1) One line uses X as the predictor, and Y as the criterion
(2) A second line uses Y as the predictor, and X as the criterion

This means that you have to be very careful to note in your input data the cells that contain X as the predictor, and Y as the criterion. If you get these cells mixed up and reverse them, you will create the wrong line for your data and you will have botched the problem terribly.

This is why we STRONGLY RECOMMEND IN THIS BOOK that you always put the X data (i.e., the predictor variable) on the LEFT of your table, and the Y data (i.e., the criterion variable) on the RIGHT of your table on your spreadsheet so that you don't get these variables mixed up.

Also note that the correlation, r, will be exactly the same correlation no matter which variable you call the predictor variable and which variable you call the criterion variable. The correlation coefficient just summarizes the relationship between two variables, and doesn't care which one is the predictor and which one is the criterion.

Let's suppose that you would like to use the years of experience as the predictor variable, and you would like to use it to predict the salary of an electrical engineer. Since the correlation between these two variables is *+.81*, this shows there is a strong, positive relationship and that the number of years of relevant business experience is a good predictor of pay.

1. Open the file that you saved earlier in this chapter: PAY10

6.3.1 *Using Excel to Create a Chart and the Regression Line Through the Data Points*

Objective: To create a chart and the regression line summarizing the relationship between YEARS and PAY

2. Click and drag the mouse to highlight both columns of numbers (B9:C20), *but do not highlight the labels above the data points.*

Highlight the data set: B9:C20
Insert (top left of screen)
Highlight: Scatter chart icon (immediately above the word: "Charts" at the top center of your screen)
Click on the down arrow on the right of the chart icon
Highlight the top left scatter chart icon (see Fig. 6.14)

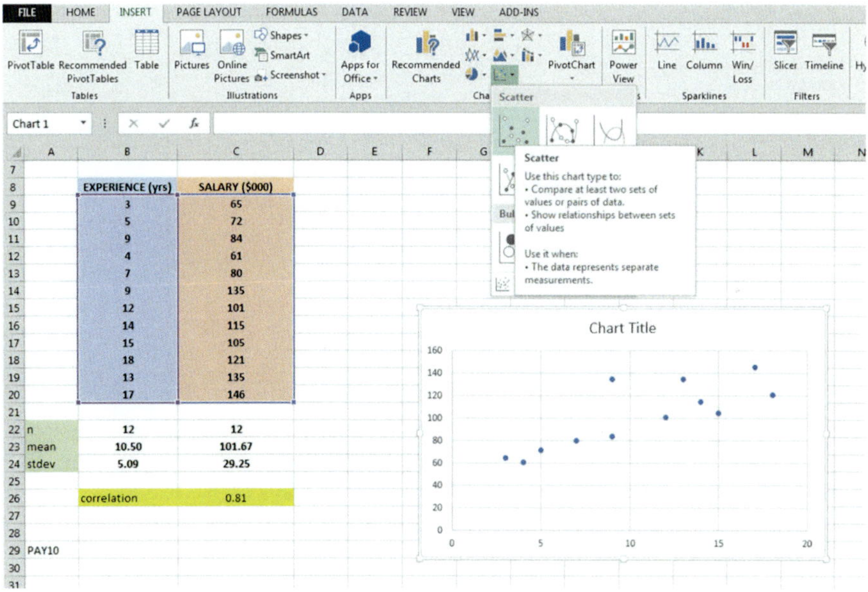

Fig. 6.14 Example of Selecting a Scatter Chart

Click on the top left chart to select it
Click on the "+icon" to the right of the chart (CHART ELEMENTS)
Click on the check mark next to the "Chart Title" **and also** next to "Gridlines" to remove these check marks (see Fig. 6.15)

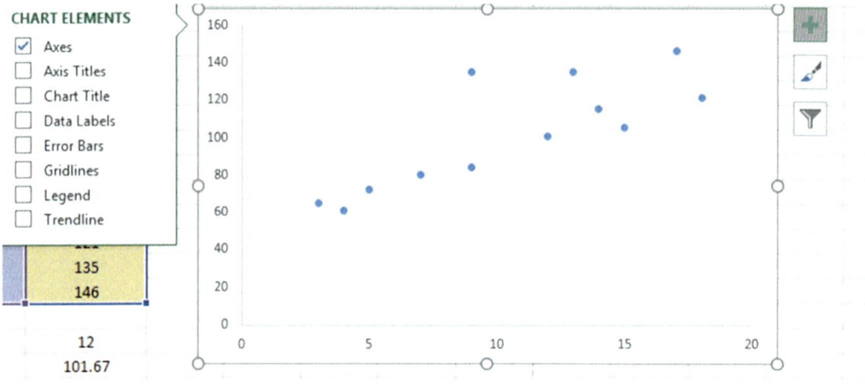

Fig. 6.15 Example of Chart Elements Selected

Click on the box next to: "Chart Title" and then click on the arrow to its right. Then, click on: "Above chart".

Note that the words: "Chart Title" are now in a box at the top of the chart (see Fig. 6.16).

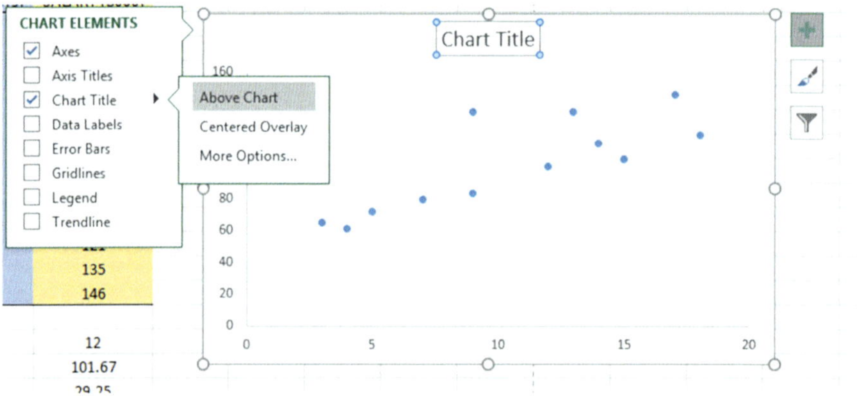

Fig. 6.16 Example of Chart Title Selected

Enter the following Chart Title to the right of "$\mathbf{f_x}$" at the top of your screen:

RELATIONSHIP BETWEEN PAY AND EXPERIENCE FOR ELECTRICAL ENGINEERS (see Fig. 6.17)

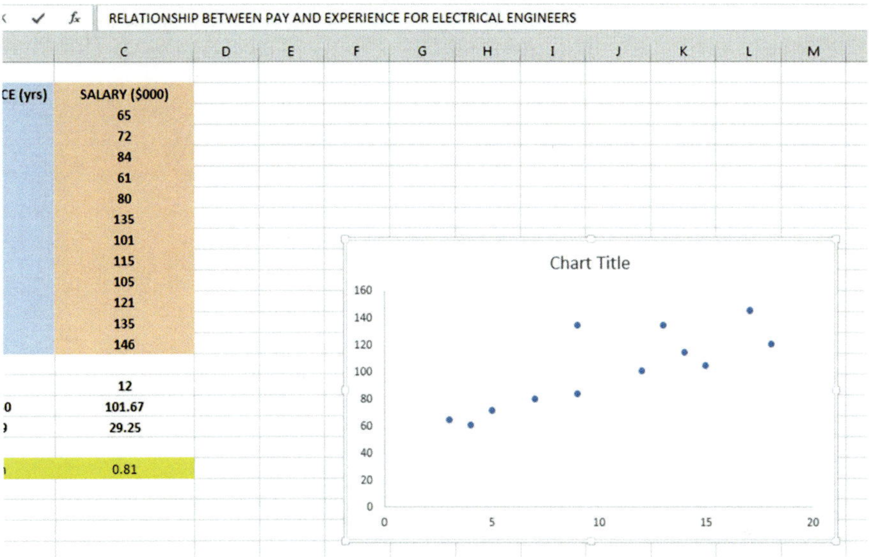

Fig. 6.17 Example of Creating a Chart Title

Hit the Enter Key to enter this chart title onto the chart

Click *inside the chart at the top right corner of the chart* to "deselect" the box around the Chart Title (see Fig. 6.18)

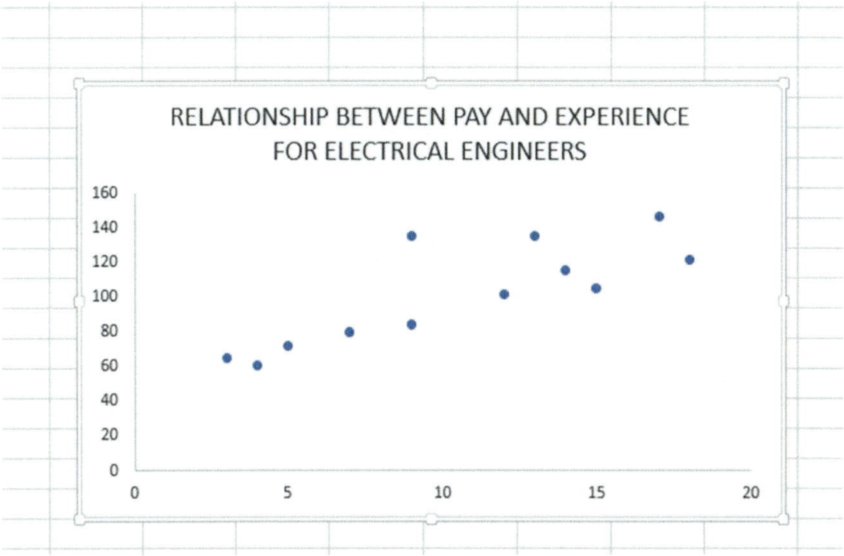

Fig. 6.18 Example of a Chart Title Inserted onto the Chart

Click on the "+ box" to the right of the chart
Add a check mark to the left of "Axis Titles" (This will create an "Axis Title" box on the y-axis of the chart).
Click on the right arrow for: "Axis titles" and then click on: "Primary Horizontal" to remove the check mark in its box (This will create the y-axis title)
Enter the following y-axis title to the right of $\mathbf{f_x}$ at the top of your screen:
GROSS PAY ($000)

Then, hit the Enter Key to enter this y-axis title onto the chart.
Click *inside the chart at the top right corner of the chart* to "deselect" the box around the y-axis title (see Fig. 6.19).

Fig. 6.19 Example of Adding a y-axis Title to the Chart

Click on the "+ box" to the right of the chart
Highlight: "Axis Titles" and click on its right arrow
Click on the words: "Primary Horizontal" to add a check mark to its box (This Creates an "Axis Title" box on the x-axis of the chart)
Enter the following x-axis title to the right of $\mathbf{f_x}$ at the top of your screen:
YEARS OF EXPERIENCE

Then, hit the Enter Key to add this x-axis title to the chart.
Click *inside the chart at the top right corner of the chart* to "deselect" the box around the x-axis title (see Fig. 6.20)

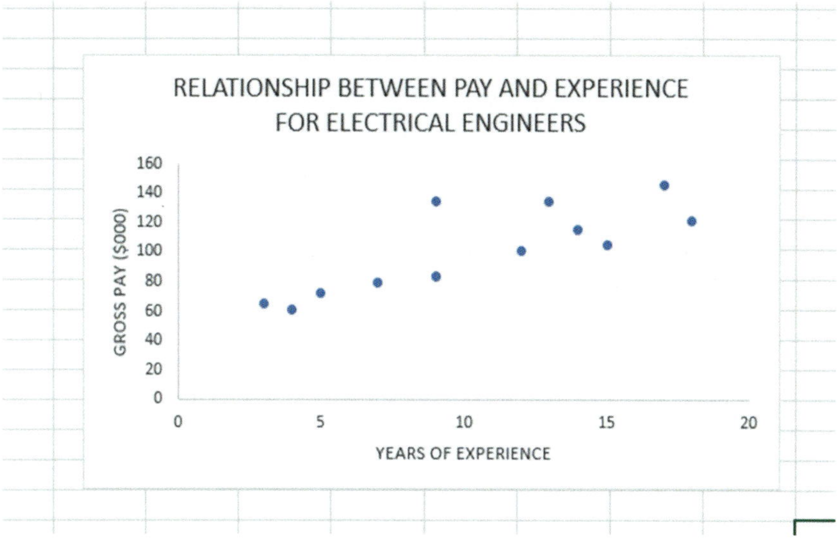

Fig. 6.20 Example of a Chart Title, an x-axis Title, and a y-axis Title

Now, let's draw the regression line onto the chart. This regression line is called the "least-squares regression line" and it is the "best-fitting" straight line through the data points.

6.3.1.1 Drawing the Regression Line Through the Data Points in the Chart

Objective: To draw the regression line through the data points on the chart

Right-click on any one of the data points inside the chart
Highlight: Add Trendline (see Fig. 6.21)

Fig. 6.21 Dialog Box for Adding a Trendline to the Chart

Click on: Add Trendline

Linear (be sure the "linear" button near the top is selected on the "Format Trendline" dialog box; see Fig. 6.22)

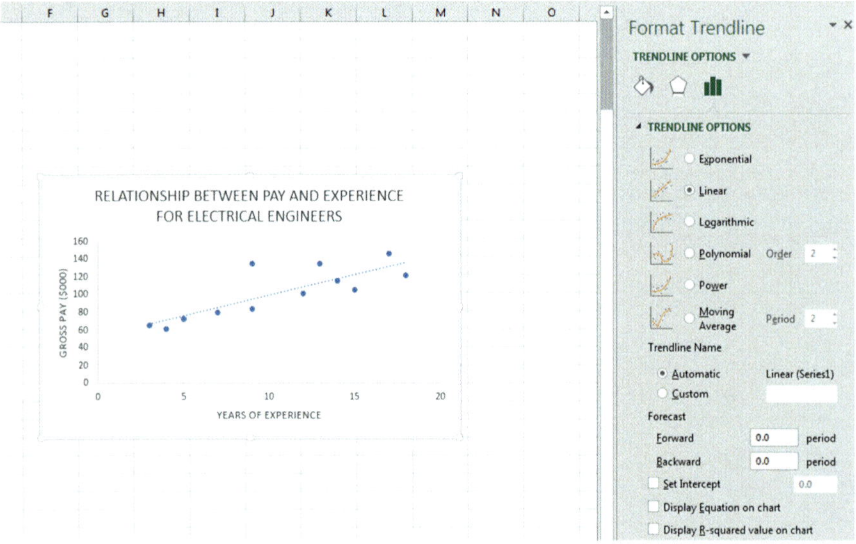

Fig. 6.22 Dialog Box for a Linear Trendline

Click on the X at the top right of the "Format Trendline" dialog box to close this dialog box
Click on any blank cell *outside* the chart to "deselect" the chart
Save this file as: PAY11

Your spreadsheet should look like the spreadsheet in Fig. 6.23.

PAY AND EXPERIENCE FOR ELECTRICAL ENGINEERS

Is there a relationship between the gross pay of electrical engineers
and their years of relevant business experience?

	EXPERIENCE (yrs)	SALARY ($000)
	3	65
	5	72
	9	84
	4	61
	7	80
	9	135
	12	101
	14	115
	15	105
	18	121
	13	135
	17	146
n	12	12
mean	10.50	101.67
stdev	5.09	29.25
	correlation	0.81

PAY11

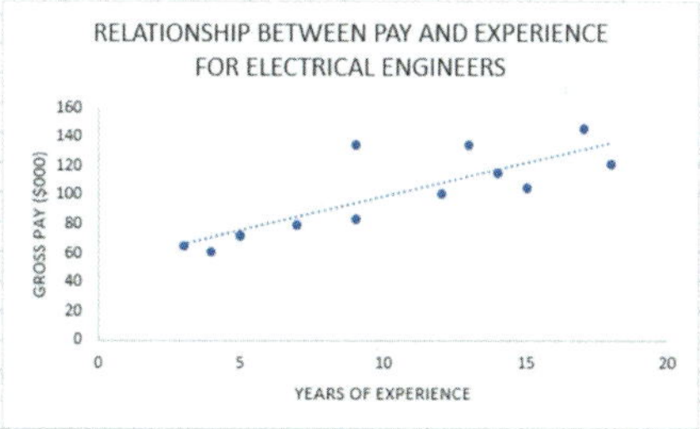

Fig. 6.23 Final Chart with the Trendline Fitted Through the Data Points of the Scatterplot

6.3.1.2 Moving the Chart Below the Table in the Spreadsheet

Objective: To move the chart below the table

Left-click your mouse on *any white space to the right of the top title inside the chart*, keep the left-click down, and drag the chart down and to the left so that the top left corner of the chart is in cell A29, then take your finger off the left-click of the mouse (see Fig. 6.24).

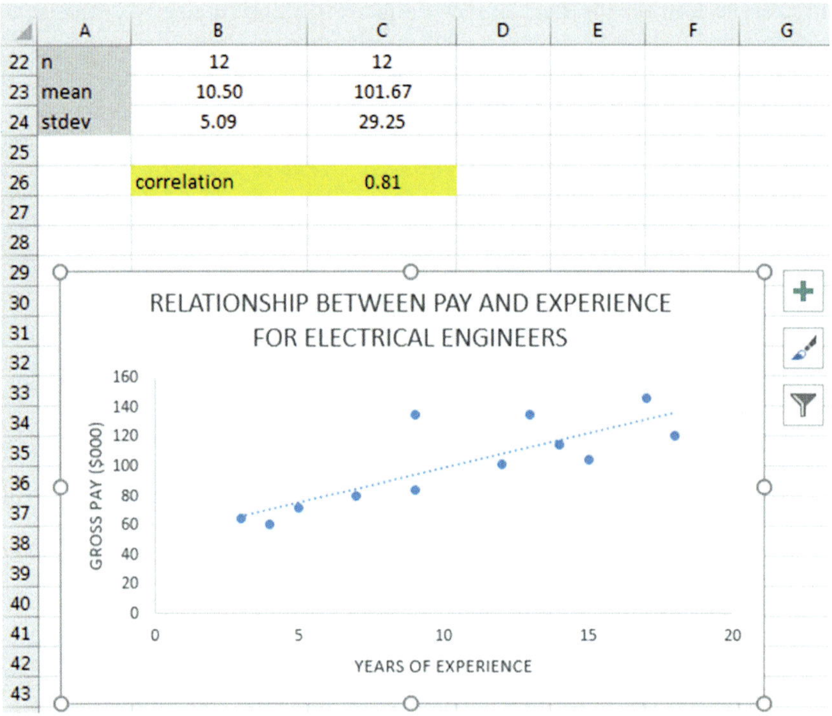

Fig. 6.24 Example of Moving the Chart Below the Table

6.3.1.3 Making the Chart "Longer" so That It Is "Taller"

Objective: To make the chart "longer" so that it is taller

Left-click your mouse on the bottom-center of the chart to create an "up-and-down-arrow" sign, hold the left-click of the mouse down and drag the bottom of the chart down to row 48 to make the chart longer, and then take your finger off the mouse.

6.3.1.4 Making the Chart "Wider"

Objective: To make the chart "wider"

Put the pointer at the middle of the right-border of the chart to create a "left-to-right arrow" sign, and then left-click your mouse and hold the left-click down while you drag the right border of the chart to the middle of Column H to make the chart wider.

Now, click on any blank cell outside the chart to "deselect" the chart (see Fig. 6.25).

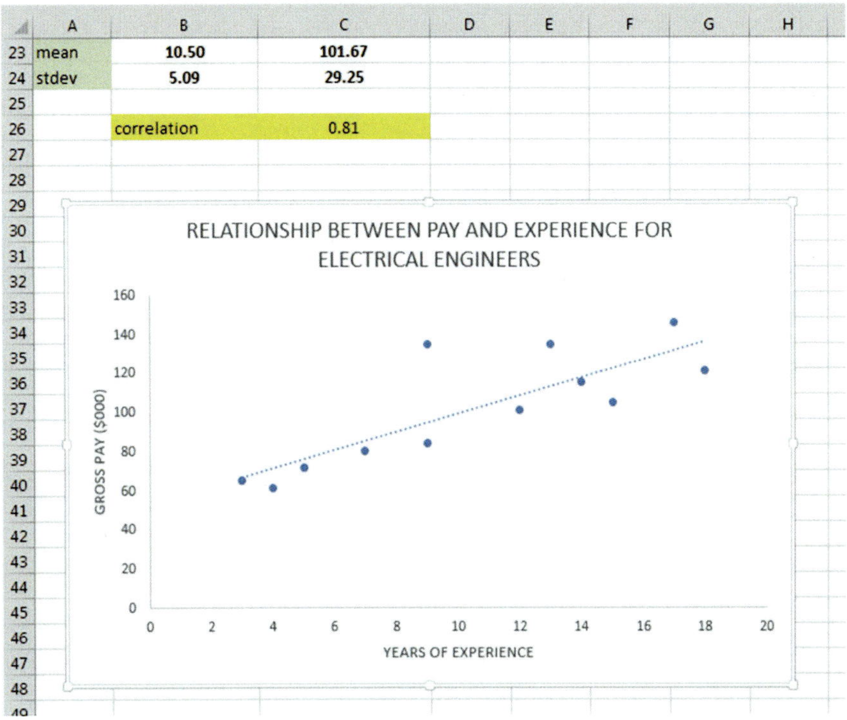

Fig. 6.25 Example of a Chart that is Enlarged to Fit the Cells: A29:H48

Now, click on any blank cell *outside* the chart to "deselect" the chart

Save this file as: PAY12

Note: If you printed this spreadsheet now, it is "too big" to fit onto one page, and would "dribble over" onto four pages of printout because the scale needs to be reduced below 100 % in order for this worksheet to fit onto only one page. You need to complete the steps below to print out some, or all, of this spreadsheet.

6.4 Printing a Spreadsheet So That the Table and Chart Fit onto One Page

Objective: To print the spreadsheet so that the table and the chart fit onto one page

Page Layout (top of screen)

Change the scale at the middle icon near the top of the screen "Scale to Fit" by clicking on the down-arrow until it reads "90 %" so that the table and the chart will fit onto one page on your printout (see Fig. 6.26):

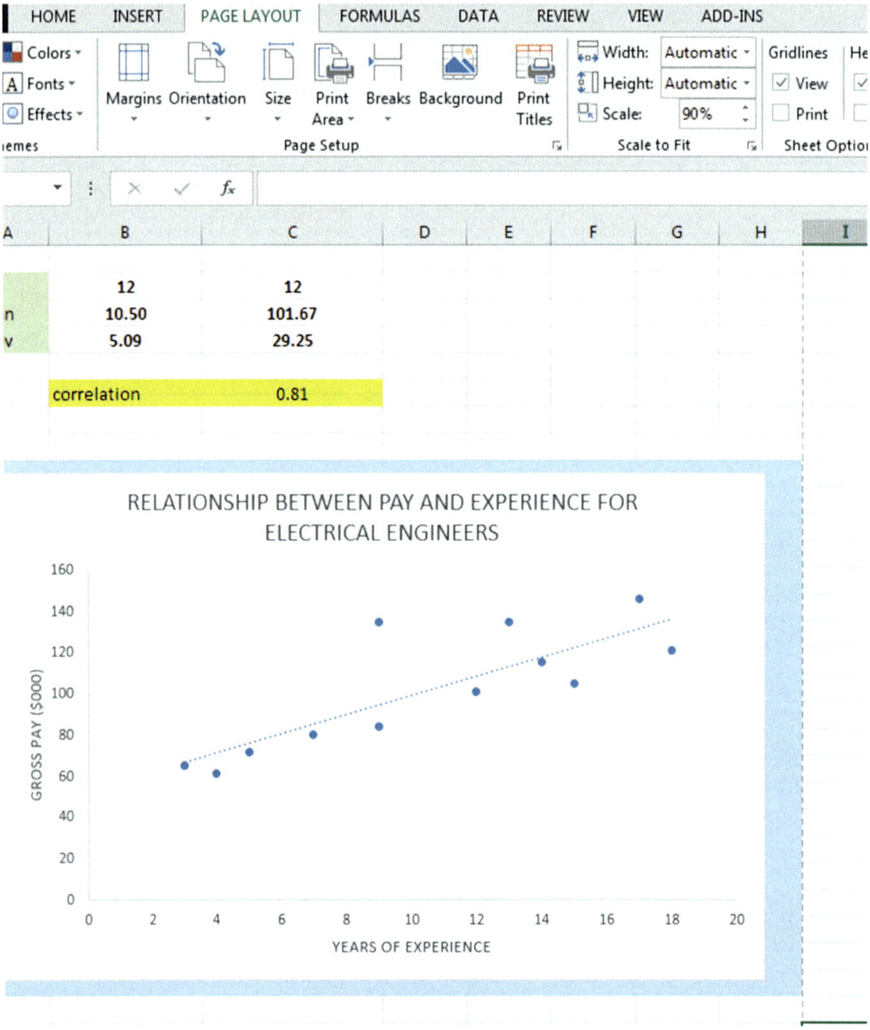

Fig. 6.26 Example of the Page Layout for Reducing the Scale of the Chart to 90 % of Normal Size

File
Print
Print (see Fig. 6.27)
Save your file as: PAY13

PAY AND EXPERIENCE FOR ELECTRICAL ENGINEERS

Is there a relationship between the gross pay of electrical engineers and their years of relevant business experience?

	EXPERIENCE (yrs)	SALARY ($000)
	3	65
	5	72
	9	84
	4	61
	7	80
	9	135
	12	101
	14	115
	15	105
	18	121
	13	135
	17	146
n	12	12
mean	10.50	101.67
stdev	5.09	29.25
	correlation	0.81

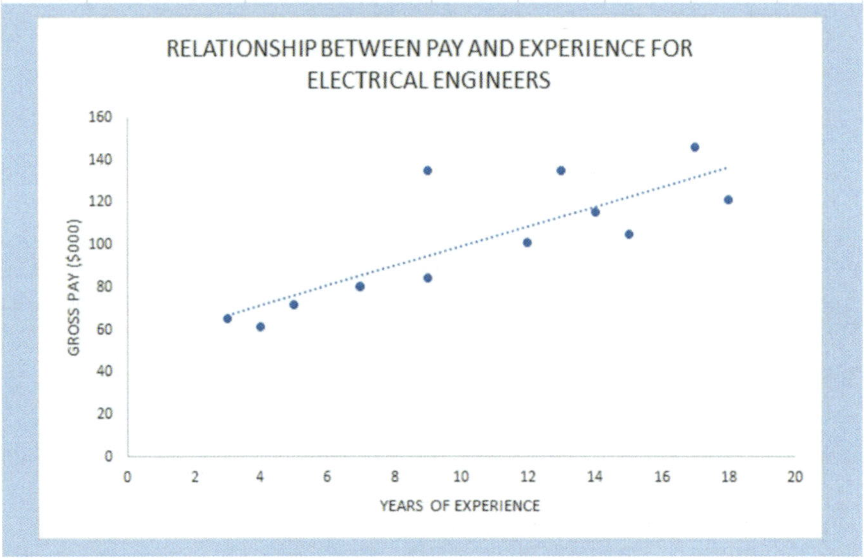

Fig. 6.27 Final Spreadsheet of a Table and a Chart (90 % Scale to Fit Size)

6.5 Finding the Regression Equation

The main reason for charting the relationship between X and Y (i.e., YEARS as X and PAY as Y in our example) is to see if there is a strong enough relationship between X and Y so that the regression equation that summarizes this relationship can be used to predict Y for a given value of X.

Since we know that the correlation between the YEARS and PAY is *+.81*, this tells us that it makes sense to use YEARS to predict PAY based on past data.

We now need to find the regression equation that is the equation of the "best-fitting straight line" through the data points.

Objective: To find the regression equation summarizing the relationship between X and Y.

In order to find this equation, we need to check to see if your version of Excel contains the "Data Analysis ToolPak" necessary to run a regression analysis.

6.5.1 Installing the Data Analysis ToolPak into Excel

Objective: To install the Data Analysis ToolPak into Excel

Since there are currently four versions of Excel in the marketplace (2007, 2010, 2013, 2016) we will now give a brief explanation of how to install the Data Analysis ToolPak into each of four versions of Excel.

6.5.1.1 Installing the Data Analysis ToolPak into Excel 2016

Open a new Excel spreadsheet

Click on: Data (at the top of your screen)

Look at the top of your monitor screen. Do you see the words: "Data Analysis" at the far right of the screen? If you do, the Data Analysis ToolPak for Excel 2016 was correctly installed when you installed Office 2016, and you should skip ahead to Sect. 6.5.2.

If the words: "Data Analysis" are not at the top right of your monitor screen, then the ToolPak component of Excel 2016 was not installed when you installed Office 2016 onto your computer. If this happens, you need to follow these steps:

File
Options (bottom left of screen)
Note: This creates a dialog box with "Excel Options" at the top left of the box
Add-Ins (on left of screen)
Manage: Excel Add-Ins (at the bottom of the dialog box)
Go (at bottom center of dialog box)
Highlight: Analysis ToolPak (in the Add-Ins dialog box)
Put a check mark to the left of Analysis Toolpak
OK (at the right of this dialog box)
Data

You now should have the words: "Data Analysis" at the top right of your screen to show that this feature has been installed correctly

Note: If these steps do not work, you should try these steps instead:
File/Options (bottom left)/Add-ins/Analysis ToolPak/Go/
click to the left of Analysis ToolPak to add a check mark/OK

If you need help doing this, ask your favorite "computer techie" for help.
You are now ready to skip ahead to Sect. 6.5.2

6.5.1.2 Installing the Data Analysis ToolPak into Excel 2013

Open a new Excel spreadsheet

Click on: Data (at the top of your screen)

Look at the top of your monitor screen. Do you see the words: "Data Analysis" at the far right of the screen? If you do, the Data Analysis ToolPak for Excel 2013 was correctly installed when you installed Office 2013, and you should skip ahead to Sect. 6.5.2.

If the words: "Data Analysis" are not at the top right of your monitor screen, then the ToolPak component of Excel 2013 was not installed when you installed Office 2013 onto your computer. If this happens, you need to follow these steps:

File
Options (bottom left of screen)
Note: This creates a dialog box with "Excel Options" at the top left of the box
Add-Ins (on left of screen)
Manage: Excel Add-Ins (at the bottom of the dialog box)
Go (at bottom center of dialog box)
Highlight: Analysis ToolPak (in the Add-Ins dialog box)
Put a check mark to the left of Analysis Toolpak
OK (at the right of this dialog box)
Data

You now should have the words: "Data Analysis" at the top right of your screen to show that this feature has been installed correctly

If you get a prompt asking you for the "installation CD," put this CD in the CD drive and click on: OK

Note: If these steps do not work, you should try these steps instead:
File/Options (bottom left)/Add-ins/Analysis ToolPak/Go/
click to the left of Analysis ToolPak to add a check mark/OK

If you need help doing this, ask your favorite "computer techie" for help.

You are now ready to skip ahead to Sect. 6.5.2

6.5.1.3 Installing the Data Analysis ToolPak into Excel 2010

Open a new Excel spreadsheet
Click on: Data (at the top of your screen)

Look at the top of your monitor screen. Do you see the words: "Data Analysis" at the far right of the screen? If you do, the Data Analysis ToolPak for Excel 2010 was correctly installed when you installed Office 2010, and you should skip ahead to Sect. 6.5.2.

If the words: "Data Analysis" are not at the top right of your monitor screen, then the ToolPak component of Excel 2010 was not installed when you installed Office 2010 onto your computer. If this happens, you need to follow these steps:

File
Options
Excel options (creates a dialog box)
Add-Ins
Manage: Excel Add-Ins (at the bottom of the dialog box)
Go
Highlight: Analysis ToolPak (in the Add-Ins dialog box)
OK
Data (You now should have the words: "Data Analysis" at the top right of your screen)

If you get a prompt asking you for the "installation CD," put this CD in the CD drive and click on: OK

Note: If these steps do not work, you should try these steps instead:
File/Options (bottom left)/Add-ins/Analysis ToolPak/Go/
click to the left of Analysis ToolPak to add a check mark/OK

If you need help doing this, ask your favorite "computer techie" for help.

You are now ready to skip ahead to Sect. 6.5.2.

6.5.1.4 Installing the Data Analysis ToolPak into Excel 2007

Open a new Excel spreadsheet
Click on: Data (at the top of your screen)

If the words "Data Analysis" do not appear at the top right of your screen, you need to install the Data Analysis ToolPak using the following steps:

Microsoft Office button (top left of your screen)
Excel options (bottom of dialog box)
Add-ins (far left of dialog box)
Go (to create a dialog box for Add-Ins)
Highlight: Analysis ToolPak
OK (If Excel asks you for permission to proceed, click on: Yes)
Data (You should now have the words: "Data Analysis" at the top right of your screen)

If you need help doing this, ask your favorite "computer techie" for help.
You are now ready to skip ahead to Sect. 6.5.2.

6.5.2 Using Excel to Find the SUMMARY OUTPUT of Regression

You have now installed *ToolPak*, and you are ready to find the regression equation for the "best-fitting straight line" through the data points by using the following steps:
Open the Excel file: PAY13 (if it is not already open on your screen)

Note: If this file is already open, and there is a "border" around the chart, you need to click on any empty cell outside of the chart to deselect the chart.

Now that you have installed *Toolpak*, you are ready to find the regression equation summarizing the relationship between YEARS and PAY used in your data set.

Remember that you gave the name: *YEARS* to the X data (the predictor), and the name: *PAY* to the Y data (the criterion) in a previous section of this chapter (see Sect. 6.2)

Data (top of screen)
Data analysis (far right at top of screen; see Fig. 6.28)

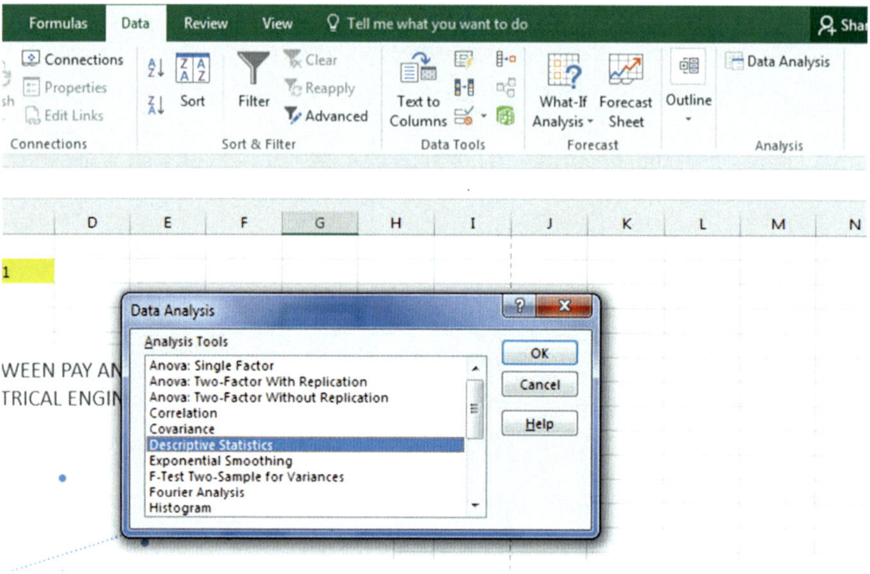

Fig. 6.28 Example of Using the Data/Data Analysis Function of Excel

Scroll down the dialog box using the down arrow and highlight: Regression (see Fig. 6.29)

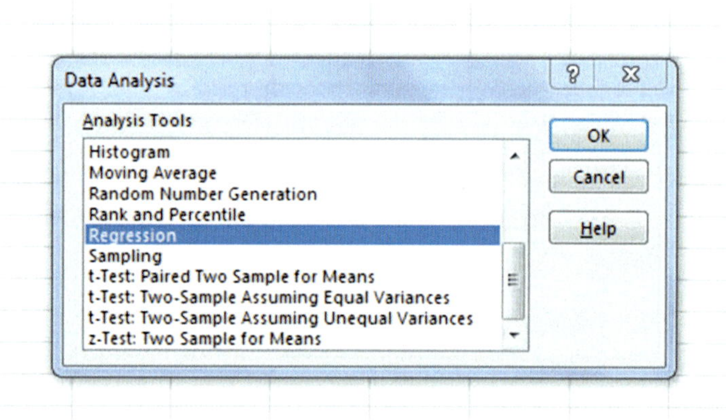

Fig. 6.29 Dialogue Box for Creating the Regression Function in Excel

OK

Input Y Range: PAY
Input X Range: YEARS

Click on the "button" to the left of Output Range to select this, and enter
A52 in the box as the place on your spreadsheet to insert the
Regression analysis in cell A52.
OK

The *SUMMARY OUTPUT* should now be in cells: A52: I69

Widen column A so that all of the words in the SUMMARY OUTPUT are readable.

Now, change the data in the following two cells to Number format (two decimal places) by first clicking on "Home" at the top left of your screen:

B55
B68

Next, change this cell to four decimal places: B69

Now, change the format for all other numbers that are in decimal format to number format, three decimal places, and center all numbers within their cells.

Next, widen all columns so that all of the labels fit inside the column widths.

Print the file so that it fits onto one page. (*Hint: Change the scale under "Page Layout" to 65 % to make it fit.*) Your file should be like the file in Fig. 6.30.

PAY AND EXPERIENCE FOR ELECTRICAL ENGINEERS

Is there a relationship between the gross pay of electrical engineers and their years of relevant business experience?

EXPERIENCE (yrs)	SALARY ($000)
3	65
5	72
9	84
4	61
7	80
9	135
12	101
14	115
15	105
18	121
13	135
17	146

n	12	12
mean	10.50	101.67
stdev	5.09	29.25

correlation	0.81

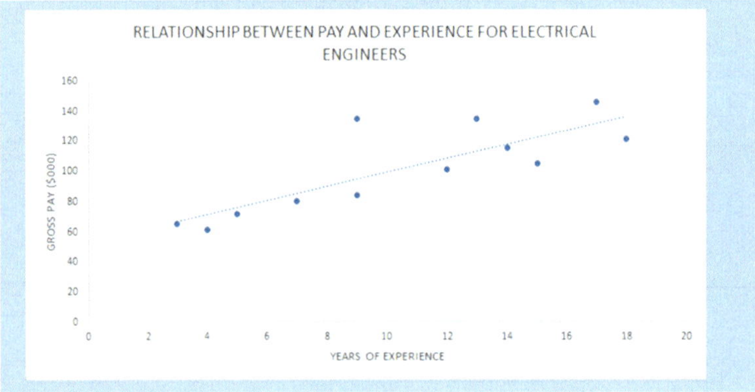

SUMMARY OUTPUT

Regression Statistics	
Multiple R	0.81
R Square	0.662
Adjusted R Square	0.628
Standard Error	17.847
Observations	12

ANOVA

	df	*SS*	*MS*	*F*	*Significance F*
Regression	1	6225.347	6225.347	19.544	0.001
Residual	10	3185.319	318.532		
Total	11	9410.667			

	Coefficients	*Standard Error*	*t Stat*	*P-value*	*Lower 95%*	*Upper 95%*	*Lower 95.0%*	*Upper 95.0%*
Intercept	52.59	12.238	4.298	0.002	25.325	79.861	25.325	79.861
X Variable 1	4.6737	1.057	4.421	0.001	2.318	7.029	2.318	7.029

Fig. 6.30 Final Spreadsheet of Correlation and Simple Linear Regression including the SUMMARY OUTPUT for the Data

Save the resulting file as:. PAY14

Note the following problem with the summary output.

Whoever wrote the computer program for this version of Excel made a mistake and gave the name: "Multiple R" to cell A55.

This is not correct. Instead, cell A55 should say: "correlation r" since this is the notation that we are using for the correlation between X and Y.

You can now use your printout of the regression analysis to find the regression equation that is the best-fitting straight line through the data points.

But first, let's review some basic terms.

6.5.2.1 Finding the y-Intercept, a, of the Regression Line

The point on the y-axis at which the regression line would intersect the y-axis if it were extended to reach the y-axis is called the "y-intercept" and *we will use the letter "a" to stand for the y-intercept of the regression line*. The y-intercept on the SUMMARY OUTPUT of Fig. 6.30 is *+52.59 and appears in cell B68*. This means that if you were to draw an imaginary line continuing down the regression line toward the y-axis that this imaginary line would cross the y-axis at 52.59. This is why it is called the "y-intercept."

6.5.2.2 Finding the Slope, b, of the Regression Line

The "tilt" of the regression line is called the "slope" of the regression line. It summarizes to what degree the regression line is either above or below a horizontal line through the data points. If the correlation between X and Y were zero, the regression line would be exactly horizontal to the X-axis and would have a zero slope.

If the correlation between X and Y is positive, the regression line would "slope upward to the right" above the x-axis. Since the regression line in Fig. 6.30 slopes upward to the right, the slope of the regression line is +4.6737 as given in cell *B69*. *We will use the notation "b" to stand for the slope of the regression line*. (Note that Excel calls the slope of the line: "X Variable 1" in the Excel printout).

Since the correlation between YEARS and PAY was +*.81*, you can see that the regression line for these data "slopes upward to the right" through the data points. Note that the SUMMARY OUTPUT of the regression line in Fig.6.30 gives a correlation, r, of *.81* in cell *B55*.

If the correlation between X and Y were negative, the regression line would "slope down to the right" above the x-axis. This would happen whenever the correlation between X and Y is a negative correlation that is between zero and minus one (0 and −1).

6.5.3 Finding the Equation for the Regression Line

To find the regression equation for the straight line that can be used to predict PAY, we only need two numbers in the SUMMARY OUTPUT in Fig. 6.30: *B68 and B69*.

$$\text{The format for the regression line is :} \qquad Y = a + bX \qquad (6.3)$$

where a = *the y-intercept* (52.59 in our example in cell B68)
and b = *the slope of the line* (+4.6737 in our example in cell B69)
Therefore, the equation for the best-fitting regression line for our example is:

$$\text{Y} = \text{a} + \text{b X}$$
$$\boxed{\text{Y} = 52.59 + 4.6737\ \text{X}}$$

Remember that Y is the PAY that we are trying to predict, using the number of years of experience as the predictor, X.

Let's try an example using this formula to predict the PAY of an electrical engineer.

6.5.4 Using the Regression Line to Predict the y-Value for a Given x-Value

Objective: To find the predicted PAY of an electrical engineer who has had 12 years of relevant business experience

Since the number of years of experience (i.e., X = 12), substituting this number into our regression equation gives:

$$\text{Y} = 52.59 + 4.6737\ (12)$$
$$\text{Y} = 52.59 + 56.08$$
$$\text{Y} = 108.67 \text{ or } \$108,670 \text{ since PAY is measured in thousands of dollars}$$

Important note: If you look at your chart and move directly upwards in your chart from 12 years of experience until you hit the regression line, you will see that you hit this line just ABOVE 100 on the y-axis to the left when you draw a line horizontal to the x-axis (actually, it is exactly 108.67), the result from above for predicting the PAY for 12 years of experience.

Now, let's do a second example and predict the PAY of an engineer who had 8 years of business experience.

$$Y = 52.59 + 4.6737\ X$$

$$Y = 52.59 + 4.6737\ (8)$$

$$Y = 52.59 + 37.39$$

$$Y = 89.98 \text{ or } \$89,980 \text{ since pay is measured in thousands of dollars}$$

Important note: If you look at your chart and move directly upwards in your chart from 8 years of experience until you hit the regression line, you will see that you hit this line just above 80 on the y-axis to the left (actually it is exactly 89.98), the result from above for predicting the pay of an engineer who had 8 years of relevant business experience.

For a more detailed discussion of regression, see Black (2010), Pease et al. (2013), and Whetzel and Wheaton (2007).

6.6 Adding the Regression Equation to the Chart

Objective: To Add the Regression Equation to the Chart

If you want to include the regression equation within the chart next to the regression line, you can do that, but a word of caution first.

Throughout this book, we are using the regression equation for one predictor and one criterion to be the following:

$$Y = a + b\,X \tag{6.3}$$

where a = y-intercept and
b = slope of the line

See, for example, the regression equation in Sect. 6.5.3 where the y-intercept was *a* = *52.59* and the slope of the line was *b* = *+4.6737* to generate the following regression equation:

$$Y = 52.59 + 4.6737\ X$$

However, Excel 2016 uses a slightly different regression equation (which is in a different order but is logically identical to the one used in this book) when you add a regression equation to a chart:

$$Y = bX + a \tag{6.4}$$

where a = y-intercept and
b = slope of the line

Note that this equation is identical to the one we are using in this book with the terms arranged in a different sequence.

For the example we used in Sect. 6.5.3, Excel 2016 would write the regression equation on the chart as:

$$Y = 4.6737\ X + 52.59$$

This is the format that will result when you add the regression equation to the chart using Excel 2016 using the following steps:

Open the file: PAY14 (*that you saved in Sect. 6.5.2*)
Click just *inside the outer border of the chart in the top right corner* to add the "border" around the chart in order to "select the chart" for changes you are about to make
Right-click on any of the data-points in the chart
Highlight: Add Trendline, and click on it to select this command
The "Linear button" near the top of the dialog box will be selected (on its left)

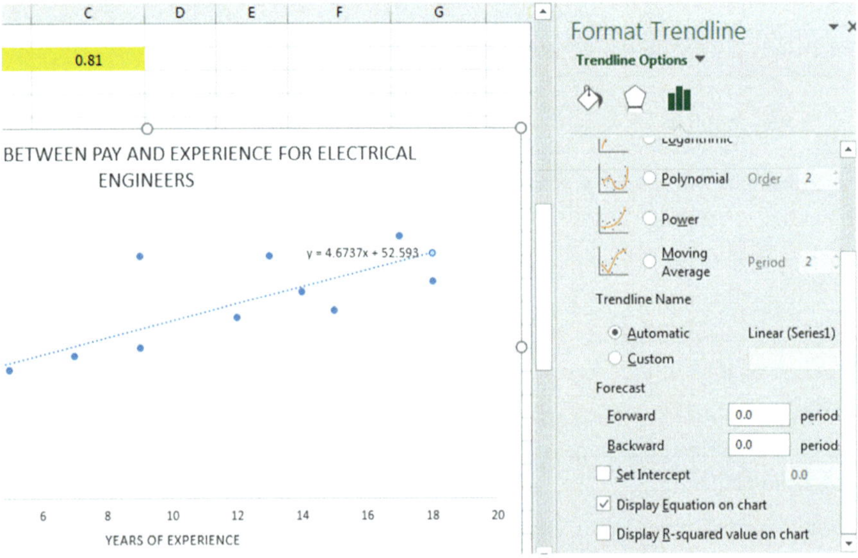

Fig. 6.31 Dialog Box for Adding the Regression Equation to the Chart Next to the Regression Line on the Chart

Scroll down this dialog box and click on: Display Equation on chart (near the bottom of the dialog box; see Fig. 6.31)
Click on the X at the top right of the "Format Trendline" dialog box to remove this box.
Click on any empty cell *outside of the chart* to deselect the chart.

PAY AND EXPERIENCE FOR ELECTRICAL ENGINEERS

Is there a relationship between the gross pay of electrical engineers and their years of relevant business experience?

	EXPERIENCE (yrs)	SALARY ($000)
	3	65
	5	72
	9	84
	4	61
	7	80
	9	135
	12	101
	14	115
	15	105
	18	121
	13	135
	17	146
n	12	12
mean	10.50	101.67
stdev	5.09	29.25
	correlation	0.81

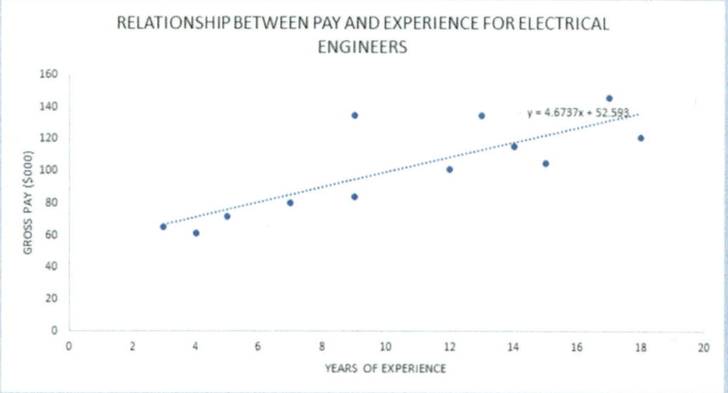

SUMMARY OUTPUT

Regression Statistics	
Multiple R	0.81
R Square	0.662
Adjusted R Square	0.628
Standard Error	17.847
Observations	12

ANOVA

	df	*SS*	*MS*	*F*	*Significance F*
Regression	1	6225.347	6225.347	19.544	0.001
Residual	10	3185.319	318.532		
Total	11	9410.667			

	Coefficients	*Standard Error*	*t Stat*	*P-value*	*Lower 95%*	*Upper 95%*	*Lower 95.0%*	*Upper 95.0%*
Intercept	52.59	12.238	4.298	0.002	25.325	79.861	25.325	79.861
X Variable 1	4.6737	1.057	4.421	0.001	2.318	7.029	2.318	7.029

Fig. 6.32 Example of a Chart with the Regression Equation Displayed Next to the Regression Line

Note that the regression equation on the chart is in the following form next to the regression line on the chart (see Fig. 6.32).

$$Y = 4.6737\ X + 52.59$$

Save this file as: PAY15, and print it out so that it fits onto one page.

6.7 How to Recognize Negative Correlations in the SUMMARY OUTPUT Table

Important note: Since Excel does not recognize negative correlations in the SUMMARY OUTPUT results, but treats all correlations as if they were positive correlations (this was a mistake made by the programmer), you need to be careful to note that there may be a negative correlation between X and Y even if the printout says that the correlation is a positive correlation.

You will know that the correlation between X and Y is a negative correlation when these two things occur:

(1) THE SLOPE, b, IS A NEGATIVE NUMBER. This can only occur when there is a negative correlation.
(2) THE CHART CLEARLY SHOWS A DOWNWARD SLOPE IN THE REGRESSION LINE, which can only occur when the correlation between X and Y is negative.

6.8 Printing Only Part of a Spreadsheet Instead of the Entire Spreadsheet

Objective: To print part of a spreadsheet separately instead of printing the entire spreadsheet

There will be many occasions when your spreadsheet is so large in the number of cells used for your data and charts that you only want to print part of the spreadsheet separately so that the print will not be so small that you cannot read it easily.

We will now explain how to print only part of a spreadsheet onto a separate page by using three examples of how to do that using the file, PAY15, that you created in Sect. 6.6: (1) printing only the table and the chart on a separate page, (2) printing only the chart on a separate page, and (3) printing only the SUMMARY OUTPUT of the regression analysis on a separate page.

Note: If the file: PAY15 is not open on your screen, you need to open it now.

If the "border" is around the outside of the chart, click on any white space outside of the chart to deselect the chart.

Let's describe how to do these three goals with three separate objectives:

6.8.1 Printing Only the Table and the Chart on a Separate Page

Objective: To print only the table and the chart on a separate page

1. Left-click your mouse starting at the top left of the table *in cell A3* and drag the mouse *down and to the right so that all of the table and all of the chart are highlighted in light blue on your computer screen from cell A3 to cell H48* (the light blue cells are called the "selection" cells).
2. File
   Print
   Print Active Sheet (hit the down arrow on the right)
   Print selection
   Print

The resulting printout should contain only the table of the data and the chart resulting from the data.

Then, click on any empty cell in your spreadsheet to deselect the table and chart.

6.8.2 Printing Only the Chart on a Separate Page

Objective: To print only the chart on a separate page

1. Click on any "white space" *just inside the outside border of the chart in the top right corner of the chart* to create the "border" around all of the borders of the chart in order to "select" the chart.
2. File
   Print
   Print selected chart
   Print selected chart (again)
   Print

The resulting printout should contain only the chart resulting from the data.

Important note: After each time you print a chart by itself on a separate page, you should immediately click on any white space OUTSIDE the chart to remove the "border" from the chart. When the border is on the outside borders of the chart, this tells Excel that you want to print only the chart by itself. Do this now!

6.8.3 Printing Only the SUMMARY OUTPUT of the Regression Analysis on a Separate Page

Objective: To print only the SUMMARY OUTPUT of the regression analysis on a separate page

1. Left-click your mouse at the cell just above SUMMARY OUTPUT in *cell A52* on the left of your spreadsheet and drag the mouse *down and to the right* until all of the regression output is highlighted in dark blue on your screen from A52 to I69.
2. File
   Print
   Print active sheets (hit the down arrow on the right)
   Print selection
   Print

The resulting printout should contain only the summary output of the regression analysis on a separate page.

Finally, click on any empty cell on the spreadsheet to "deselect" the regression table.

6.9 End-of-Chapter Practice Problems

1. Suppose that you have been asked by an HR manager at Engineering Company XYZ to help her to develop a recruiting budget for newly-hired engineers. She wants to predict the average recruiting costs for these hires as a function of the salary that was accepted by the newly-hired engineers based on data from the previous six months. You have decided to use a correlation and simple linear regression analysis, and to test your Excel skills, you have collected the data of a random sample of newly-hired engineers. These hypothetical data appear in Fig. 6.33.

ENGINEERING COMPANY XYZ	
What is the relationship between the accepted salary of newly-hired engineers and the recruiting cost for those engineers?	
SALARY ($000)	**RECRUITING COST ($)**
45	5700
81	6200
75	6725
64	7150
69	8540
65	8930
72	9120
76	9560
97	10500
86	11630
92	12400
97	13900
89	14500
103	15800
102	16500

Fig. 6.33 Worksheet Data for Chap. 6: Practice Problem #1

(a) create an Excel spreadsheet using RECRUITING COST ($) as the criterion and SALARY ($000) as the predictor using the following format:

- Top title: RELATIONSHIP BETWEEN SALARY AND RECRUITING COST
- x-axis title: SALARY ($000)
- y-axis title: RECRUITING COST ($)
- Re-size the chart so that it is 7 columns wide and 25 rows long
- Delete the legend
- Delete the gridlines
- Move the chart below the table

(b) Create the *least-squares regression line* for these data on the scatterplot.

(c) Use Excel's *regression* function to find the equation for the least-squares regression line for these data and display the results below the chart on your spreadsheet.

(d) Use number format (two decimal places) for the correlation and the y-intercept on the SUMMARY OUTPUT, and use number format (four decimal places) for all of the other decimal figures in the SUMMARY OUTPUT.

(e) Print the input data and the chart so that this information fits onto one page.
(f) Then, print the regression output table so that this information fits onto a separate page.
(g) Save the file as: RECRUITING2

Answer the following questions using your Excel printout:

1. What is the correlation r ?
2. What is the y-intercept *a* ?
3. What is the slope b?
4. What is the regression equation (use two decimal places for the y-intercept and four decimal places for the slope)?
5. Use the regression equation to predict the RECRUITING COST you would expect for a SALARY of $80,000.

2. Suppose that HR manager at COMPANY ABC, a large multi-institutional organization, wants to analyze the data from a recent "Morale Survey" with managers at different locations, and that you have been asked to design this email survey. You have not completed the design of the survey, but you do know that you want to include items that ask managers how satisfied they are with their jobs (ITEM #30), and also their likelihood of leaving the employment at ABC sometime during the next two years (ITEM #18).

Suppose that you want to study the relationship between these twos survey items.

Create an Excel spreadsheet and enter the data using JOB SATISFACTION as the independent (predictor) variable, and LIKELY TO LEAVE ABC as the dependent (criterion) variable. You decide to test your Excel skills on last year's data using the hypothetical data presented in Fig. 6.34.

COMPANY ABC

MORALE SURVEY

Item #18 "How likely are you to leave your employment at ABC sometime in the next two years?"

1	2	3	4	5	6	7
very unlikely						very likely

Item #30 "Overall, how satisfied are you with your current job at ABC?"

1	2	3	4	5	6	7
very dissatisfied						very satisfied

JOB SATISFACTION	LIKELY TO LEAVE ABC
Item 30	Item 18
2	5
6	6
4	3
3	2
5	4
4	7
3	6
2	5
1	6
4	7
5	4
3	3
6	2
7	1
5	2
4	3
3	1
4	7
2	6
1	6

Fig. 6.34 Worksheet Data for Chap. 6: Practice Problem #2

Create an Excel spreadsheet and enter the data using JOB SATISFACTION as the independent variable (predictor) and LIKELY TO LEAVE ABC as the dependent variable (criterion).

(a) create an *XY scatterplot* of these two sets of data such that:

- top title: RELATIONSHIP BETWEEN JOB SATISFACTION AND
- LIKELIHOOD OF LEAVING ABC
- x-axis title: JOB SATISFACTION
- y-axis title: LIKELIHOOD OF LEAVING ABC
- re-size the chart so that it is 7 columns wide and 25 rows long
- delete the legend
- delete the gridlines
- move the chart below the table

(b) Create the *least-squares regression line* for these data on the scatterplot.
(c) Use Excel to run the regression statistics to find the *equation for the least-squares regression line* for these data and display the results below the chart on your spreadsheet. Use number format (two decimal places) for the correlation, r, and three decimal places for both the y-intercept and the slope of the line. Change all other decimal figures to four decimal places.
(d) Print the input data and the chart so that this information fits onto one page.
(e) Then, print out the regression output table so that this information fits onto a separate page.

By hand:

(1a) Circle and label the value of the *y-intercept* and the *slope* of the regression line on the regression output table that you just printed.
(2b) *Read from the graph* the likelihood of leaving ABC you would predict for a JOB SATISFACTION score of 6, and write your answer in the space immediately below:

____

(f) save the file as: SATIS16

Answer the following questions using your Excel printout:

1. What is the correlation?
2. What is the y-intercept?
3. What is the slope of the line?
4. What is the regression equation for these data (use three decimal places for the y-intercept and the slope)?
5. Use that regression equation to predict the LIKELIHOOD OF LEAVING ABC you would expect for a JOB SATISFACTION score of 5.

(Note that this correlation is not the multiple correlation as the Excel table indicates, but is merely the correlation, r, instead.)
But how does Excel treat *negative correlations*?

Important note: Since Excel does not recognize negative correlations in the SUMMARY OUTPUT but treats all correlations as if they were positive correlations, you need to be careful to note when there is a negative correlation between the two variables under study.

You know that the correlation is negative when:

(1) *The slope, b, is a negative number, which can only occur when there is a negative correlation.*
(2) *The chart clearly shows a downward slope in the regression line, which can only happen when the correlation is negative.*

Note that you found a negative correlation of −.39 between JOB SATISFACTION and LIKELIHOOD OF LEAVING ABC. You know that the correlation is a negative correlation for two reasons: (1) the regression line slopes downward and to the right on the chart, signaling a negative correlation, and (2) the slope is −0.483 which also tells you that the correlation is a negative correlation.

3. Suppose that you wanted to study the relationship between DIET (measured in calories allowed per day) and WEIGHT LOSS (measured in kilograms, kg) for adult women between the ages of 30 and 40 who are overweight for their height and body structure, and who all weigh roughly the same number of kilograms before undertaking the weight loss program. You want to test your Excel skills on a random sample of these women based on their weight change over the past four months to make sure that you can do this type of research. The hypothetical data appear in Fig. 6.35:

RELATIONSHIP BETWEEN DIET AND WEIGHT LOSS	
ADULT WOMEN AGES 30-40	
DIET (calories allowed per day)	WEIGHT LOSS (kg)
900	16.0
1050	12.0
1150	8.0
1275	6.0
1420	3.0
1530	5.5
1610	9.5
1710	2.5
1820	6.0
1875	9.0
1930	6.0
2100	3.0

Fig. 6.35 Worksheet Data for Chap. 6: Practice Problem #3

Create an Excel spreadsheet and enter the data using DIET (calories allowed per day) as the independent variable (predictor) and WEIGHT LOSS (kg) as the dependent variable (criterion). Underneath the table, use Excel's =*correl* function to find the correlation between these two variables. Label the correlation and place it underneath the table; then round off the correlation to two decimal places.

(a) create an *XY scatterplot* of these two sets of data such that:

- top title: RELATIONSHIP BETWEEN DIET AND WEIGHT LOSS
- x-axis title: DIET (calories allowed per day)
- y-axis title: WEIGHT LOSS (kg)
- move the chart below the table
- re-size the chart so that it is 8 columns wide and 25 rows long
- delete the legend
- delete the gridlines

(b) Create the *least-squares regression line* for these data on the scatterplot, and add the regression equation to the chart.

(c) Use Excel to run the regression statistics to find the *equation for the least-squares regression line* for these data and display the results below the chart on your spreadsheet. Use number format (two decimal places) for the correlation and three decimal places for all other decimal figures, including the coefficients.

(d) Print just the input data and the chart so that this information fits onto one page. Then, print the regression output table on a separate page so that it fits onto that separate page.
(e) save the file as: DIET3
Answer the following questions using your Excel printout:

1. What is the correlation between DIET and WEIGHT LOSS?
2. What is the y-intercept?
3. What is the slope of the line?
4. What is the regression equation?
5. Use the regression equation to predict the WEIGHT LOSS you would expect for a woman who was practicing a DIET of 1500 calories allowed a day. Show your work on a separate sheet of paper.

References

Aamodt M, Surrette M, and Cohen D. Understanding statistics: a guide for I/O psychologists and human resource professionals. Belmont: WADSWORTH CENGAGE Learning; 2007.

Black K. Business statistics: for contemporary decision making. 6th ed. Hoboken: John Wiley & Sons, Inc.; 2010.

Davis J H. Statistics for compensation: a practical guide to compensation analysis. Hoboken: John Wiley & Sons; 2011

Levine D, Stephan D, Krehbiel T, Berenson M. Statistics for managers using microsoft excel. 6th ed. Boston: Prentice Hall Pearson; 2011.

Pease G, Byerly B, and Fitz-enz J. Human capital analytics: how to harness the potential of your organization's greatest asset. Hoboken: John Wiley & Sons; 2013.

Whetzel D L and Wheaton G R (Eds.). Applied measurement: industrial psychology in human resources management. Mahwah: Lawrence Erlbaum Associates; 2007.

Zikmund W G, Babin B J. Exploring marketing research. 10th ed. Mason: South-Western Cengage Learning; 2010.

Chapter 7
Multiple Correlation and Multiple Regression

There are many times in human resource management when you want to predict a criterion, Y, but you want to find out if you can develop a better prediction model by using *several predictors* in combination (e.g. X_1, X_2, X_3, etc.) instead of a single predictor, X.

The resulting statistical procedure is called "multiple correlation and multiple regression" because it uses two or more predictors in combination to predict Y, instead of a single predictor, X. Each predictor is "weighted" differently based on its separate correlation with Y and its correlation with the other predictors. The job of multiple correlation is to produce a regression equation that will weight each predictor differently and in such a way that the combination of predictors does a better job of predicting Y than any single predictor by itself. We will call the multiple correlation: R_{xy}.

You will recall (see Sect. 6.5.3) that the regression equation that predicts Y when only one predictor, X, is used is:

$$Y = a + bX \tag{7.1}$$

You will remember from Chap. 6 that the correlation, r, ranges from -1 to $+1$. However, the multiple correlation, R_{xy}, only ranges from zero to plus one (0 to +1). R_{xy} is never a negative number!

7.1 Multiple Regression Equation

The multiple regression equation follows a similar format and is:

$$Y = a + b_1X_1 + b_2X_2 + b_3X_3 + etc.\ depending\ on\ the\ number\ of\ predictors\ used \tag{7.2}$$

T.J. Quirk, J. Palmer-Schuyler, *Excel 2016 for Human Resource Management Statistics*, Excel for Statistics, DOI 10.1007/978-3-319-40063-1_7

The "weight" given to each predictor in the equation is represented by the letter "b" with a subscript to correspond to the same subscript on the predictors.

For more information about multiple correlation, see Davis (2011) and Aamodt *et al.* (2007).

Important note: In order to do multiple regression, you need to have installed the "Data Analysis ToolPak" that was described in Chap. 6 (see Sect. 6.5.1). If you did not install this, you need to do so now.

Let's try a practice problem.

The Graduate Record Examinations (GRE) are a standardized test that is an admissions requirement for many U.S. graduate schools that offer a Master's degree in Human Resource Management (HRM). The GRE is intended to measure general academic preparedness, regardless of specialization field. The GRE test produces three subtest scores: (1) GRE VERBAL REASONING (scale 130–170), (2) GRE QUANTITATIVE REASONING (scale 130–170), and (3) ANALYTICAL WRITING (scale 0–6).

Suppose that you have been asked by a director of an M.A. program in HRM to find out the relationship between these variables based on last year's entering graduate class and the ability of the GRE to predict first-year grade-point average (GPA).

You have decided to use the three subtest scores as the predictors, X_1, X_2, and X_3 and the first-year grade-point average (FIRST-YEAR GPA) as the criterion, Y. To test your Excel skills, you have randomly selected a small group of students from last year's entering HRM graduate class, and have recorded their scores on these variables.

Let's use the following notation:

Y	FIRST-YEAR GPA
X_1	GRE VERBAL
X_2	GRE QUANTITATIVE
X_3	GRE WRITING

Suppose, further, that you have collected the following hypothetical data summarizing these scores (see Fig. 7.1):

GRADUATE RECORD EXAMINATIONS (GRE)

How well does the GRE predict first-year GPA in an M.A. program iin Human Resources Managment?

FIRST-YEAR GPA	GRE VERBAL	GRE QUANTITATIVE	GRE WRITING
3.25	160	161	5
3.42	156	158	4
2.85	156	157	2
2.65	154	153	1
3.65	166	166	6
3.16	159	160	3
3.56	166	163	4
2.35	155	154	2
2.86	153	154	3
2.95	158	157	4
3.15	158	159	4
3.45	160	160	5

Fig. 7.1 Worksheet Data for GRE versus FIRST-YEAR GPA (Practical Example)

Create an Excel spreadsheet for these data using the following cell reference:

A2: GRADUATE RECORD EXAMINATIONS (GRE)
A4: How well does the GRE predict first-year GPA in an M.A. program in Human Resources Management?
A6: FIRST-YEAR GPA
A7: 3.25
B6: GRE VERBAL
C6: GRE QUANTITATIVE
D6: GRE WRITING
D18: 5

Next, change the column width to match the above table, and change all GPA figures to number format (two decimal places).

Now, fill in the additional data in the chart such that:

A18: 3.45
B18: 160
D18: 5

Then, center all numbers in your table

Important note: Be sure to double-check all of your numbers in your table to be sure that they are correct, or your spreadsheets will be incorrect.

Save this file as: GRE14

Before we do the multiple regression analysis, we need to try to make one important point very clear:

Important: When we used one predictor, X, to predict one criterion, Y, we said that you need to make sure that the X variable is ON THE LEFT in your table, and the Y variable is ON THE RIGHT in your table so that you don't get these variables mixed up (see Sect. 6.3).

However, in multiple regression, you need to follow this rule which is exactly the opposite:

When you use several predictors in multiple regression, it is essential that the criterion you are trying to predict, Y, be ON THE FAR LEFT, and that all of the predictors are TO THE RIGHT of the criterion, Y, in your table so that you know which variable is the criterion, Y, and which variables are the predictors. If you make this a habit, you will save yourself a lot of grief.

Notice in the table above, that the criterion Y (FIRST-YEAR GPA) is on the far left of the table, and the three predictors (GRE VERBAL, GRE QUANTITATIVE, and GRE WRITING) are to the right of the criterion variable. If you follow this rule, you will be less likely to make a mistake when conducting multiple regression.

7.2 Finding the Multiple Correlation and the Multiple Regression Equation

Objective: To find the multiple correlation and multiple regression equation using Excel.

You do this by the following commands:

Data
Click on: Data Analysis (far right top of screen)
Regression (scroll down to this in the box; see Fig. 7.2)

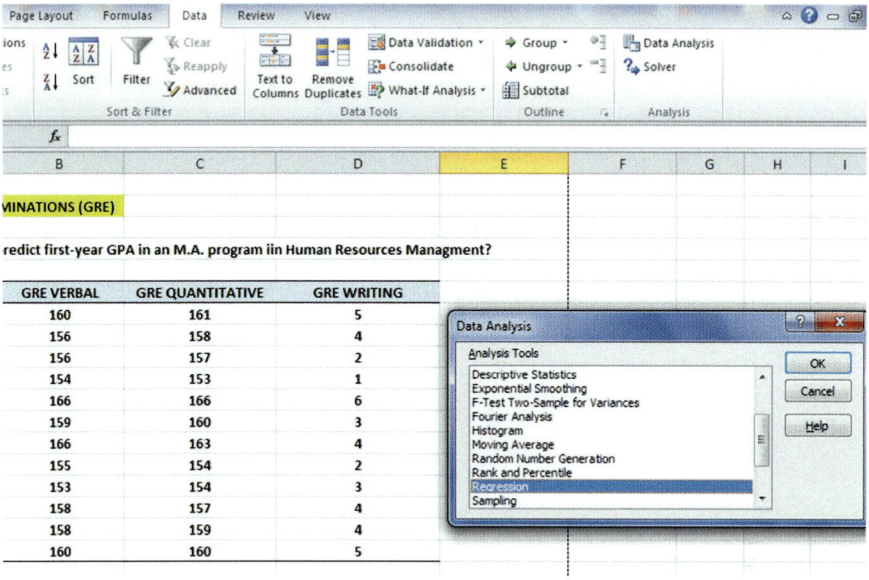

Fig. 7.2 Dialogue Box for Regression Function

OK

Input Y Range: A6:A18
Input X Range: B6:D18

Note that both the input Y Range and the Input X Range above both include the label at the top of the columns.

Click on the Labels box to *add a check mark* to it (because you have included the column labels in row 6)

Output Range (click on the button to its left, and enter): A20 (see Fig. 7.3)

Important note: Excel automatically assigns a dollar sign $ in front of each column letter and each row number so that you can keep these ranges of data constant for the regression analysis.

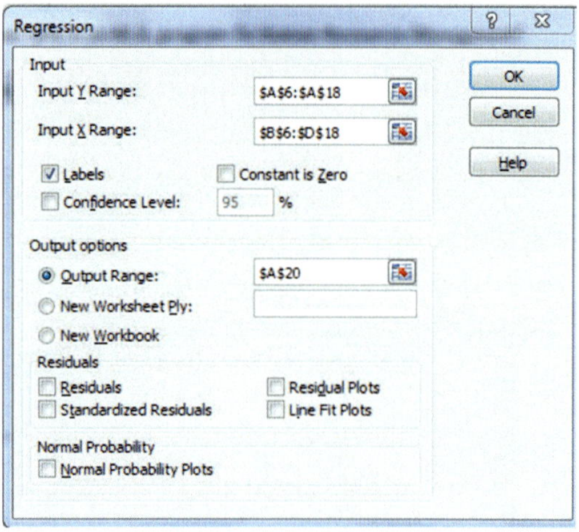

Fig. 7.3 Dialogue Box for GRE vs. FIRST-YEAR GPA Data

OK (see Fig. 7.4 to see the resulting SUMMARY OUTPUT)

GRADUATE RECORD EXAMINATIONS (GRE)

How well does the GRE predict first-year GPA in an M.A. program iin Human Resources Managment?

FIRST-YEAR GPA	GRE VERBAL	GRE QUANTITATIVE	GRE WRITING
3.25	160	161	5
3.42	156	158	4
2.85	156	157	2
2.65	154	153	1
3.65	166	166	6
3.16	159	160	3
3.56	166	163	4
2.35	155	154	2
2.86	153	154	3
2.95	158	157	4
3.15	158	159	4
3.45	160	160	5

SUMMARY OUTPUT

Regression Statistics	
Multiple R	0.905532671
R Square	0.819989418
Adjusted R Square	0.752485449
Standard Error	0.194101687
Observations	12

ANOVA

	df	*SS*	*MS*	*F*	*Significance F*
Regression	3	1.372962948	0.457654316	12.14727723	0.002390367
Residual	8	0.301403719	0.037675465		
Total	11	1.674366667			

	Coefficients	*Standard Error*	*t Stat*	*P-value*	*Lower 95%*
Intercept	-7.620664262	4.260893504	-1.788513197	0.111492356	-17.4463023
GRE VERBAL	-0.022937928	0.044772044	-0.512327035	0.622263259	-0.126182446
GRE QUANTITATIVE	0.088853291	0.059724909	1.487709111	0.175144874	-0.048872596
GRE WRITING	0.078000329	0.075711817	1.030226623	0.333041348	-0.096591433

Fig. 7.4 Regression SUMMARY OUTPUT of GRE vs. FIRST-YEAR GPA Data

Next, format cell B23 in number format (two decimal places)

Next, format the following four cells in Number format (three decimal places):

B36
B37
B38
B39

Change all other decimal figures to four decimal places, and center all figures within their cells.

Save the file as: GRE16

Now, print the file so that it fits onto one page by changing the scale to *75 % size*.

The resulting regression analysis is given in Fig. 7.5.

Once you have the SUMMARY OUTPUT, you can determine the multiple correlation and the regression equation that is the best-fit line through the data

GRADUATE RECORD EXAMINATIONS (GRE)

How well does the GRE predict first-year GPA in an M.A. program in Human Resources Managment?

FIRST-YEAR GPA	GRE VERBAL	GRE QUANTITATIVE	GRE WRITING
3.25	160	161	5
3.42	156	158	4
2.85	156	157	2
2.65	154	153	1
3.65	166	166	6
3.16	159	160	3
3.56	166	163	4
2.35	155	154	2
2.86	153	154	3
2.95	158	157	4
3.15	158	159	4
3.45	160	160	5

SUMMARY OUTPUT

Regression Statistics	
Multiple R	0.91
R Square	0.8200
Adjusted R Square	0.7525
Standard Error	0.1941
Observations	12

ANOVA

	df	*SS*	*MS*	*F*	*Significance F*
Regression	3	1.3730	0.4577	12.1473	0.0024
Residual	8	0.3014	0.0377		
Total	11	1.6744			

	Coefficients	*Standard Error*	*t Stat*	*P-value*	*Lower 95%*
Intercept	-7.621	4.2609	-1.7885	0.1115	-17.4463
GRE VERBAL	-0.023	0.0448	-0.5123	0.6223	-0.1262
GRE QUANTITATIVE	0.089	0.0597	1.4877	0.1751	-0.0489
GRE WRITING	0.078	0.0757	1.0302	0.3330	-0.0966

Fig. 7.5 Final Spreadsheet for GRE vs. FIRST-YEAR GPA Regression Analysis

points using GRE VERBAL, GRE QUANTITATIVE, and GRE WRITING as the three predictors, and FIRST-YEAR GPA as the criterion.

Note on the SUMMARY OUTPUT where it says: "Multiple R." This term is correct since this is the term Excel uses for the multiple correlation, which is +0.91. This means, that from these data, the combination of GRE VERBAL, GRE QUANTITATIVE, and GRE WRITING scores together form a very strong positive relationship in predicting FIRST-YEAR GPA.

To find the regression equation, *notice the coefficients at the bottom of the SUMMARY OUTPUT in cells B36–B39*:

Intercept: a (this is the y-intercept)	*−7.621*
GRE VERBAL SCORE*:* b_1	*−0.023*
GRE QUANTITATIVE SCORE: b_2	*0.089*
GRE WRITING SCORE: b_3	0.078

Since the general form of the multiple regression equation is:

$$Y = a + b_1X_1 + b_2X_2 + b_3X_3 \quad (7.2)$$

we can now write the multiple regression equation for these data:

$$Y = -7.621 - 0.023X_1 + 0.089X_2 + 0.078X_3$$

7.3 Using the Regression Equation to Predict FIRST-YEAR GPA

Objective: To find the predicted FIRST-YEAR GPA using a GRE VERBAL Score of 158, a GRE QUANTITATIVE Score of 163, and a GRE WRITING Score of 4

Plugging these three numbers into our regression equation gives us:

Y = −7.621 − 0.023(158) + 0.089(163) + 0.078(4)
Y = −7.621 − 3.634 + 14.507 + 0.312
Y = 3.56 (since GPA scores are typically measured in two decimals)

If you want to learn more about the theory behind multiple regression, see Keller (2009).

7.4 Using Excel to Create a Correlation Matrix in Multiple Regression

The final step in multiple regression is to find the correlation between all of the variables that appear in the regression equation.

In our example, this means that we need to find the correlation between each of the six pairs of variables:

To do this, we need to use Excel to create a "correlation matrix." This matrix summarizes the correlations between all of the variables in the problem.

Objective: To use Excel to create a correlation matrix between the four variables in this example.

To use Excel to do this, use these steps:
Data (top of screen under "Home" at the top left of screen)

Data Analysis
Correlation (scroll *up* to highlight this formula; see Fig. 7.6)

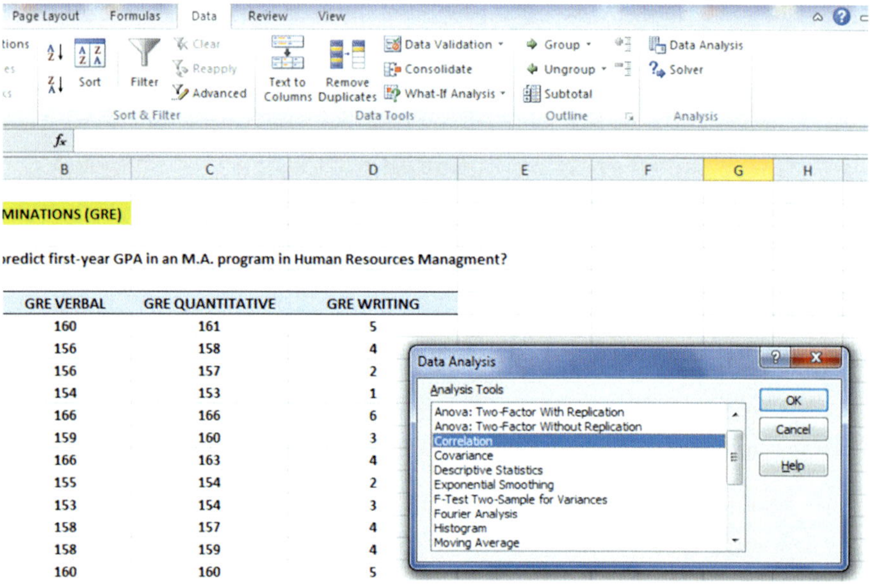

Fig. 7.6 Dialogue Box for GRE vs. FIRST-YEAR GPA Correlations

OK

Input range: A6:D18

(Note that this input range includes the labels at the top of the FOUR variables (FIRST-YEAR GPA, GRE VERBAL, GRE QUANTITATIVE, and GRE WRITING) as well as all of the figures in the original data set).
Grouped by: Columns
Put a check in the box for: Labels in the First Row (since you included the labels at the top of the columns in your input range of data above)
Output range (click on the button to its left, and enter): A42 (see Fig. 7.7)

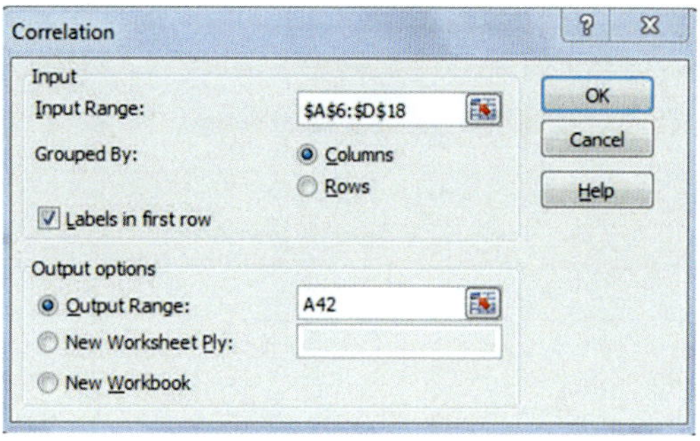

Fig. 7.7 Dialogue Box for Input/Output Range for Correlation Matrix

OK

The resulting correlation matrix appears in A42:E46 (See Fig. 7.8).

42		FIRST-YEAR GPA	GRE VERBAL	GRE QUANTITATIVE	GRE WRITING
43	FIRST-YEAR GPA	1			
44	GRE VERBAL	0.790556617	1		
45	GRE QUANTITATIVE	0.882548207	0.94457432	1	
46	GRE WRITING	0.834890495	0.723159288	0.826269747	1
47					

Fig. 7.8 Resulting Correlation Matrix for GRE vs. FIRST-YEAR GPA Data

Next, format all of the numbers in the correlation matrix that are in decimals to two decimals places. And, also, make column D wider so that the GRE QUANTITIVE score label fits inside cell D42.

Save this Excel file as: GRE15

The final spreadsheet for these scores appears in Fig. 7.9.

GRADUATE RECORD EXAMINATIONS (GRE)

How well does the GRE predict first-year GPA in an M.A. program in Human Resources Managment?

FIRST-YEAR GPA	GRE VERBAL	GRE QUANTITATIVE	GRE WRITING
3.25	160	161	5
3.42	156	158	4
2.85	156	157	2
2.65	154	153	1
3.65	166	166	6
3.16	159	160	3
3.56	166	163	4
2.35	155	154	2
2.86	153	154	3
2.95	158	157	4
3.15	158	159	4
3.45	160	160	5

SUMMARY OUTPUT

Regression Statistics	
Multiple R	0.91
R Square	0.8200
Adjusted R Square	0.7525
Standard Error	0.1941
Observations	12

ANOVA

	df	*SS*	*MS*	*F*	*Significance F*
Regression	3	1.3730	0.4577	12.1473	0.0024
Residual	8	0.3014	0.0377		
Total	11	1.6744			

	Coefficients	*Standard Error*	*t Stat*	*P-value*	*Lower 95%*
Intercept	-7.621	4.2609	-1.7885	0.1115	-17.4463
GRE VERBAL	-0.023	0.0448	-0.5123	0.6223	-0.1262
GRE QUANTITATIVE	0.089	0.0597	1.4877	0.1751	-0.0489
GRE WRITING	0.078	0.0757	1.0302	0.3330	-0.0966

	FIRST-YEAR GPA	*GRE VERBAL*	*GRE QUANTITATIVE*	*GRE WRITING*
FIRST-YEAR GPA	1			
GRE VERBAL	0.79	1		
GRE QUANTITATIVE	0.88	0.94	1	
GRE WRITING	0.83	0.72	0.83	1

Fig. 7.9 Final Spreadsheet for GRE vs. FIRST-YEAR GPA Regression and the Correlation Matrix

Note that the number "1" along the diagonal of the correlation matrix means that the correlation of each variable with itself is a perfect, positive correlation of 1.0.

Correlation coefficients are always expressed in just two decimal places.

You are now ready to read the correlation between the six pairs of variables:

The correlation between GRE VERBAL and FIRST-YEAR GPA is: +.79

The correlation between GRE QUANTITATIVE and FIRST-YEAR GPA is: +.88

The correlation between GRE WRITING and FIRST-YEAR GPA is: +.83

The correlation between GRE VERBAL and GRE QUANTITATIVE is: +.94

The correlation between GRE VERBAL and GRE WRITING is: +.72

The correlation between GRE QUANTITATIVE and GRE WRITING is: +.83

This means that the best single predictor of FIRST-YEAR GPA is the GRE QUANTITATIVE SCORE with a correlation of +.88. Adding the other two predictor variables, GRE VERBAL and GRE WRITING, improved the prediction by only 0.03 to 0.91, resulting in only a slightly better prediction. GRE QUANTITATIVE scores are an excellent predictor of FIRST-YEAR GPA all by themselves.

If you want to learn more about the correlation matrix, see Levine et al. (2011).

7.5 End-of-Chapter Practice Problems

1. The Graduate Management Admission Test (GMAT) is a three-and-a-half hour exam that is accepted by almost 6,000 Business and Management programs in more than 80 countries as part of the admission application for people who want to obtain a graduate degree. This test is taken by more than 200,000 applicants each year. Suppose that a major university that offers an M.A. in Human Resources Management requires a GMAT score as part of the application process to this program, wants to know how well GMAT scores of applicants predict their Grade-Point Average (GPA) at the end of their first year of graduate school. The GMAT has four subtest scores: (1) Verbal (score range 0–60), (2) Quantitative (score range 0–60), (3) Analytical writing (score range 0–6 in 0.5 intervals), and (4) Integrated Reasoning (score range 1–8) You have decided to use these four subtest scores as predictors of first-year GPA, and to check your skills in Excel, you have created the hypothetical data given in Fig. 7.10.

GRADUATE MANAGEMENT ADMISSION TEST (GMAT)

How well does the GMAT predict first-year GPA in an HRM program?

FIRST-YEAR GPA	VERBAL	QUANTITATIVE	ANALYTICAL WRITING	INTEGRATED REASONING
3.25	50	45	4.0	4
3.67	56	48	4.5	6
2.8	54	51	5.0	5
3.05	52	53	5.5	4
3.45	51	54	4.0	3
3.33	48	58	3.0	7
2.75	46	59	4.5	8
2.95	45	57	5.5	5
2.6	52	51	6.0	6
3.67	57	50	4.5	4
3.75	53	48	3.0	7
3.42	46	46	4.0	6
3.15	42	48	5.0	7
3.26	38	49	4.0	5
2.96	41	52	5.5	4

Fig. 7.10 Worksheet Data for Chap. 7: Practice Problem #1

(a) create an Excel spreadsheet using FIRST-YEAR GPA as the criterion (Y), and the other variables as the four predictors of this criterion (X_1 = VERBAL, X_2 = QUANTITATIVE, X_3 = ANALYTICAL WRITING, and X_4 = INTEGRATED REASONING).
(b) Use Excel's *multiple regression* function to find the relationship between these five variables and place the SUMMARY OUTPUT below the table.
(c) Use number format (two decimal places) for the multiple correlation on the Summary Output, and use three decimal places for the coefficients in the SUMMARY OUTPUT.
(d) Save the file as: GMAT16
(e) Print the table and regression results below the table so that they fit onto one page.

Answer the following questions using your Excel printout:

1. What is the multiple correlation R_{xy}?
2. What is the y-intercept a?
3. What is the coefficient for VERBAL, b_1?
4. What is the coefficient for QUANTITATIVE, b_2?
5. What is the coefficient for ANALYTICAL WRITING, b_3?
6. What is the coefficient for INTEGRATED REASONING, b_4?
7. What is the multiple regression equation?
8. Predict the FIRST-YEAR GPA you would expect for a VERBAL score of 52, a QUANTITATIVE SCORE OF 48, an ANALYTICAL WRITING SCORE of 4.5, and an INTEGRATED REASONING SCORE OF 6.

(f) Now, go back to your Excel file and create a correlation matrix for these five variables, and place it underneath the SUMMARY OUTPUT.
(g) Re-save this file as: GMAT16
(h) Now, print out *just this correlation matrix* on a separate sheet of paper.

Answer to the following questions using your Excel printout. (Be sure to include the plus or minus sign for each correlation):

9. What is the correlation between VERBAL and FIRST-YEAR GPA?
10. What is the correlation between QUANTITATIVE and FIRST-YEAR GPA?
11. What is the correlation between ANALYTICAL WRITING and FIRST-YEAR GPA?
12. What is the correlation between INTEGRATED REASONING and FIRST-YEAR GPA?
13. What is the correlation between VERBAL and QUANTITATIVE?
14. What is the correlation between QUANTITATIVE and ANALYTICAL WRITING?
15. What is the correlation between ANALYTICAL WRITING and INTEGRATED REASONING?

16. What is the correlation between QUANTITATIVE and INTEGRATED REASONING?
17. Discuss which of the four predictors is the best predictor of FIRST-YEAR GPA.
18. Explain in words how much better the four predictor variables combined predict FIRST-YEAR GPA than the best single predictor by itself.

2. Suppose that you work for a company that claims to base the pay raises of its managers on performance level rather on simply the years of experience at the company. The company measures "performance" by using a rating by the manager's supervisor on a 5-point scale that ranges from 1 = Unsatisfactory to 5 = Outstanding. The company measures "experience" by the total number of years of relevant business experience of the manager, both at this company and also at former companies. The educational level of the manager is measured as the total number of undergraduate or graduate degrees obtained by the manager. Let's find out what happens when you use the hypothetical data that is presented in Fig. 7.11.

Research question:	"Is there a relationship between performance, experience, education and pay raise?"		
PERCENT RAISE	PERFORMANCE RATING	YEARS OF EXPERIENCE	NO. DEGREES
6	4	12	4
4	5	10	5
2	3	5	1
5	5	8	3
3	3	4	2
2	2	6	1
6	5	12	4
3	3	6	2
2	1	3	1
4	3	10	3

Fig. 7.11 Worksheet Data for Chap. 7: Practice Problem #2

(a) Create an Excel spreadsheet using PERCENT RAISE as the criterion (Y), and the other variables as the three predictors of this criterion.
(b) Use Excel's *multiple regression* function to find the relationship between these variables and place it below the table.
(c) Use number format (two decimal places) for the multiple correlation on the Summary Output, number format (four decimal places) for the coefficients, and two decimal places for all other decimal figures in the SUMMARY OUTPUT.
(d) Print the table and regression results below the table so that they fit onto one page.
(e) By hand on this printout, *circle and label:*

(1a) multiple correlation R_{xy}
(2b) coefficients for the y-intercept, PERFORMANCE RATING, YEARS OF EXPERIENCE, and NO. DEGREES

(f) Save this file as: Raise2
(g) Now, go back to your Excel file and create a correlation matrix for these four variables, and place it underneath the SUMMARY OUTPUT. *Change each correlation to just two decimals.* Save this file again as: Raise3
(h) Now, print out *just this correlation matrix in portrait mode* on a separate sheet of paper.

Answer the following questions using your Excel printout:

1. What is the multiple correlation R_{xy}?
2. What is the y-intercept a?
3. What is the coefficient for PERFORMANCE RATING b_1?
4. What is the coefficient for YEARS OF EXPERIENCE b_2?
5. What is the coefficient for NO. DEGREES b_3?
6. What is the multiple regression equation?
7. Underneath this regression equation by hand, predict the PERCENT RAISE you would expect for a PERFORMANCE RATING score of 4, 12 YEARS OF EXPERIENCE, and 3 DEGREES.

Answer the following questions using your Excel printout. Be sure to include the plus or minus sign for each correlation:

8. What is the correlation between PERFORMANCE RATING and PERCENT RAISE?
9. What is the correlation between YEARS OF EXPERIENCE and PERCENT RAISE?
10. What is the correlation between NO. DEGREES and PERCENT RAISE?
11. What is the correlation between PERFORMANCE RATING and YEARS OF EXPERIENCE?
12. Discuss which of the three predictors is the best predictor of PERCENT RAISE.
13. Explain in words how much better the three predictor variables combined predict PERCENT RAISE than the best single predictor by itself.

3. The performance rating given to a manager at an organization is frequently a basis for that manager's promotion opportunities, perceived value to the organization, and, sometimes, even that manager's salary raise. Suppose that you want to study the relationship between the number of years of relevant business experience of a manager, the number of undergraduate or graduate degrees earned by that manager, and that manager's performance rating (rated on a scale where 1 = Poor and 7 = Excellent) at a large, high-tech company. You decide to test your Excel skills on a small sample of mid-level managers at your company to study this relationship.

These hypothetical data appear in Fig. 7.12.

Research question:	"Are experience and education good predictors of performance?"	
PERFORMANCE RATING	**EXPERIENCE**	**NO. DEGREES**
7	20	3
6	15	2
4	8	2
1	5	0
2	6	1
6	18	3
5	6	2
7	10	3
4	11	2
5	12	3
4	8	4
6	14	3
5	9	2

Fig. 7.12 Worksheet Data for Chap. 7: Practice Problem #3

(a) create an Excel spreadsheet using PERFORMANCE RATING as the criterion, and both the number of years of relevant business experience and the number of undergraduate/graduate degrees earned by the manager as the predictors.
(b) Save the file as: Performance2
(c) Use Excel's *multiple regression* function to find the relationship between these three variables and place the SUMMARY OUTPUT below the table.
(d) Use number format (two decimal places) for the multiple correlation, and four decimals for the y-intercept, EXPERIENCE, and NO. DEGREES coefficients on the SUMMARY OUTPUT. Use number format (three decimal places) for the other decimal figures in the SUMMARY OUTPUT.
(e) Print the table and regression results below the table so that they fit onto one page.

Answer the following questions using your Excel printout:

1. What is multiple correlation R_{xy}?
2. What is the y-intercept a?
3. What is the coefficient for EXPERIENCE b_1?
4. What is the coefficient for NO. DEGREES b_2?
5. What is the multiple regression equation?
6. Predict the PERFORMANCE RATING you would expect for a manager with 10 years of relevant business experience and three undergraduate/graduate degrees.

(f) Now, go back to your Excel file and create a correlation matrix for these three variables, and place it underneath the SUMMARY OUTPUT on your spreadsheet.
(g) Save this file as: Performance3
(h) Now, print out *just this correlation matrix* on a separate sheet of paper.

Answer the following questions using your Excel printout. Be sure to include the plus or minus sign for each correlation:

7. What is the correlation between EXPERIENCE and PERFORMANCE RATING?
8. What is the correlation between NO. DEGREES and PERFORMANCE RATING?
9. What is the correlation between EXPERIENCE and NO. DEGREES?
10. Discuss which of the two predictors is the better predictor of PERFORMANCE RATING.
11. Explain in words how much better the two predictor variables combined predict PERFORMANCE RATING than the better single predictor by itself.

References

Aamodt M, Surrette M, and Cohen D. Understanding statistics: a guide for I/O psychologists and human resource professionals. Belmont: WADSWORTH CENGAGE Learning; 2007.

Davis JH. Statistics for compensation: a practical guide to compensation analysis. Hoboken: John Wiley & Sons; 2011.

Keller G. Statistics for management and economics. 8th ed. Mason: South-Western Cengage Learning; 2009.

Levine D, Stephan D, Krehbiel T, Berenson M. Statistics for managers using Microsoft Excel. 6th ed. Boston: Pearson Prentice Hall; 2011.

Chapter 8
One-Way Analysis of Variance (ANOVA)

So far in this 2016 Excel Guide, you have learned how to use a one-group t-test to compare the sample mean to the population mean, and a two-group t-test to test for the difference between two sample means. *But what should you do when you have more than two groups and you want to determine if there is a significant difference between the means of these groups?*

The answer to this question is: *Analysis of Variance (ANOVA).*

The ANOVA test allows you to test for the difference between the means when you have *three or more groups* in your research study. The null hypothesis is that all of the population means are equal. The research hypothesis is that at least two of the population means are significantly different from one another. To conduct an ANOVA test, you need to assume both that the populations are normally distributed and also that they have equal standard deviations.

Important note: In order to do One-way Analysis of Variance, you need to have installed the "Data Analysis Toolpak" that was described in Chap. 6 (see Sect. 6.5.1). If you did not install this, you need to do that now.

Employee Job Satisfaction Surveys are commonplace in many companies and are typically conducted annually by the Human Resource Department to determine the attitude of employees toward the company and toward their job within the company.

Suppose that you are working in an HR department of a large company that has three divisions (A, B, C) and that you have been asked to analyze the data from a recent online employee satisfaction survey that was completed by non-supervisory employees. Each employee was asked to rate his or her attitude toward the company and toward his or her job on 5-point Likert scales where 1 = Strongly Disagree, 2 = Disagree, 3 = Undecided, 4 = Agree, and 5 = Strongly Agree.

T.J. Quirk, J. Palmer-Schuyler, *Excel 2016 for Human Resource Management Statistics*, Excel for Statistics, DOI 10.1007/978-3-319-40063-1_8

The survey contained 20 items such that there were four items in each of five categories: (1) Attitude toward top management and its leadership (e.g. "Top management is doing a good job of leading this company"), (2) Communications (e.g. "I have a good communication relationship with my supervisor"), (3) Employee Development Opportunities (e.g. "There are sufficient opportunities for me to develop my abilities and skills in this company"), (4) Company Culture (e.g. "This company is a good place to work"), and (5) Job Responsibilities (e.g. "I have a good understanding of my current job responsibilities at this company"). The ratings on these 20 items were summed to produce a total score for Job Satisfaction (range: 20–100).

You have been asked to analyze the data to determine if there was any significant difference in Job Satisfaction scores between the three divisions. Note that it is not necessary for each division to have the same number of employees or to have the same sample size in order for ANOVA to be used on the data. Statisticians delight in this fact by stating that: "ANOVA is a very robust test." (Statisticians love that term!)

To test your Excel skills using ANOVA, you have decided to take a random sample of non-supervisory employees from each division to create the hypothetical data given in Fig. 8.1

Fig. 8.1 Worksheet Data for Job Satisfaction (Practical Example)

COMPANY XYZ

EMPLOYEE SATISFACTION SURVEY

DIVISION A	DIVISION B	DIVISION C
90	89	86
86	82	84
84	87	85
76	88	79
58	91	75
79	79	71
82	76	75
83	74	76
86	85	74
78	83	78
90	84	73
92	89	79
94	91	81
85	93	83
87		84
76		

Create an Excel spreadsheet for these data in this way:

A2: COMPANY XYZ
A4: EMPLOYEE SATISFACTION SURVEY
A6: DIVISION A
B6: DIVISION B
C6: DIVISION C
A7: 90

Enter the other information into your spreadsheet table. When you have finished entering these data, the last cell on the left should have 76 in cell A22, and the last cell on the right should have 84 in cell C21. Widen the columns to match the width of the labels and then center the numbers in each of the columns. Use number format (zero decimals) for all numbers.

Important note: Be sure to double-check all of your figures in the table to make sure that they are exactly correct or you will not be able to obtain the correct answer for this problem!

Save this file as: Survey5

8.1 Using Excel to Perform a One-Way Analysis of Variance (ANOVA)

Objective: To use Excel to perform a one-way ANOVA test.

You are now ready to perform an ANOVA test on these data using the following steps:

Data (at top of screen)
Data Analysis (far right at top of screen)
ANOVA: Single Factor (*scroll up to this formula and highlight it*; see Fig. 8.2)

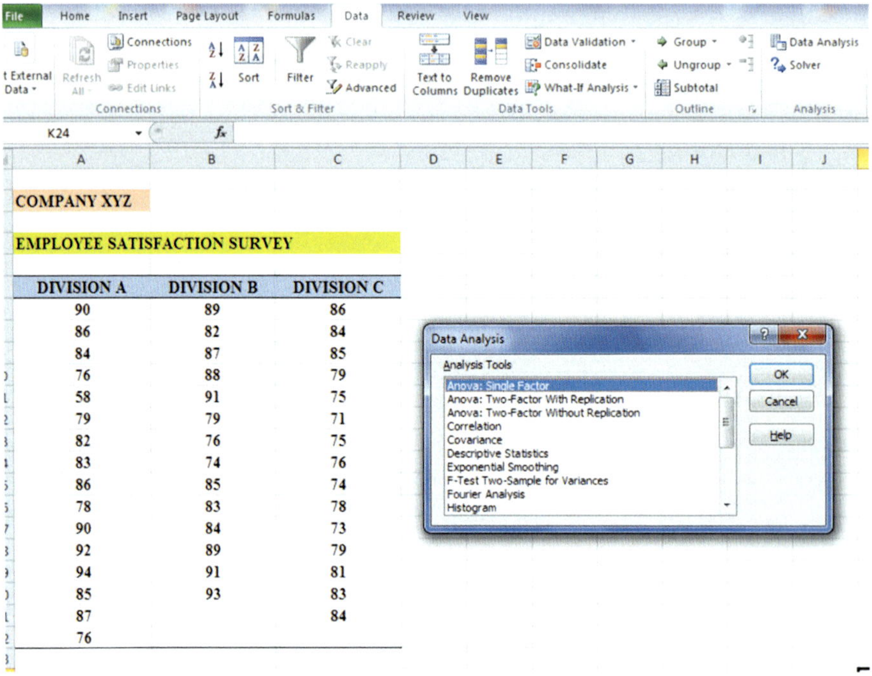

Fig. 8.2 Dialog Box for Data Analysis: ANOVA Single Factor

OK

Input range: A6:C22 (note that you have included in this range the column titles that are in row 6)

Important note: Whenever the data set has a different sample size in the groups being compared, the INPUT RANGE that you define must start at the column title of the first group on the left and go to the last column on the right to the lowest row that has a figure in it in the entire data matrix so that the INPUT RANGE has the "shape" of a rectangle when you highlight it. Since DIVISION A has 76 in cell A22, your "rectangle" must include row 22!

Grouped by: Columns
Put a check mark in: Labels in First Row
Output range (click on the button to its left): A24 (see Fig. 8.3)

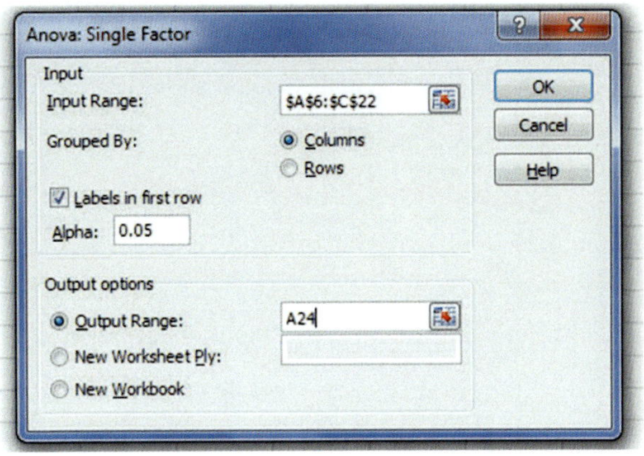

Fig. 8.3 Dialog Box for ANOVA: Single Factor Input/Output Range

OK

Center all of the numbers in the ANOVA table, and round off all numbers that are decimals to two decimal places.

Save this file as: Survey6

You should have generated the table given in Fig. 8.4.

	A	B	C	D	E	F	G
19	94	91	81				
20	85	93	83				
21	87		84				
22	76						
23							
24	Anova: Single Factor						
25							
26	SUMMARY						
27	*Groups*	*Count*	*Sum*	*Average*	*Variance*		
28	DIVISION A	16	1326	82.88	73.58		
29	DIVISION B	14	1191	85.07	33.30		
30	DIVISION C	15	1183	78.87	22.98		
31							
32							
33	ANOVA						
34	*Source of Variation*	*SS*	*df*	*MS*	*F*	*P-value*	*F crit*
35	Between Groups	289.37	2	144.68	3.27	0.05	3.22
36	Within Groups	1858.41	42	44.25			
37							
38	Total	2147.78	44				
39							

Fig. 8.4 ANOVA Results for Job Satisfaction Surveys

Print out both the data table and the ANOVA summary table so that all of this information fits onto one page. (Hint: Set the Page Layout/Fit to Scale to *95 % size*).

As a check on your analysis, you should have the following in these cells:

A24: ANOVA: Single Factor
D29: 85.07
D36: 44.25
E35: 3.27
G35: 3.22

Now, let's discuss how you should interpret this table:

8.2 How to Interpret the ANOVA Table Correctly

Objective: To interpret the ANOVA table correctly

ANOVA allows you to test for the differences between means when you have three or more groups of data. This ANOVA test is called the F-test statistic, and is typically identified with the letter: F.

The formula for the F-test is this:

F = Mean Square between groups (MS_b) divided by Mean Square within groups (MS_w)

$$F = MS_b / MS_w \tag{8.1}$$

The derivation and explanation of this formula is beyond the scope of this *Excel Guide*. In this *Excel Guide*, we are attempting to teach you *how to use Excel to conduct statistical tests*, and we are not attempting to teach you the statistical theory that is behind the ANOVA formulas. For a detailed explanation of ANOVA, see Polit (2010) and Aamodt *et al.* (2007).

Note that cell D35 contains $MS_b = 144.68$, while cell D36 contains $MS_w = 44.25$.

When you divide these two figures using their cell references in Excel, you get the answer for the F-test of 3.27 which is in cell E35. (Remember, Excel is more accurate than your calculator!) Let's discuss now the meaning of the figure: $F = 3.27$.

In order to determine whether this figure for F of 3.27 indicates a significant difference between the means of the three groups, the first step is to write the null hypothesis and the research hypothesis for the Job Satisfaction scores in each of the three divisions.

In our initial visit comparisons, the null hypothesis states that the population means of the three groups are equal, while the research hypothesis states that the population means of the three groups are not equal, and that there is, therefore, a significant difference between the population means of the three groups. Which of these two hypotheses should you accept based on the ANOVA results?

8.3 Using the Decision Rule for the ANOVA F-Test

To state the hypotheses, let's refer to DIVISION A as Group 1, DIVISION B as Group 2, and DIVISION C as Group 3. The hypotheses would then be:

H_0: $\mu_1 = \mu_2 = \mu_3$
H_1: $\mu_1 \neq \mu_2 \neq \mu_3$

The answer to this question is analogous to the decision rule used in this book for both the one-group t-test and the two-group t-test. You will recall that this rule (See Sect. 4.1.6 and Sect. 5.1.8) was:

If the absolute value of t is less than the critical t, you accept the null hypothesis.

or

If the absolute value of t is greater than the critical t, you reject the null hypothesis, and accept the research hypothesis.

Now, here is the decision rule for ANOVA:

Objective: To learn the decision rule for the ANOVA F-test

The decision rule for the ANOVA F-test is the following:

If the value for F is less than the critical F-value, accept the null hypothesis.

or

If the value of F is greater than the critical F-value, reject the null hypothesis, and accept the research hypothesis.

Note that Excel tells you the critical F-value in cell G35: 3.22
Therefore, our decision rule for the Job Satisfaction scores ANOVA test is this:

Since the value of F of 3.27 is greater than the critical F-value of 3.22, we reject the null hypothesis and accept the research hypothesis.

Therefore, our conclusion, in plain English, is:

There was a significant difference between the three divisions in their Job Satisfaction scores.

Note that it is not necessary to take the absolute value of F of 3.27. The F-value can never be less than one, and so it can never be a negative value which requires us to take its absolute value in order to treat it as a positive value.

It is important to note that ANOVA tells us that there was a significant difference between the population means of the three groups, *but it does not tell us which pairs of groups were significantly different from each other.*

8.4 Testing for the Difference Between Two Groups Using the ANOVA t-Test

To answer that question, we need to do a different test called the ANOVA t-test.

Objective: To test the difference between the means of two groups using an ANOVA t-test when the ANOVA F-test results indicate a significant difference between the population means.

Since we have three groups of data (one group for each of the three divisions), we would have to perform three separate ANOVA t-tests to determine which pairs of groups were significantly different. This requires that we would have to perform a separate ANOVA t-test for the following pairs of groups:

(1) DIVISION A vs. DIVISION B
(2) DIVISION A vs. DIVISION C
(3) DIVISION B vs. DIVISION C

We will do just one of these pairs of tests, DIVISION B vs. DIVISION C, to illustrate the way to perform an ANOVA t-test comparing these two divisions. The ANOVA t-test for the other two pairs of groups would be done in the same way.

8.4.1 Comparing Division B vs. Division C in Job Satisfaction Using the ANOVA t-Test

Objective: To compare DIVISION B vs. DIVISION C in Job Satisfaction scores using the ANOVA t-test.

The first step is to write out the null hypothesis and the research hypothesis for these two divisions.

For the ANOVA t-test, the null hypothesis is that the population means of the two groups are equal, while the research hypothesis is that the population means of the two groups are not equal (i.e., there is a significant difference between these two means). Since we are comparing DIVISION B (Group 2) vs. DIVISION C (Group 3), these hypotheses would be:

H_0: $\mu_2 = \mu_3$
H_1: $\mu_2 \neq \mu_3$

For Group 2 vs. Group 3, the formula for the ANOVA t-test is:

$$ANOVA\ t = \frac{\overline{X}_1 - \overline{X}_2}{s.e._{ANOVA}} \tag{8.2}$$

where

$$s.e._{ANOVA} = \sqrt{MS_w\left(\frac{1}{n_1} + \frac{1}{n_2}\right)} \tag{8.3}$$

Important note: Formula 8.3 uses n_1 and n_2, but since we are comparing Group 2 and Group 3, you should use n_2 and n_3 in your use of this formula.

The steps involved in computing this ANOVA t-test are:

1. Find the difference of the sample means for the two groups: (85.07 − 78.87 = 6.20).
2. Find $1/n_2 + 1/n_3$ (since both groups have a different number of scores in them, this becomes: 1/14 + 1/15 = 0.07 + 0.07 = 0.14)
3. Multiply MS_w times the answer for step 2: (44.25 × 0.14 = 6.20)
4. Take the square root of step 3: SQRT (6.20) = 2.49
5. Divide Step 1 by Step 4 to find ANOVA t: (6.20/2.49 = 2.49)

Note: Since Excel computes all calculations to 16 decimal places, when you use Excel for the above computations, your answer will be 2.51 in two decimal places. Excel's answer will be much more accurate because it always uses 16 decimal places in its computations.

Now, what do we do with this ANOVA t-test result of 2.51? In order to interpret this value of 2.51 correctly, we need to determine the critical value of t for the ANOVA t-test. To do that, we need to find the degrees of freedom for the ANOVA t-test as follows:

8.4.1.1 Finding the Degrees of Freedom for the ANOVA t-Test

Objective: To find the degrees of freedom for the ANOVA t-test.

The degrees of freedom (df) for the ANOVA t-test is found as follows:

df = take the total sample size of all of the groups and subtract the number of groups in your study ($n_{TOTAL} - k$ where k = the number of groups)

In our example, the total sample size of the three groups is 45 since there are 16 employees in Group 1, 14 employees in Group 2, and 15 employees in Group 3, and since there are three groups, 45 − 3 gives a degrees of freedom for the ANOVA t-test of 42.

If you look up df = 42 in the t-table in Appendix E in the degrees of freedom column (df), which is the *second column on the left of this table*, you will find that the critical t-value is 1.96.

Important note: Be sure to use the degrees of freedom column (df) in Appendix E for the ANOVA t-test critical t value

8.4.1.2 Stating the Decision Rule for the ANOVA t-Test

Objective: To learn the decision rule for the ANOVA t-test

Interpreting the result of the ANOVA t-test follows the same decision rule that we used for both the one-group t-test (see Sect. 4.1.6) and the two-group t-test (see Sect. 5.1.8):

If the absolute value of t is less than the critical value of t, we accept the null hypothesis.

or

If the absolute value of t is greater than the critical value of t, we reject the null hypothesis and accept the research hypothesis.

Since we are using a type of t-test, we need to take the absolute value of t. Since the absolute value of 2.51 is greater than the critical t-value of 1.96, we reject the null hypothesis (that the population means of the two groups are equal) and accept the research hypothesis (that the population means of the two groups are significantly different from one another).

This means that our conclusion, in plain English, is as follows:

The average Job Satisfaction score for non-supervisory employees in DIVISION B was significantly higher than the average Job Satisfaction score for non-supervisory employees in DIVISION C (85.07 vs. 78.87).

8.4.1.3 Performing an ANOVA t-Test Using Excel Commands

Now, let's do these calculations for the ANOVA t-test using Excel with the file you created earlier in this chapter: Survey6

A41: DIVISION B vs. DIVISION C
A43: 1/n DIVISION B + 1/n DIVISION C
A45: s.e. DIVISION B vs. DIVISION C
A47: ANOVA t-test
C43: =(1/14 + 1/15) (no spaces between symbols)
C45: =SQRT(D36*C43)
C47: =(D29 – D30)/C45 (no spaces between symbols)

You should now have the following results in these cells when you round off all these figures in the ANOVA t-test to two decimal points:

C43: 0.14
C45: 2.47
C47: 2.51

Save this final result under the file name: Survey7

Print out the resulting spreadsheet so that it fits onto one page like Fig. 8.5 (Hint: Reduce the Page Layout/Scale to Fit to *90 %*).

COMPANY XYZ

EMPLOYEE SATISFACTION SURVEY

DIVISION A	DIVISION B	DIVISION C
90	89	86
86	82	84
84	87	85
76	88	79
58	91	75
79	79	71
82	76	75
83	74	76
86	85	74
78	83	78
90	84	73
92	89	79
94	91	81
85	93	83
87		84
76		

Anova: Single Factor

SUMMARY

Groups	Count	Sum	Average	Variance
DIVISION A	16	1326	82.88	73.58
DIVISION B	14	1191	85.07	33.30
DIVISION C	15	1183	78.87	22.98

ANOVA

Source of Variation	SS	df	MS	F	P-value	F crit
Between Groups	289.37	2	144.68	3.27	0.05	3.22
Within Groups	1858.41	42	44.25			
Total	2147.78	44				

DIVISION B vs. DIVISION C

1/n DIVISION B + 1/n DIVISION C	0.14
s.e. DIVISION B vs. DIVISION C	2.47
ANOVA t-test	2.51

Fig. 8.5 Final Spreadsheet of Job Satisfaction for Division B vs. Division C

For a more detailed explanation of the ANOVA t-test, see Scott and Mazhindu (2005) and Black (2010).

Important note: You are only allowed to perform an ANOVA t-test comparing the means of two groups when the F-test produces a significant difference between the means of all of the groups in your study.

It is improper to do any ANOVA t-test when the value of F is less than the critical value of F. Whenever F is less than the critical F, this means that there was no difference between the means of the groups, and, therefore, any test conducted to see if there is a difference between the means of any two groups would capitalize on chance differences between the two groups.

8.5 End-of-Chapter Practice Problems

1. Suppose that you worked for a large engineering company with locations in various cities within the USA. "Employee turnover" is a critical factor in the success of every business since talented and experienced employees are difficult to replace if they decide to leave the company. Suppose that you have collected the turnover rate data presented in Fig. 8.6 by randomly sampling your company's locations for each of the four departments of your company. You have been asked to analyze the data to determine if there was a significant difference in the turnover rate between the four departments over the past year.

COMPANY XYZ			
TURNOVER RATE (in percent) LAST YEAR			
ENGINEERING	MANUFACTURING	ADMINISTRATION	SALES
8	11	8	6
10	19	9	12
11	17	15	8
12	16	10	6
9	18	11	7
8	12	9	9
10	13	14	8
11	15	9	10
12	16	10	12
8	14	11	11
7	16	12	8
6	19		9
8	18		6
6			7
7			8
			10

Fig. 8.6 Worksheet Data for Chap. 8: Practice Problem #1

(a) Enter these data on an Excel spreadsheet.
(b) Perform a *one-way ANOVA test* on these data, and show the resulting ANOVA table *underneath* the input data for the four departments.
(c) If the F-value in the ANOVA table is significant, create an Excel formula to compute the ANOVA t-test comparing the average for MANUFACTURING against SALES and show the results below the ANOVA table on the spreadsheet (put the standard error and the ANOVA t-test value on separate lines of your spreadsheet, and use one decimal place for each value)
(d) Print out the resulting spreadsheet so that all of the information fits onto one page
(e) Save the spreadsheet as: Turnover8

Now, write the answers to the following questions using your Excel printout:

1. What are the null hypothesis and the research hypothesis for the ANOVA F-test?
2. What is MS_b on your Excel printout?
3. What is MS_w on your Excel printout?
4. Compute $F = MS_b/MS_w$ using your calculator.
5. What is the critical value of F on your Excel printout?
6. What is the result of the ANOVA F-test?
7. What is the conclusion of the ANOVA F-test in plain English?
8. If the ANOVA F-test produced a significant difference between the four departments in turnover rate during the past year, what is the null hypothesis and the research hypothesis for the ANOVA t-test comparing MANUFACTURING versus SALES?
9. What is the mean (average) for MANUFACTURING on your Excel printout?
10. What is the mean (average) for SALES on your Excel printout?
11. What are the degrees of freedom (df) for the ANOVA t-test comparing MANUFACTURING versus SALES?
12. What is the critical t value for this ANOVA t-test in Appendix E for these degrees of freedom?
13. Compute the $s.e._{ANOVA}$ using your calculator.
14. Compute the ANOVA t-test value comparing MANUFACTURING versus SALES using your calculator.
15. What is the result of the ANOVA t-test comparing MANUFACTURING versus SALES?
16. What is the conclusion of the ANOVA t-test comparing MANUFACTURING versus SALES in plain English?

Note: Since there are four departments and they comprise six pairs of departments between them, you need to do six ANOVA t-tests to determine what the significant differences are between the four departments in turnover rate during the past year. *Since you have just completed the ANOVA t-test comparing MANUFACTURING versus SALES, you would also need to do the ANOVA t-test comparing:*

ENGINEERING versus MANUFACTURING
ENGINEERING versus ADMINISTRATION
ENGINEERING versus SALES
MANUFACTURING versus ADMINISTRATION
ADMINISTRATION versus SALES

in order to write a conclusion summarizing these six ANOVA t-tests overall.

2. In an organization with many different departments in different locations, the retention rate of customers in different departments of the organization is an important factor in the success of the organization. If you measure "retention rate" by the percent of customers for a department at the beginning of the year that were still customers at the end of that year, you can compare the departments in your organization in terms of their customer retention rate. Suppose you decide to take a random sample of locations of your organization, and to record the retention rate for each location during the past year for each of three departments.

   Note that each department can have a different number of locations in order for ANOVA to be used on the data.

   Suppose that your random sample produces the hypothetical data given in Fig. 8.7.

Fig. 8.7 Worksheet Data for Chap. 8: Practice Problem #2

RETENTION RATE (last year in percent)

PRODUCTION	SALES	ENGINEERING
58	79	80
66	92	89
65	84	87
59	86	88
58	88	86
61	89	84
63	90	80
62	92	82
65	89	86
66	91	83
	82	89
	79	

   (a) Enter these data on an Excel spreadsheet.
   (b) Perform a *one-way ANOVA test* on these data, and show the resulting ANOVA table *underneath* the input data for the three departments. Round off all decimal figures to two decimal places, and center all numbers in the ANOVA table.

(c) If the F-value in the ANOVA table is significant, create an Excel formula to compute the ANOVA t-test comparing retention rate for PRODUCTION against the retention rate for ENGINEERING, and show the results below the ANOVA table on the spreadsheet (put the standard error and the ANOVA t-test value on separate lines of your spreadsheet, and use two decimal places for each value)
(d) Print out the resulting spreadsheet so that all of the information fits onto one page
(e) Save the spreadsheet as: Retention6

Now, write the answers to the following questions using your Excel printout:

1. What are the null hypothesis and the research hypothesis for the ANOVA F-test?
2. What is MS_b on your Excel printout?
3. What is MS_w on your Excel printout?
4. Compute $F = MS_b/MS_w$ using your calculator.
5. What is the critical value of F on your Excel printout?
6. What is the result of the ANOVA F-test?
7. What is the conclusion of the ANOVA F-test in plain English?
8. If the ANOVA F-test produced a significant difference between the three departments in their retention rate, what is the null hypothesis and the research hypothesis for the ANOVA t-test comparing PRODUCTION versus ENGINEERING?
9. What is the mean (average) retention rate for PRODUCTION on your Excel printout?
10. What is the mean (average) retention rate for ENGINEERING on your Excel printout?
11. What are the degrees of freedom (df) for the ANOVA t-test comparing PRODUCTION versus ENGINEERING?
12. What is the critical t value for this ANOVA t-test in Appendix E for these degrees of freedom?
13. Compute the $s.e._{ANOVA}$ using Excel for PRODUCTION versus ENGINEERING.
14. Compute the ANOVA t-test value comparing PRODUCTION versus ENGINEERING using Excel.
15. What is the result of the ANOVA t-test comparing PRODUCTION versus ENGINEERING?
16. What is the conclusion of the ANOVA t-test comparing PRODUCTION versus ENGINEERING in plain English?

3. When universities in the USA want to hire qualified faculty, they typically advertise for the position on a Web site for professional organizations that include job openings on the Web site so that members of the organizations can become informed about possible job matches in their career search. If a university wants to hire a new qualified faculty member to teach Human Resource

Management, there are three popular Web sites that provide this job listing: (1) The American Society for Training and Development (ASTD), (2) The Society for Human Resource Management (SHRM), and (3) The Chronicle of Higher Education. Suppose that a university wants to determine if there was a difference in applications received from these three Web sites when the past eight professors of HRM were hired by that university. The hypothetical data for this study are given in Fig. 8.8.

Fig. 8.8 Worksheet Data for Chap. 8: Practice Problem #3

SOURCE OF HR TEACHING APPLICATIONS			
	NUMBER OF APPLICATIONS		
HR POSITION	CHRONICLE	SHRM	ASTD
1	85	68	86
2	64	64	89
3	92	65	102
4	54	62	116
5	68	63	101
6	67	61	98
7	55	60	95
8	82	59	94

(a) Enter these data on an Excel spreadsheet.
(b) Perform a *one-way ANOVA test* on these data, and show the resulting ANOVA table *underneath* the input data for the three Web sites.
(c) If the F-value in the ANOVA table is significant, create an Excel formula to compute the ANOVA t-test comparing the average applications for SHRM against the average applications for ASTD, and show the results below the ANOVA table on the spreadsheet (put the standard error and the ANOVA t-test value on separate lines of your spreadsheet, and use two decimal places for each value)
(d) Print out the resulting spreadsheet so that all of the information fits onto one page
(e) Save the spreadsheet as: Placement6

Now, write the answers to the following questions using your Excel printout:

1. What are the null hypothesis and the research hypothesis for the ANOVA F-test?
2. What is MS_b on your Excel printout?
3. What is MS_w on your Excel printout?
4. Compute $F = MS_b/MS_w$ using your calculator.
5. What is the critical value of F on your Excel printout?
6. What is the result of the ANOVA F-test?
7. What is the conclusion of the ANOVA F-test in plain English?

8. If the ANOVA F-test produced a significant difference between the three Web sites in the number of job applications received for an HRM opening, what is the null hypothesis and the research hypothesis for the ANOVA t-test comparing SHRM versus ASTD?
9. What is the mean (average) number of applications for SHRM on your Excel printout?
10. What is the mean (average) number of applications for ASTD on your Excel printout?
11. What are the degrees of freedom (df) for the ANOVA t-test comparing SHRM versus ASTD?
12. What is the critical t value for this ANOVA t-test in Appendix E for these degrees of freedom?
13. Compute the $s.e._{ANOVA}$ using your calculator for SHRM versus ASTD.
14. Compute the ANOVA t-test value comparing SHRM versus ASTD using your calculator.
15. What is the result of the ANOVA t-test comparing SHRM versus ASTD?
16. What is the conclusion of the ANOVA t-test comparing SHRM versus ASTD in plain English?

References

Aamodt M, Surrette M, and Cohen D. Understanding statistics: a guide for I/O psychologists and human resource professionals. Belmont: WADSWORTH CENGAGE Learning; 2007.

Black K. Business statistics: for contemporary decision making. 6th ed. Hoboken: John Wiley & Sons, Inc.; 2010.

Polit DF. Statistics for data analysis for nursing research. 2nd ed. Upper Saddle River: Pearson Education Inc.; 2010.

Scott I, Mazhindu D. Statistics for health care professionals: an introduction. Thousand Oaks: Sage; 2005.

Appendices

Appendix A: Answers to End-of-Chapter Practice Problems

T.J. Quirk, J. Palmer-Schuyler, *Excel 2016 for Human Resource Management Statistics*, Excel for Statistics, DOI 10.1007/978-3-319-40063-1

Chapter 1: Practice Problem #1 Answer (see Fig. A.1)

HUMAN RESOURCES MORALE SURVEY

Item #21: **"Management is doing a good job of keeping employee morale at a high level."**

1	2	3	4	5	6	7
Disagree						Agree

Rating		
3		
6		
5		
7	n	23
2		
3		
6	Mean	4.52
5		
4		
7	STDEV	1.73
6		
1		
3	s.e.	0.36
2		
4		
5		
6		
4		
5		
3		
6		
4		
7		

Fig. A.1 Answer to Chap. 1: Practice Problem #1

Chapter 1: Practice Problem #2 Answer (see Fig. A.2)

DEPARTMENT D (last month)			
ON-TIME PERFORMANCE (%)			
95			
94		n	16
93			
98			
100		Mean	96.9
95			
96			
98		STDEV	2.1
99			
96			
97		s.e.	0.5
95			
98			
99			
100			
98			

Fig. A.2 Answer to Chap. 1: Practice Problem #2

Chapter 1: Practice Problem #3 Answer (see Fig. A.3)

ABSENCE RATE				
MONTH	MONTHLY ABSENCE RATE (%)			
JAN	2.5			
FEB	2.8		n	12
MAR	2.6			
APR	3.1			
MAY	3.4		Mean	2.8
JUN	2.7			
JUL	2.6			
AUG	2.4		STDEV	0.3
SEP	3.1			
OCT	3.0			
NOV	2.8		s.e.	0.1
DEC	2.7			

Fig. A.3 Answer to Chap. 1: Practice Problem #3

Chapter 2: Practice Problem #1 Answer (see Fig. A.4)

Fig. A.4 Answer to Chap. 2: Practice Problem #1

FRAME NUMBERS	Duplicate frame numbers	RANDOM NO.
1	7	0.443
2	50	0.652
3	23	0.007
4	13	0.863
5	6	0.495
6	14	0.187
7	60	0.528
8	37	0.028
9	61	0.534
10	33	0.660
11	43	0.490
12	4	0.159
13	8	0.493
14	5	0.776
15	59	0.079
16	39	0.150
17	63	0.825
18	35	0.219
19	49	0.784
20	1	0.045
21	57	0.969
22	12	0.887
[illegible]	[illegible]	[illegible]
[illegible]	[illegible]	[illegible]
61	11	0.481
62	42	0.123
63	54	0.082

Chapter 2: Practice Problem #2 Answer (see Fig. A.5)

Fig. A.5 Answer to Chap. 2: Practice Problem #2

FRAME NO.	Duplicate frame no.	Random number
1	58	0.602
2	50	0.651
3	43	0.558
4	42	0.469
5	86	0.406
6	24	0.669
7	22	0.104
8	11	0.585
9	104	0.008
10	105	0.676
11	61	0.537
12	41	0.714
13	79	0.336
14	93	0.154
15	85	0.215
16	54	0.294
17	16	0.217
18	77	0.734
19	15	0.702
20	112	0.624
1	28	
9.		0.750
100	96	0.827
101	48	0.673
102	108	0.972
103	109	0.233
104	33	0.041
105	3	0.304
106	90	0.362
107	110	0.596
108	62	0.234
109	88	0.520
110	60	0.740
111	98	0.112
112	94	0.349
113	59	0.002
114	67	0.360

Chapter 2: Practice Problem #3 Answer (see Fig. A.6)

FRAME NUMBERS	Duplicate frame numbers	Random number
1	58	0.003
2	7	0.255
3	37	0.115
4	49	0.532
5	26	0.134
6	65	0.833
7	48	0.394
8	63	0.064
9	15	0.580
10	25	0.914
11	21	0.911
12	36	0.917
13	43	0.344
14	11	0.307
15	10	0.216
16	39	0.827
17	72	0.648
18	59	0.234
19	16	0.177
20	54	0.368
21	52	0.952
22	3	0.893
23	45	0.253
24	4	0.006
25	76	0.504
26	19	0.564
27	46	0.385
28	24	0.046
29	69	0.611
30	8	0.856
31	[illegible]	[illegible]
	[illegible]	[illegible]
66	14	0.262
67	13	0.597
68	38	0.945
69	17	0.679
70	57	0.344
71	60	0.649
72	9	0.710
73	20	0.367
74	18	0.417
75	5	0.494

Fig. A.6 Answer to Chap. 2: Practice Problem #3

Chapter 3: Practice Problem #1 Answer (see Fig. A.7)

COST PER INTERVIEW						
Question:	"Does our COST PER INTERVIEW for prospective job candidates come close to the $120.00 per interview that we budgeted?					
		Null hypothesis:		μ	=	$120
COST PER INTERVIEW ($)		Research hypothesis:		μ	≠	$120
127						
128		n		22		
135						
118						
110		Mean		$128.32		
129						
127						
134		STDEV		$7.29		
142						
135						
129		s.e.		$1.55		
128						
117						
128		95% confidence interview				
135						
131			Lower limit:		$125.08	
134						
132			Upper limit:		$131.55	
119						
125						
126		Draw a picture of this confidence interval				
134						

$120 ----------------	$125.08 ----------------------------	$128.32 ------------	---$131.55
ref. value	lower limit	Mean	upper limit

Result: Since the reference value of $120 is outside of the confidence interval, we reject the null hypothesis and accept the research hypothesis.

Conclusion: Our COST PER INTERVIEW during this past quarter was significantly more than $120, and was probably closer to $128.

Fig. A.7 Answer to Chap. 3: Practice Problem #1

Chapter 3: Practice Problem #2 Answer (see Fig. A.8)

COST PER EXTERNAL HIRE

Question: "Does our COST PER EXTERNAL HIRE for prospective job candidates come close to the $6500.00 per external hire that we budgeted?

Null hypothesis:	μ	=	$6,500
Research hypothesis:	μ	≠	$6,500

COST PER EXTERNAL HIRE ($)
6800
7100
7050
6855
6480
6610
6725
6250
6130
6050
6200
6350
6475
6250
6175
6325
6260
6410
6530
6675
6750
6450
6870
6420
6150
6275

n	26
Mean	$6,485
STDEV	$292
s.e.	$57

95% confidence interview

Lower limit:	$6,367
Upper limit:	$6,603

Draw a picture of this confidence interval

$6,367 ----------------	$6485 ----	-----$6500 ----------------	---$6603
lower limit	Mean	ref. value	upper limit

Result: Since the reference value of $6500 is inside of the confidence interval, we accept the null hypothesis.

Conclusion: Our COST PER EXTERNAL HIRE during this past year was $6500.

Fig. A.8 Answer to Chap. 3: Practice Problem #2

Chapter 3: Practice Problem #3 Answer (see Fig. A.9)

Webster University

End of M.A. Program in Human Resource Management Exit Survey

Item #23: "Overall, how would you rate the quality of the M.A. Program in Human Resource Management?"

1	2	3	4	5	6	7
Poor						Excellent

RATING				
3	Null hypothesis:	μ	=	4
6				
5	Research hypothesis:	μ	≠	4
7				
4				
5	n	22		
6				
4	Mean	5.59		
6				
7	STDEV	1.22		
5				
7	s.e.	0.26		
4				
7				
7	95% confidence interval			
6				
6		Lower limit:	5.05	
6				
5		Upper limit:	6.13	
4				
6				
7	Draw a picture of this confidence interval			

----4------ ---------------5.05- ----------- -------5.59 ----------- ------- 6.13 -- -----------

Ref Value	Lower Limit	Mean	Upper Limit

Result: Since the reference value is outside of the confidence interval, we reject the null hypothesis and accept the research hypothesis.

Conclusion: M.A. students nearing the end of their HRM program rated the overall quality of the program as significantly positive.

Note: In the English language, it is not correct to say that something is "significantly excellent" since something is either excellent or it is not excellent. To avoid this language pitfall, it is much better to refer to a positive opinion as "significantly positive."

Fig. A.9 Answer to Chap. 3: Practice Problem #3

Chapter 4: Practice Problem #1 Answer (see Fig. A.10)

TURNOVER RATE FOR THE CALL CENTERS

MONTH	TURNOVER (%)
JAN	22
FEB	24
MAR	20
APR	19
MAY	18
JUN	24
JUL	23
AUG	25
SEP	21
OCT	20
NOV	19
DEC	18

Null lypothesis:	μ	=	20%
Research hypothesis:	μ	≠	20%

n	12
MEAN	21.08
STDEV	2.47
s.e.	0.71
critical t	2.201
t-test	1.52

Result: Since the absolute value of 1.52 is less than the critical t of 2.201, we accept the null hypothesis.

Conclusion: The average turnover rate for the Call Centers this past year was 20 percent.

Fig. A.10 Answer to Chap. 4: Practice Problem #1

Chapter 4: Practice Problem #2 Answer (see Fig. A.11)

HR WEBINAR TRAINING PROGRAM ON HEALTH AND SAFETY ISSUES

Item #10: **""Overall, how would you rate the quality of the HR Webinar Training Program dealing with Health and Saftey issues?"**

1	2	3	4	5	6	7	
very			4.05			very	
poor			Mean			good	
	DATA						
	3		Null hypothesis:		μ	=	4
	4						
	5		Research hypothesis:		μ	≠	4
	2						
	4						
	3		n		20		
	5						
	6						
	7		Mean		4.05		
	4						
	3						
	5		STDEV		1.36		
	4						
	3						
	3		s.e.		0.30		
	5						
	4						
	6		critical t		2.093		
	2						
	3						
			t-test		0.16		

Result: Since the absolute value of 0.16 is less than the critical t of 2.093, we accept the null hypothesis.

Conclusion: Participants in the HR Webinar Training Program on Health and Saftey Issues rated the overall quality of the program as neither positive nor negative.

Fig. A.11 Answer to Chap. 4: Practice Problem #2

Chapter 4: Practice Problem #3 Answer (see Fig. A.12)

SEXUAL HARASSMENT COMPLAINTS

MONTH	NO. OF COMPLAINTS
JAN	22
FEB	24
MAR	21
APR	18
MAY	16
JUN	26
JUL	27
AUG	22
SEP	24
OCT	19
NOV	21
DEC	24

Null hypothesis:	μ	=	25 per month
Research hypothesis:	μ	≠	25 per month

n	12
Mean	22.00
STDEV	3.25
s.e.	0.94
critical t	2.201
t-test	-3.20

Result: Since the absolute value of – 3.20 is greater than the critical t of 2.201, we reject the null hypothesis and accept the research hypothesis.

Conclusion: The average number of sexual harassment complaints per month this year was significantly less than the 25 complaints per month last year, and was probably closer to 22 complaints per month this year.

Fig. A.12 Answer to Chap. 4: Practice Problem #3

Chapter 5: Practice Problem #1 Answer (see Fig. A.13)

HR TRAINING PROGRAM

$H_0: \mu_1 = \mu_2$

$H_1: \mu_1 \neq \mu_2$

"REDUCING SEXUAL HARASSMENT IN THE WORKPLACE"

Item #24: "Overall, how would you rate the quality of the HR Training Program on the topic: Reducing Sexual Harassment in the Workplace?"

1	2	3	4	5	6	7	8	9
very poor								very good

SUPERVISORS	NON-SUPERVISORS
6	7
5	6
7	5
8	6
4	4
5	8
6	5
7	9
6	8
9	6
8	7
6	4
7	6
5	5
6	6
5	5
7	7
4	8
8	4
6	9
9	3
	4
	5

GROUP	n	Mean	STDEV
1 SUPERVISORS	21	6.38	1.47
2 NON-SUPERVISORS	23	5.96	1.69

Null hypothesis: $\mu_1 = \mu_2$

Research hypothesis: $\mu_1 \neq \mu_2$

(n1 - 1) x STDEV1 squared	42.95
(n2 - 1) x STDEV2 squared	62.96
n1 + n2 - 2	42
1/n1 + 1/n2	0.09
s.e.	0.48
critical t	1.96
t-test	0.89

Result: Since the absolute value of 0.89 is less than the critical t of 1.96, we accept the null hypothesis.

Conclusion: There was no difference in the ratings of the quality of the HR Training Program on "Reducing Sexual Harassment in the Workplace" between supervisors and non-supervisors.

Fig. A.13 Answer to Chap. 5: Practice Problem #1

Chapter 5: Practice Problem #2 Answer (see Fig. A.14)

HR TRAINING PROGRAM

1-800 CUSTOMER SERVICE REPS

GROUP	n	Mean	STDEV
1 EXPERIMENTAL GROUP	34	6.24	1.12
2 CONTROL GROUP	37	4.37	1.54

Null hypothesis:	μ_1	=	μ_2
Research hypothesis:	μ_1	≠	μ_2

STDEV1 squared / n1	0.04
STDEV2 squared / n2	0.06
D16 + D18	0.10
s.e.	0.32
critical t	1.96
t-test	5.88

Result: Since the absolute value of 5.88 is greater than the critical t of 1.96, we reject the null hypthesis and accept the research hypothesis.

Conclusion: The Experimental Group of Customer Service reps had significantly higher scores on the quality of service that they provided to customers than the Control Group of Customer Service reps (6.24 vs. 4.37).

Fig. A.14 Answer to Chap. 5: Practice Problem #2

Chapter 5: Practice Problem #3 Answer (see Fig. A.15)

M.A. IN HUMAN RESOURCES MANAGEMENT

GPA of students who have completed all required core courses

Group	n	Mean	STDEV
1 Males	47	3.15	0.42
2 Females	56	3.45	0.37

$H_0: \mu_1 = \mu_2$

$H_1: \mu_1 \neq \mu_2$

STDEV1 squared / n1	0.004
STDEV2 squared / n2	0.002
E12 + E14	0.006
s.e.	0.079
critical t	1.96
t-test	-3.811

Result: Since the absolute value of − 3.811 is greater than the critical t of 1.96, we reject the null hypothesis and accept the research hypothesis.

Conclusion: Female students in the M.A. program for Human Resources Management had a significantly higher GPA after completing all the required core courses in the program than Male students (3.45 vs. 3.15).

Fig. A.15 Answer to Chap. 5: Practice Problem #3

Chapter 6: Practice Problem #1 Answer (see Fig. A.16)

ENGINEERING COMPANY XYZ

What is the relationship between the accepted salary of newly-hired engineers and the recruiting cost for those engineers?

SALARY ($000)	RECRUITING COST ($)
45	5700
81	6200
75	6725
64	7150
69	8540
65	8930
72	9120
76	9560
97	10500
86	11630
92	12400
97	13900
89	14500
103	15800
102	16500

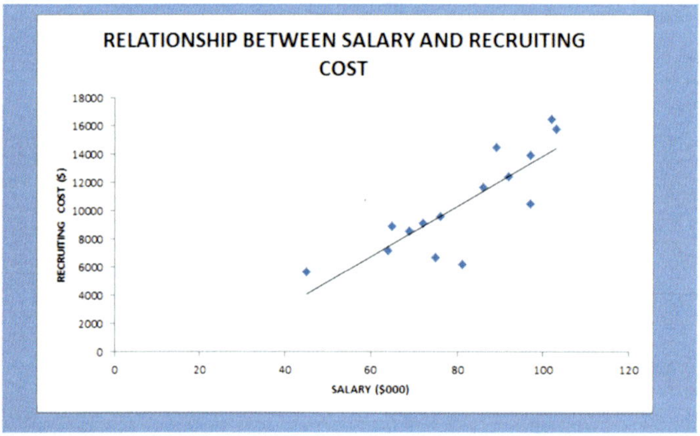

SUMMARY OUTPUT

Regression Statistics	
Multiple R	0.83
R Square	0.6966
Adjusted R Square	0.6733
Standard Error	2007.0678
Observations	15

ANOVA

	df	*SS*	*MS*	*F*	*Significance F*
Regression	1	120258413.8332	120258413.8	29.8532	0.0001
Residual	13	52368176.1668	4028321.2436		
Total	14	172626590.0000			

	Coefficients	*Standard Error*	*t Stat*	*P-value*	*Lower 95%*
Intercept	-3958.83	2692.4231	-1.4704	0.1653	-9775.4537
X Variable 1	178.5139	32.6721	5.4638	0.0001	107.9303

Fig. A.16 Answer to Chap. 6: Practice Problem #1

Chapter 6: Practice Problem #1 (continued)

1. $r = +.83$
2. $a = \text{y-intercept} = -3958.83$
3. $b = \text{slope} = 178.5139$
4. $Y = a + bX$
   $Y = -3958.83 + 178.5139\ X$
5. $Y = -3958.83 + 178.5139\ (80)$
   $Y = -3958.83 + 14,281.11$
   $Y = \$10,322$

Chapter 6: Practice Problem #2 Answer (see Fig. A.17)

COMPANY ABC

MORALE SURVEY

Item #18: "How likely are you to leave your employment at ABC sometime in the next two years?"

1	2	3	4	5	6	7
very unlikely						very likely

Item #30: "Overall, how satisfied are you with your current job at ABC?"

1	2	3	4	5	6	7
very dissatisfied						very satisfied

JOB SATISFACTION	LIKELY TO LEAVE ABC
ITEM 30	ITEM 18
2	5
6	6
4	3
3	2
5	4
4	7
3	6
2	5
1	6
4	7
5	4
3	3
6	2
7	1
5	2
4	3
3	1
4	7
2	6
1	6

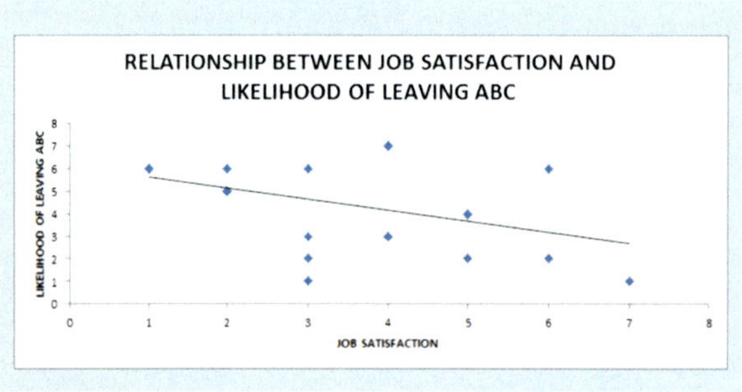

SUMMARY OUTPUT

Regression Statistics	
Multiple R	0.39
R Square	0.1517
Adjusted R Square	0.1046
Standard Error	1.9441
Observations	20

ANOVA

	df	*SS*	*MS*	*F*	*Significance F*
Regression	1	12.1655	12.1655	3.2187	0.0896
Residual	18	68.0345	3.7797		
Total	19	80.2000			

	Coefficients	*Standard Error*	*t Stat*	*P-value*	*Lower 95%*
Intercept	6.086	1.0864	5.6022	0.0000	3.8038
X Variable 1	-0.483	0.2691	-1.7941	0.0896	-1.0481

Fig. A.17 Answer to Chap. 6: Practice Problem #2

Chapter 6: Practice Problem #2 (continued)

(2b) about 3.1

1. r = −.39 (note the negative correlation!)
2. a = y-intercept = 6.086
3. b = slope = −0.483 (note the negative slope!)
4. Y = a + b X
   Y = 6.086 − 0.483 X
5. Y = 6.086 − 0.483 (5)
   Y = 6.086 − 2.415
   Y = 3.7

Chapter 6: Practice Problem #3 Answer (see Fig. A.18)

RELATIONSHIP BETWEEN DIET AND WEIGHT LOSS

ADULT WOMEN AGES 30-40

DIET (calories allowed per day)	WEIGHT LOSS (kg)
900	16.0
1050	12.0
1150	8.0
1275	6.0
1420	3.0
1530	5.5
1610	9.5
1710	2.5
1820	6.0
1875	9.0
1930	6.0
2100	3.0

correlation	-0.64

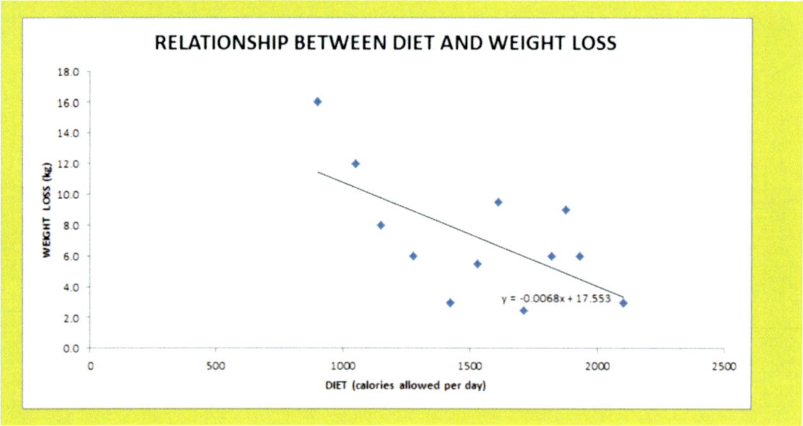

SUMMARY OUTPUT

Regression Statistics	
Multiple R	0.64
R Square	0.413
Adjusted R Square	0.354
Standard Error	3.198
Observations	12

ANOVA

	df	SS	MS	F	Significance F
Regression	1	71.946	71.946	7.034	0.024
Residual	10	102.284	10.228		
Total	11	174.229			

	Coefficients	Standard Error	t Stat	P-value	Lower 95%	Upper 95%
Intercept	17.553	4.008	4.379	0.001	8.622	26.483
X Variable 1	-0.007	0.003	-2.652	0.024	-0.012	-0.001

Fig. A.18 Answer to Chap. 6: Practice Problem #3

Chapter 6: Practice Problem #3 (continued)

1. r = –.64 (note the negative correlation!)
2. a = y-intercept = 17.553
3. b = slope = –0.007 (note the negative slope!)
4. Y = a + b X
   Y = 17.553 – 0.007 X
5. Y = 17.553 – 0.007 (1500)
   Y = 17.553 – 10.5
   Y = 7.1 kg weight loss

Chapter 7: Practice Problem #1 Answer (see Fig. A.19)

GRADUATE MANAGEMENT ADMISSION TEST (GMAT)

How well does the GMAT predict first-year GPA in an HRM program?

FIRST-YEAR GPA	VERBAL	QUANTITATIVE	ANALYTICAL WRITING	INTEGRATED REASONING
3.25	50	45	4.0	4
3.67	56	48	4.5	6
2.8	54	51	5.0	5
3.05	52	53	5.5	4
3.45	51	54	4.0	3
3.33	48	58	3.0	7
2.75	46	59	4.5	8
2.95	45	57	5.5	5
2.6	52	51	6.0	6
3.67	57	50	4.5	4
3.75	53	48	3.0	7
3.42	46	46	4.0	6
3.15	42	48	5.0	7
3.26	38	49	4.0	5
2.96	41	52	5.5	4

SUMMARY OUTPUT

Regression Statistics	
Multiple R	0.83
R Square	0.6878
Adjusted R Square	0.5629
Standard Error	0.2335
Observations	15

ANOVA

	df	*SS*	*MS*	*F*	*Significance F*
Regression	4	1.2005	0.3001	5.5070	0.0132
Residual	10	0.5450	0.0545		
Total	14	1.7456			

	Coefficients	*Standard Error*	*t Stat*	*P-value*	*Lower 95%*
Intercept	5.263	1.0522	5.0016	0.0005	2.9183
VERBAL	0.013	0.0113	1.1662	0.2706	-0.0120
QUANTITATIVE	-0.023	0.0151	-1.5471	0.1529	-0.0570
ANALYTICAL WRITING	-0.275	0.0734	-3.7486	0.0038	-0.4389
INTEGRATED REASONING	-0.047	0.0459	-1.0283	0.3280	-0.1494

	FIRST-YEAR GPA	*VERBAL*	*QUANTITATIVE*	*ANALYTICAL WRITING*	*INTEGRATED REASONING*
FIRST-YEAR GPA	1				
VERBAL	0.31	1			
QUANTITATIVE	-0.42	-0.12	1		
ANALYTICAL WRITING	-0.69	-0.06	0.12	1	
INTEGRATED REASONING	-0.09	-0.14	0.17	-0.26	1

Fig. A.19 Answer to Chap. 7: Practice Problem #1

Chapter 7: Practice Problem #1 (continued)

1. Multiple correlation = .83
2. y-intercept = 5.263
3. $b_1 = 0.013$
4. $b_2 = -0.023$
5. $b_3 = -0.275$
6. $b_4 = -0.047$
7. $Y = a + b_1X_1 + b_2X_2 + b_3X_3 + b_4X_4$
   $Y = 5.263 + 0.013\ X_1 - 0.023\ X_2 - 0.275\ X_3 - 0.047\ X_4$
8. $Y = 5.263 + 0.013\ (52) - 0.023\ (48) - 0.275\ (4.5) - 0.047\ (6)$
   $Y = 5.263 + .676 - 1.104 - 1.237 - 0.282$
   $Y = 5.939 - 2.623$
   $Y = 3.32$
9. 0.31
10. −0.42
11. −0.69
12. −0.09
13. −0.12
14. 0.12
15. −0.26
16. 0.17
17. The best predictor of first-year GPA was ANALYTICAL WRITING ($r = -.69$). Note: Be sure to ignore the negative sign for this predictor!
18. The four predictors combined predict first-year GPA at $R_{xy} = .83$, and this is much better than the best single predictor by itself.

Chapter 7: Practice Problem #2 Answer (see Fig. A.20)

Research question:	"Is there a relationship between performance, experience, education and pay raise?"		
PERCENT RAISE	PERFORMANCE RATING	YEARS OF EXPERIENCE	NO. DEGREES
6	4	12	4
4	5	10	5
2	3	5	1
5	5	8	3
3	3	4	2
2	2	6	1
6	5	12	4
3	3	6	2
2	1	3	1
4	3	10	3

SUMMARY OUTPUT

Regression Statistics	
Multiple R	0.91
R Square	0.83
Adjusted R Square	0.74
Standard Error	0.80
Observations	10

ANOVA

	df	*SS*	*MS*	*F*	*Significance F*
Regression	3	18.25	6.08	9.48	0.01
Residual	6	3.85	0.64		
Total	9	22.10			

	Coefficients	*Standard Error*	*t Stat*	*P-value*	*Lower 95%*
Intercept	0.1297	0.82	0.16	0.88	-1.88
PERFORMANCE RATING	0.3436	0.37	0.94	0.38	-0.55
YEARS OF EXPERIENCE	0.3001	0.16	1.85	0.11	-0.10
NO. DEGREES	0.0468	0.46	0.10	0.92	-1.07

	PERCENT RAISE	*PERFORMANCE RATING*	*YEARS OF EXPERIENCE*	*NO. DEGREES*
PERCENT RAISE	1			
PERFORMANCE RATING	0.80	1		
YEARS OF EXPERIENCE	0.88	0.74	1	
NO. DEGREES	0.83	0.84	0.86	1

Fig. A.20 Answer to Chap. 7: Practice Problem #2

Chapter 7: Practice Problem #2 (continued)

1. $R_{xy} = .91$
2. a = y-intercept = 0.1297
3. $b_1 = 0.3436$
4. $b_2 = 0.3001$
5. $b_3 = 0.0468$
6. $Y = a + b_1X_1 + b_2X_2 + b_3X_3$
   $Y = 0.1297 + 0.3436\ X_1 + 0.3001\ X_2 + 0.0468\ X_3$
7. $Y = 0.1297 + 0.3436\ (4) + 0.3001\ (12) + 0.0468\ (3)$
   $Y = 0.1297 + 1.3744 + 3.6012 + 0.1404$
   $Y = 5.25\%$ raise
8. +0.80
9. +0.88
10. +0.83
11. +0.74
12. The best predictor of PERCENT RAISE was YEARS OF EXPERIENCE ($r = +.88$)
13. The three predictors combined predict PERCENT RAISE much better ($R_{xy} = .91$) than the best single predictor by itself ($r = .88$)

Chapter 7: Practice Problem #3 Answer (see Fig. A.21)

Research question:	"Are experience and education good predictors of performance?"	
PERFORMANCE RATING	**EXPERIENCE**	**NO. DEGREES**
7	20	3
6	15	2
4	8	2
1	5	0
2	6	1
6	18	3
5	6	2
7	10	3
4	11	2
5	12	3
4	8	4
6	14	3
5	9	2

SUMMARY OUTPUT

Regression Statistics	
Multiple R	0.84
R Square	0.703
Adjusted R Square	0.644
Standard Error	1.066
Observations	13

ANOVA

	df	*SS*	*MS*	*F*	*Significance F*
Regression	2	26.940	13.470	11.850	0.002
Residual	10	11.367	1.137		
Total	12	38.308			

	Coefficients	*Standard Error*	*t Stat*	*P-value*	*Lower 95%*
Intercept	0.8482	0.858	0.989	0.346	-1.064
EXPERIENCE	0.1916	0.077	2.496	0.032	0.021
NO. DEGREES	0.7922	0.350	2.266	0.047	0.013

	PERFORMANCE RATING	*EXPERIENCE*	*NO. DEGREES*
PERFORMANCE RATING	1		
EXPERIENCE	0.74	1	
NO. DEGREES	0.72	0.52	1

Fig. A.21 Answer to Chap. 7: Practice Problem #3

Chapter 7: Practice Problem #3 (continued)

1. Multiple correlation = .84
2. a = y-intercept = 0.8482
3. $b_1 = 0.1916$
4. $b_2 = 0.7922$
5. $Y = a + b_1X_1 + b_2X_2$
   $Y = 0.8482 + 0.1916\ X_1 + 0.7922\ X_2$
6. $Y = 0.8482 + 0.1916\ (10) + 0.7922\ (3)$
   $Y = 0.8482 + 1.916 + 2.377$
   $Y = 5$
7. +0.74
8. +0.72
9. +0.52
10. The better predictor of PERFORMANCE RATING was EXPERIENCE (r = .74).
11. The two predictors combined predicted PERFORMANCE RATING much better at $R_{xy} = .84$.

Chapter 8: Practice Problem #1 Answer (see Fig. A.22)

COMPANY XYZ

TURNOVER RATE (in percent) LAST YEAR

ENGINEERING	MANUFACTURING	ADMINISTRATION	SALES
8	11	8	6
10	19	9	12
11	17	15	8
12	16	10	6
9	18	11	7
8	12	9	9
10	13	14	8
11	15	9	10
12	16	10	12
8	14	11	11
7	16	12	8
6	19		9
8	18		6
6			7
7			8
			10

Anova: Single Factor

SUMMARY

Groups	*Count*	*Sum*	*Average*	*Variance*
ENGINEERING	15	133	8.9	4.1
MANUFACTURING	13	204	15.7	6.7
ADMINISTRATION	11	118	10.7	4.8
SALES	16	137	8.6	4.0

ANOVA

Source of Variation	*SS*	*df*	*MS*	*F*	*P-value*	*F crit*
Between Groups	447.3	3	149.1	30.8	1.6E-11	2.8
Within Groups	246.6	51	4.8			
Total	693.9	54				

MANUFACTURING vs. SALES

1/n MANUFACTURING + 1/n SALES	0.1
s.e. MANUFACTURING vs. SALES	0.8
ANOVA t-test	8.7

Fig. A.22 Answer to Chap. 8: Practice Problem #1

Chapter 8: Practice Problem #1 (continued)

Let Group 1 = ENGINEERING, Group 2 = MANUFACTURING, Group 3 = ADMINISTRATION and Group 4 = SALES

1. H_0: $\mu_1 = \mu_2 = \mu_3 = \mu_4$
   H_1: $\mu_1 \neq \mu_2 \neq \mu_3 \neq \mu_4$
2. $MS_b = 149.1$
3. MSw = 4.8
4. F = 149.1/4.8 = 31.1
5. critical F = 2.8
6. Result: Since 30.8 is greater than 2.8, we reject the null hypothesis and accept the research hypothesis
7. There was a significant difference between the four departments in TURNOVER RATE.

   MANUFACTURING vs. SALES

8. H_0: $\mu_2 = \mu_4$
   H_1: $\mu_2 \neq \mu_4$
9. 15.7
10. 8.6
11. df = 55 – 4 = 51
12. critical t = 1.96
13. 1/13 + 1/16 = 0.077 + 0.063 = 0.14

$$\text{s.e.} = \text{SQRT}\ (4.8{*}0.14) = \text{SQRT}(\ 0.672) = 0.82$$

14. ANOVA t = (15.7 – 8.6)/0.82 = 8.66
15. Result: Since the absolute value of 8.66 is greater than 1.96, we reject the null hypothesis and accept the research hypothesis
16. Conclusion: MANUFACTURING had a significantly higher TURNOVER RATE than SALES (15.7 % vs. 8.6 %).

Chapter 8: Practice Problem #2 Answer (see Fig. A.23)

RETENTION RATE (last year in percent)

PRODUCTION	SALES	ENGINEERING
58	79	80
66	92	89
65	84	87
59	86	88
58	88	86
61	89	84
63	90	80
62	92	82
65	89	86
66	91	83
	82	89
	79	

Anova: Single Factor

SUMMARY

Groups	*Count*	*Sum*	*Average*	*Variance*
PRODUCTION	10	623	62.30	10.23
SALES	12	1041	86.75	22.39
ENGINEERING	11	934	84.91	11.09

ANOVA

Source of Variation	*SS*	*df*	*MS*	*F*	*P-value*	*F crit*
Between Groups	3891.29	2	1945.64	129.92	1.68E-15	3.32
Within Groups	449.26	30	14.98			
Total	4340.55	32				

PRODUCTION vs. ENGINEERING	
1/n PRODUCTION + 1/n ENGINEERING	0.19
s.e. PRODUCTION vs. ENGINEERING	1.69
ANOVA t-test	-13.37

Fig. A.23 Answer to Chap. 8: Practice Problem #2

Chapter 8: Practice Problem #2 (continued)

Let PRODUCTION = Group A, SALES = Group B, and ENGINEERING = Group C

1. Null hypothesis: $\mu_A = \mu_B = \mu_C$
   Research hypothesis: $\mu_A \neq \mu_B \neq \mu_C$
2. $MS_b = 1945.64$
3. $MS_w = 14.98$
4. F = 1945.64/14.98 = 129.88
5. critical F = 3.32
6. Since the F-value of 129.88 is greater than the critical F value of 3.32, we reject the null hypothesis and accept the research hypothesis.
7. There was a significant difference between the three departments in their RETENTION RATE.
8. Null hypothesis: $\mu_A = \mu_C$
   Research hypothesis: $\mu_A \neq \mu_C$
9. 62.30
10. 84.91
11. df = 33 − 3 = 30
12. critical t = 2.042
13. 1/10 + 1/11 = 0.10 + 0.09 = 0.19
    s.e. = SQRT(14.98 * 0.19) = SQRT(2.85) = 1.69
14. t = (62.30 − 84.91)/1.69 = −22.61/1.69 = −13.38
15. Since the absolute value of −13.38 is greater than the critical t of 2.042, we reject the hull hypothesis and accept the research hypothesis.
16. ENGINEERING had a significantly higher RETENTION RATE than PRODUCTION (85 % vs. 62 %).

Chapter 8: Practice Problem #3 Answer (see Fig. A.24)

SOURCE OF HR TEACHING APPLICATIONS			
	NUMBER OF APPLICATIONS		
HR POSITION	CHRONICLE	SHRM	ASTD
1	85	68	86
2	64	64	89
3	92	65	102
4	54	62	116
5	68	63	101
6	67	61	98
7	55	60	95
8	82	59	94

Anova: Single Factor

SUMMARY

Groups	Count	Sum	Average	Variance
HR POSITION	8	36	4.50	6.00
CHRONICLE	8	567	70.88	196.70
SHRM	8	502	62.75	8.50
ASTD	8	781	97.63	85.41

ANOVA

Source of Variation	SS	df	MS	F	P-value	F crit
Between Groups	36937.63	3.00	12312.54	166.05	6.18E-18	2.95
Within Groups	2076.25	28.00	74.15			
Total	39013.88	31.00				

SHRM vs. ASTD	
1/n SHRM + 1/n ASTD	0.25
s.e. SHRM vs. ASTD	4.31
ANOVA t-test	-8.10

Fig. A.24 Answer to Chap. 8: Practice Problem #3

Chapter 8: Practice Problem #3 (continued)

Let CHRONICLE = Group 1, SHRM = Group 2, and ASTD = Group 3

1. Null hypothesis: $\mu_1 = \mu_2 = \mu_3$
   Research hypothesis: $\mu_1 \neq \mu_2 \neq \mu_3$
2. $MS_b = 12{,}312.54$
3. $MS_w = 74.15$
4. $F = 12{,}312.54/74.15 = 166.05$
5. critical $F = 2.95$
6. Result: Since the F-value of 166.05 is greater than the critical F value of 2.95, we reject the null hypothesis and accept the research hypothesis.
7. Conclusion: There was a significant difference between the three Web sites in the number of applications received.
8. Null hypothesis: $\mu_2 = \mu_3$
   Research hypothesis: $\mu_2 \neq \mu_3$
9. 62.75
10. 97.63
11. degrees of freedom = 32 − 3 = 29
12. critical t = 2.045
13. $s.e._{ANOVA} = SQRT(MS_w \times \{1/8 + 1/8\}) = SQRT(74.15 \times 0.25) = SQRT(18.54) = 4.31$
14. ANOVA $t = (62.75 - 97.63)/4.31 = -34.88/4.31 = -8.09$
15. Since the absolute value of −8.09 is greater than the critical t of 2.045, we reject the null hypothesis and accept the research hypothesis.
16. ASTD had significantly more applications for an HRM tenured faculty position than SHRM (98 vs. 63)

Appendix B: Practice Test

Chapter 1: Practice Test

Suppose that the HR manager at Macy's Department Store in New York City is concerned about the number of complaints the store manager has been receiving about the quality of service provided by clerks who work in the store's Cosmetics Department. Since this Department is one of the most profitable departments in the store, the HR manager wants to design an in-service training program for the clerks in this department in an attempt to reduce these complaints. In order to measure the effectiveness of that training program, the HR manager has asked you to create an Excel spreadsheet summarizing the number of complaints for the past 12 months so that the average number of complaints can be used to set a baserate for measuring the effectiveness of the training program. You want to try out your Excel skills on the hypothetical data in Fig. B.1.

Fig. B.1 Worksheet Data for Chap. 1 Practice Test (Practical Example)

MACY'S DEPARTMENT STORE (New York City)

COSMETICS DEPT. (No. of complaints this past year)

MONTH	NO. OF COMPLAINTS
JAN	24
FEB	32
MAR	26
APR	24
MAY	20
JUN	27
JUL	28
AUG	30
SEP	32
OCT	24
NOV	26
DEC	29

(a) Create an Excel table for these data, and then use Excel to the right of the table to find the sample size, mean, standard deviation, and standard error of the mean for these data. Label your answers, and round off the mean, standard deviation, and standard error of the mean to two decimal places.
(b) Save the file as: COMPLAINTS6

Chapter 2: Practice Test

Suppose that an HR manager who works at a large automobile manufacturer with plants in several states wants to take a random sample of 12 of the 54 mid-level managers in the company to create two focus groups to discuss the attractiveness of a possible new benefit that could be offered to these managers in the future. You have been asked to create a random sample of 12 of these managers, and you have assigned an ID number to each manager.

(a) Set up a spreadsheet of frame numbers for these managers with the heading: FRAME NUMBERS
(b) Then, create a separate column to the right of these frame numbers which duplicates these frame numbers with the title: Duplicate frame numbers.
(c) Then, create a separate column to the right of these duplicate frame numbers called RAND NO. and use the = *RAND()* function to assign random numbers to all of the frame numbers in the duplicate frame numbers column, and change this column format so that three decimal places appear for each random number.
(d) Sort the *duplicate frame numbers and random numbers* into a random order.
(e) Print the result so that the spreadsheet fits onto one page.
(f) Circle on your printout the I.D. number of the first 12 managers that you would use in your focus groups.
(g) Save the file as: RAND54

Important note: Note that everyone who does this problem will generate a different random order of managers' ID numbers since Excel assigns a different random number each time the RAND() command is used. For this reason, the answer to this problem given in this Excel Guide will have a completely different sequence of random numbers from the random sequence that you generate. This is normal and what is to be expected.

Chapter 3: Practice Test

Suppose that you have been asked to determine if the hourly rate of a certain type of technician at a specific clinic with offices in the city and county of St. Louis is comparable to the wages paid to technicians in other clinics in surrounding cities and counties. The average hourly wage currently paid to this type of technician in the city and county of St. Louis is $25.00. You have decided to test your Excel skills on a random sample of hypothetical data of other clinics outside of the city and county of St. Louis which is in Fig. B.2

Fig. B.2 Worksheet Data for Chap. 3 Practice Test (Practical Example)

CITY AND COUNTY OF ST. LOUIS
HOURLY WAGES PAID TO TECHNICIANS ($)
23.75
32.25
24.50
26.75
28.25
30.50
31.75
24.50
23.45
28.00
31.25
24.80
26.70
31.60
28.75
29.25

(a) Create an Excel table for these data, and use Excel to the right of the table to find the sample size, mean, standard deviation, and standard error of the mean for these data. Label your answers, and round off the mean, standard deviation, and standard error of the mean to two decimal places in currency format.
(b) By hand, write the null hypothesis and the research hypothesis on your printout.
(c) Use Excel's *TINV function* to find the 95 % confidence interval about the mean for these data. Label your answers. Use two decimal places for the confidence interval figures in currency format.
(d) On your printout, draw a diagram of this 95 % confidence interval by hand, including the reference value.
(e) On your spreadsheet, enter the *result.*
(f) On your spreadsheet, enter the *conclusion in plain English.*
(g) Print the data and the results so that your spreadsheet fits onto one page.
(h) Save the file as: HOURLY3

Chapter 4: Practice Test

Suppose that you work for a large health care facility with laboratory facilities at several locations in the state of Missouri. The HR manager has asked you to determine the average time it takes workers at these facilities to perform a certain laboratory procedure. You decide to use a time-and-motion study to determine if the average time to complete this procedure has changed from the last time this type of study was done for this procedure. The last time this procedure was studied, it took an average of 32 minutes to complete the procedure. You want to test your Excel skills on a small sample of data using the hypothetical data given in Fig. B.3.

TIME REQUIRED TO COMPLETE A SPECIFIC LABORATORY TEST

TIME AND MOTION DATA

Time (in minutes)
33
31
30
28
29
27
30
31
32
33
34
29
28
30
31
34
29
28
30
31
34

Fig. B.3 Worksheet Data for Chap. 4 Practice Test (Practical Example)

(a) Write the null hypothesis and the research hypothesis on your spreadsheet.
(b) Create a spreadsheet for these data, and then use Excel to find the sample size, mean, standard deviation, and standard error of the mean to the right of the data set. Use number format (two decimal places) for the mean, standard deviation, and standard error of the mean.
(c) Type the *critical t* from the t-table in Appendix E onto your spreadsheet, and label it.
(d) Use Excel to compute the t-test value for these data (use two decimal places) and label it on your spreadsheet.
(e) Type the *result* on your spreadsheet, and then type the *conclusion in plain English* on your spreadsheet.
(f) Save the file as: TIME3

Chapter 5: Practice Test

The manager of an HR department in a large multi-state manufacturing company wants to see if supervisors and non-supervisors at the company's plants have different attitudes toward the effectiveness of the supervision of plant workers at this company. You have decided to create a survey using Likert items in the form of 5-point rating scales such that 1 = Strongly Disagree, 2 = Disagree, 3 = Undecided, 4 = Agree, and 5 = Strongly Agree. You have developed a 20-item survey that deals with job satisfaction. The survey for supervisors contains items such as: "As a supervisor, I am available when needed"; "As a supervisor, I am knowledgeable about the ways in which the work of this department should be done"; "As a supervisor, I am helpful with solving problems that my subordinates have". The non-supervisors have a similar survey containing the same types of items (e.g. "My supervisor gives clear instructions to me"; "My supervisor is aware of problems that occur in our department"; "My supervisor is considerate of the feelings of the workers in this department"). The ratings of the 20 items were summed to create a total score on the survey that ranged from 20 to 100 for each group. Suppose that you want to test your Excel skills on the hypothetical data given in Fig. B.4.

RATING SCALE	5	4	3	2	1
	Strongly Agree	Agree	Undecided	Disagree	Strongly Disagree

SUPERVISORS	NON-SUPERVISORS
85	78
92	84
84	79
79	71
86	82
89	87
95	91
85	80
	79
	81
	80

Fig. B.4 Worksheet Data for Chap. 5 Practice Test (Practical Example)

(a) Write the null hypothesis and the research hypothesis.
(b) Create an Excel table that summarizes these data.
(c) Use Excel to find the standard error of the difference of the means.
(d) Use Excel to perform a *two-group t-test*. What is the value of *t* that you obtain (use two decimal places)?
(e) On your spreadsheet, type the *critical value of t* using the t-table in Appendix E.
(f) Type the *result* of the test on your spreadsheet.
(g) Type your *conclusion in plain English* on your spreadsheet.
(h) Save the file as: SUPER6
(i) Print the final spreadsheet so that it fits onto one page.

Chapter 6: Practice Test

In a large engineering company, what is the relationship between the salary of engineers as a percent of the engineers' midpoint salary (position in range) and the raise given to the engineers at the last contract? The midpoint of the range of engineers' salaries is scored as 100, and each engineer's salary is than compared to that midpoint to determine what percent of that midpoint an engineer's salary represents. The resulting number is called "position in range." Engineers whose salaries are below the midpoint have a score less than 100, and engineers whose salaries are above the midpoint have a score greater than 100. Suppose that you wanted to study this question. Analyze the hypothetical data that are given in Fig. B.5.

COMPANY XYZ

Question: **Is there a relationship between the salary of engineers as a percent of the engineers' midpoint salary (position in range) and the raise given to the engineers at the last contract?**

POSITION IN RANGE	PERCENT RAISE
83	5.5
90	5.0
100	3.0
110	1.5
86	4.0
97	3.5
102	4.0
107	1.5
112	2.0
114	2.5
116	1.5

Fig. B.5 Worksheet Data for Chap. 6 Practice Test (Practical Example)

Create an Excel spreadsheet, and enter the data.

(a) create an *XY scatterplot* of these two sets of data such that:

- top title: RELATIONSHIP BETWEEN POSITION IN RANGE AND PERCENT RAISE FOR ENGINEERS
- x-axis title: POSITION IN RANGE
- y-axis title: % RAISE
- move the chart below the table
- re-size the chart so that it is 7 columns wide and 25 rows long
- delete the legend
- delete the gridlines

(b) Create the *least-squares regression line* for these data on the scatterplot.

(c) Use Excel to run the regression statistics to find the *equation for the least-squares regression line* for these data and display the results below the chart on your spreadsheet. Add the regression equation to the chart. Use number format (two decimal places) for the correlation and number format (three decimal places) for the coefficients.

Print *just the input data and the chart* so that this information fits onto one page in portrait format.

Then, print *just the regression output table* on a separate page so that it fits onto that separate page in portrait format.

By hand:

(d) Circle and label the value of the *y-intercept* and the *slope* of the regression line on your printout.

(e) Write the regression equation *by hand* on your printout for these data (use three decimal places for the y-intercept and the slope).

(f) Circle and label the *correlation* between the two sets of scores in the regression analysis summary output table on your printout.

(g) Underneath the regression equation you wrote by hand on your printout, use the regression equation to predict the PERCENT RAISE you would expect for an engineer with a POSITION IN RANGE score of 90.

(h) *Read from the graph*, the PERCENT RAISE you would expect for an engineer with a POSITION IN RANGE score of 110, and write your answer in the space immediately below:

____

(i) save the file as: ENGINE3

Chapter 7: Practice Test

The Graduate Record Examinations (GRE) are frequently used to predict the first-year GPA of students in an M.A. program in Human Resources Management. The GRE has three subtest scores in Verbal, Quantitative, and Writing which can be used to create a multiple correlation to predict first-year GPA.

But, suppose, that you want to find out what would happen if you added undergraduate GPA as a fourth predictor. What would be the multiple correlation?

Let's find out what happens when you use the hypothetical data that is presented in Fig. B.6 that includes undergraduate GPA as a fourth predictor of first-year GPA for students in an M.A. program in HRM.

GRADUATE RECORD EXAMINATIONS (GRE)

How well does the GRE predict first-year GPA in an M.A. program in Human Resources Management?

FIRST-YEAR GPA	GRE VERBAL	GRE QUANTITATIVE	GRE WRITING	UNDERGRAD GPA
3.25	160	161	5	3.40
3.42	156	158	4	3.15
2.85	156	157	2	3.05
2.65	154	153	1	2.55
3.65	166	166	6	3.25
3.16	159	160	3	3.20
3.56	166	163	4	3.66
2.35	155	154	2	2.55
2.86	153	154	3	2.85
2.95	158	157	4	2.80
3.15	158	159	4	3.05
3.45	160	160	5	3.44

Fig. B.6 Worksheet Data for Chap. 7 Practice Test (Practical Example)

(a) Create an Excel spreadsheet using FIRST-YEAR GPA as the criterion (Y), and the other variables as the four predictors of this criterion.
(b) Use Excel's *multiple regression* function to find the relationship between these variables and place it below the table.
(c) Use number format (two decimal places) for the multiple correlation on the Summary Output, use number format (three decimal places) for the coefficients, and four decimal places for all other decimal figures in the SUMMARY OUTPUT.
(d) Print the table and regression results below the table so that they fit onto one page.
(e) By hand on this printout, *circle and label:*

    (1a) multiple correlation R_{xy}
    (2b) coefficients for the y-intercept, GRE VERBAL, GRE QUANTITATIVE, GRE WRITING, AND UNDERGRAD GPA

(f) Save this file as: GRE21
(g) Now, go back to your Excel file and create a correlation matrix for these five variables, and place it underneath the SUMMARY OUTPUT. *Change each correlation to just two decimals.* Save this file again as: GRE21
(h) Now, print out *just this correlation matrix in portrait mode* on a separate sheet of paper.

Answer the following questions using your Excel printout:

1. What is the multiple correlation R_{xy}?
2. What is the y-intercept a?
3. What is the coefficient for GRE VERBAL b_1?
4. What is the coefficient for GRE QUANTITATIVE b_2?
5. What is the coefficient for GRE WRITING b_3?
6. What is the coefficient for UNDERGRAD GPA b_4?
7. What is the multiple regression equation?
8. Underneath this regression equation by hand, predict the FIRST-YEAR GPA you would expect for a GRE VERBAL score of 159, a GRE QUANTITATIVE score of 154, A GRE WRITING score of 4, and an UNDERGRAD GPA of 3.05.

Answer the following questions using your Excel printout. Be sure to include the plus or minus sign for each correlation:

9. What is the correlation between UNDERGRAD GPA and FIRST-YEAR GPA?
10. What is the correlation between UNDERGRAD GPA and GRE VERBAL?
11. What is the correlation between UNDERGRAD GPA and GRE QUANTITATIVE?
12. What is the correlation between UNDERGRAD GPA and GRE WRITING?
13. Discuss which of the four predictors is the best predictor of FIRST-YEAR GPA.
14. Explain in words how much better the four predictor variables combined predict FIRST-YEAR GPA than the best single predictor by itself.

Chapter 8: Practice Test

Suppose that you wanted to compare the absentee rate of employees in four departments of a large manufacturing and engineering company during the past quarter: (1) ENGINEERING, (2) MANUFACTURING, (3) SALES, and (4) ADMINISTRATION. You decide to test your Excel skills on a small random sample of employees in each department, and you have created the hypothetical data given in Fig. B.7.

(a) Enter these data on an Excel spreadsheet.

PERCENT OF ABSENTEEISM IN DEPARTMENTS THIS PAST QUARTER

ENGINEERING	MANUFACTURING	SALES	ADMINISTRATION
3	6	2	4
5	8	5	8
6	10	4	6
8	7	1	7
7	9	3	2
4	10	5	3
2	12	4	1
1	5	2	6
3	12	5	8
5	8	4	5
4	7	1	4
3	6	3	
2		4	
		2	

Fig. B.7 Worksheet Data for Chap. 8 Practice Test (Practical Example)

Let ENGINEERING = Group 1, MANUFACTURING = Group 2, SALES = Group 3, and ADMINISTRATION = Group 4.

(b) On your spreadsheet, write the null hypothesis and the research hypothesis for these data

(c) Perform a *one-way ANOVA test* on these data, and show the resulting ANOVA table underneath the input data for the four departments.

(d) If the F-value in the ANOVA table is significant, create an Excel formula to compute the ANOVA t-test comparing absenteeism in MANUFACTURING versus ENGINEERING and show the results below the ANOVA table on the spreadsheet (put the standard error and the ANOVA t-test value on separate lines of your spreadsheet, and use two decimal places for each value)

(e) Print out the resulting spreadsheet so that all of the information fits onto one page

(f) On your printout, label by hand the MS (between groups) and the MS (within groups)

(g) Circle and label the value for F on your printout for the ANOVA of the input data

(h) Label by hand on the printout the mean for MANUFACTURING and the mean for ENGINEERING that were produced by your ANOVA formulas

(i) Save the spreadsheet as: ABSENT3

On a separate sheet of paper, now do the following by hand:

(j) find the critical value of F in the ANOVA Single Factor results table
(k) write a summary of the *result* of the ANOVA test for the input data
(l) write a summary of the *conclusion* of the ANOVA test in plain English for the input data
(m) write the null hypothesis and the research hypothesis comparing MANUFACTURING versus ENGINEERING.
(n) compute the degrees of freedom for the *ANOVA t-test* by hand for the four types of departments.
(o) use your calculator and Excel to compute the standard error (s.e.) of the ANOVA t-test
(p) Use your calculator and Excel to compute the ANOVA t-test value
(q) write the *critical value of t* for the ANOVA t-test using the table in Appendix E.
(r) write a summary of the *result* of the ANOVA t-test
(s) write a summary of the *conclusion* of the ANOVA t-test in plain English

Appendix C: Answers to Practice Test

Practice Test Answer: Chapter 1 (see Fig. C.1)

MACY'S DEPARTMENT STORE (New York City)

COSMETICS DEPT. (No. of complaints this past year

MONTH	NO. OF COMPLAINTS
JAN	24
FEB	32
MAR	26
APR	24
MAY	20
JUN	27
JUL	28
AUG	30
SEP	32
OCT	24
NOV	26
DEC	29

n	12
Mean	26.83
STDEV	3.59
s.e.	1.04

Fig. C.1 Practice Test Answer to Chap. 1 Problem

Practice Test Answer: Chapter 2 (see Fig. C.2)

FRAME NUMBERS	Duplicate frame numbers	RAND NO.
1	18	0.829
2	33	0.897
3	10	0.446
4	8	0.068
5	39	0.324
6	51	0.180
7	23	0.031
8	11	0.640
9	9	0.522
10	21	0.891
11	7	0.225
12	2	0.942
13	40	0.453
14	35	0.844
15	3	0.830
16	24	0.204
17	20	0.168
18	16	0.294
19	5	0.350
20	41	0.688
21		.506
	29	
40	49	0.45[illegible]
41	19	0.226
42	54	0.091
43	43	0.118
44	30	0.258
45	31	0.749
46	37	0.485
47	48	0.637
48	32	0.137
49	53	0.686
50	13	0.996
51	1	0.739
52	25	0.945
53	46	0.128
54	45	0.710

Fig. C.2 Practice Test Answer to Chap. 2 Problem

Practice Test Answer: Chapter 3 (see Fig. C.3)

CITY AND COUNTY OF ST. LOUIS

HOURLY WAGES PAID TO TECHNICIANS ($)
23.75
32.25
24.50
26.75
28.25
30.50
31.75
24.50
23.45
28.00
31.25
24.80
26.70
31.60
28.75
29.25

Null hypothesis:	μ	=	$25.00
Research hypothesis:	μ	≠	$25.00

n	16
Mean	$27.88
STDEV	$3.06
s.e.	$0.77

95% confidence interval

lower limit:	$26.25
upper limit:	$29.51

------- $25 ----------- $26.25 --------- --------- $27.88 ------------ -------$29.51---------

ref. value	lower limit	Mean	upper limit

Result: Since the reference value is outside of the confidence interval, we reject the null hypothesis and accept the research hypothesis:

Conclusion: The average hourly wage for this type of technician in the St. Louis area is significantly higher than the average wage of this clinic, and is probably closer to $27.90.

Fig. C.3 Practice Test Answer to Chap. 3 Problem

Practice Test Answer: Chapter 4 (see Fig. C.4)

TIME REQUIRED TO COMPLETE A SPECIFIC LABORATORY TEST					
TIME AND MOTION DATA					
	Time (in minutes)				
	33				
	31	**Null hypothesis:**	**μ**	**=**	**32 minutes**
	30				
	28	**Research hypothesis:**	**μ**	**≠**	**32 minutes**
	29				
	27				
	30	**n**	**21**		
	31				
	32				
	33	**Mean**	**30.57**		
	34				
	29				
	28	**STDEV**	**2.13**		
	30				
	31				
	34	**s.e.**	**0.47**		
	29				
	28				
	30	**critical t**	**2.086**		
	31				
	34				
		t-test	**-3.07**		
	Result:	**Since the absolute value of – 3.07 is greater than the critical t of 2.086, we reject the null hypothesis and accept the research hypothesis.**			
	Conclusion:	**The time required to conduct this laboratory test was significantly less than 32 minutes, and was probably closer to 31 minutes.**			

Fig. C.4 Practice Test Answer to Chap. 4 Problem

Practice Test Answer: Chapter 5 (see Fig. C.5)

SUPERVISORS	NON-SUPERVISORS
85	78
92	84
84	79
79	71
86	82
89	87
95	91
85	80
	79
	81
	80

Group	n	Mean	STDEV
1 Supervisors	8	86.88	5.00
2 Non-supervisors	11	81.09	5.15

Null hypothesis: $\mu_1 = \mu_2$

Research hypothesis: $\mu_1 \neq \mu_2$

(n1 - 1) x STDEV1 squared	174.88
(n2 - 1) x STDEV2 squared	264.91
n1 + n2 - 2	17
1/n1 + 1/n2	0.22
s.e.	2.36
critical t	2.11
t-test	2.45

Result: Since the absolute value of 2.45 is greater than the critical t of 2.11, we reject the null hypothesis and accept the research hypothesis.

Conclusion: The Job Satisfaction scores of Supervisors were significantly higher than the Job Satisfaction scores of Non-supervisors (86.88 vs. 81.09).

Fig. C.5 Practice Test Answer to Chap. 5 Problem

Practice Test Answer: Chapter 6 (see Fig. C.6)

COMPANY XYZ

Question: Is there a relationship between the salary of engineers as a percent of the engineers' midpoint salary (position in range) and the raise given to the engineers at the last contract?

POSITION IN RANGE	PERCENT RAISE
83	5.5
90	5.0
100	3.0
110	1.5
86	4.0
97	3.5
102	4.0
107	1.5
112	2.0
114	2.5
116	1.5

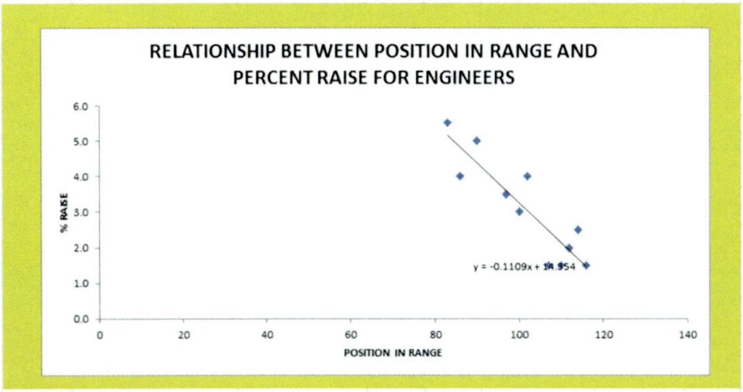

SUMMARY OUTPUT

Regression Statistics	
Multiple R	0.89
R Square	0.7937
Adjusted R	0.7708
Standard Er	0.6840
Observatio	11

ANOVA

	df	*SS*	*MS*	*F*	*Significance F*
Regression	1	16.1987	16.1987	34.6259	0.0002
Residual	9	4.2104	0.4678		
Total	10	20.4091			

	Coefficients	*Standard Error*	*t Stat*	*P-value*	*Lower 95%*	*Upper 95%*
Intercept	14.354	1.9251	7.4561	0.0000	9.9989	18.7088
X Variable	-0.111	0.0188	-5.8844	0.0002	-0.1536	-0.0683

Fig. C.6 Practice Test Answer to Chap. 6 Problem

Practice Test Answer: Chapter 6: (continued)

(d) a = y – intercept = 14.354
    b = slope = –0.111 (note the negative sign!)

(e) Y = a + b X
    Y = 14.354 – 0.111 X

(f) r = correlation = –.89 (note the negative sign!)

(g) Y = 14.354 – 0.111 (90)
    Y = 14.354 – 9.99
    Y = 4.4

(h) About 2.1

Practice Test Answer: Chapter 7 (see Fig. C.7)

GRADUATE RECORD EXAMINATIONS (GRE)

How well does the GRE predict first-year GPA in an M.A. program in Human Resources Management?

FIRST-YEAR GPA	GRE VERBAL	GRE QUANTITATIVE	GRE WRITING	UNDERGRAD GPA
3.25	160	161	5	3.40
3.42	156	158	4	3.15
2.85	156	157	2	3.05
2.65	154	153	1	2.55
3.65	166	166	6	3.25
3.16	159	160	3	3.20
3.56	166	163	4	3.66
2.35	155	154	2	2.55
2.86	153	154	3	2.85
2.95	158	157	4	2.80
3.15	158	159	4	3.05
3.45	160	160	5	3.44

GRE21

SUMMARY OUTPUT

Regression Statistics	
Multiple R	0.94
R Square	0.8825
Adjusted R Square	0.8154
Standard Error	0.1676
Observations	12

ANOVA

	df	*SS*	*MS*	*F*	*Significance F*
Regression	4	1.4777	0.3694	13.1467	0.0023
Residual	7	0.1967	0.0281		
Total	11	1.6744			

	Coefficients	*Standard Error*	*t Stat*	*P-value*	*Lower 95%*
Intercept	-3.241	4.3231	-0.7496	0.4779	-13.4632
GRE VERBAL	-0.018	0.0388	-0.4590	0.6601	-0.1094
GRE QUANTITATIVE	0.046	0.0561	0.8237	0.4373	-0.0865
GRE WRITING	0.076	0.0654	1.1589	0.2845	-0.0789
UNDERGRAD GPA	0.510	0.2642	1.9303	0.0949	-0.1147

	FIRST-YEAR GPA	GRE VERBAL	GRE QUANTITATIVE	GRE WRITING	UNDERGRAD GPA
FIRST-YEAR GPA	1				
GRE VERBAL	0.79	1			
GRE QUANTITATIVE	0.88	0.94	1		
GRE WRITING	0.83	0.72	0.83	1	
UNDERGRAD GPA	0.88	0.77	0.83	0.70	1

Fig. C.7 Practice Test Answer to Chap. 7 Problem

Practice Test Answer: Chapter 7 (continued)

1. $R_{xy} = .94$
2. $a = \text{y-intercept} = -3.241$
3. $b_1 = -0.018$
4. $b_2 = 0.046$
5. $b_3 = 0.076$
6. $b_4 = 0.510$
7. $Y = a + b_1X_1 + b_2X_2 + b_3X_3 + b_4X_4$
   $Y = -3.241 - 0.018\ X_1 + 0.046\ X_2 + 0.076\ X_3 + 0.510\ X_4$
8. $Y = -3.241 - 0.018(159) + 0.046(154) + 0.076(4) + 0.510(3.05)$
   $Y = -3.241 - 2.862 + 7.084 + 0.304 + 1.556$
   $Y = 8.944 - 6.103 = 2.84$
9. +.88
10. +.77
11. +.83
12. +.70
13. The best predictor of FIRST-YEAR GPA was GRE QUANTITATIVE and also UNDERGRADUAE GPA since both had a correlation of +.88.
14. The four predictors combined predict FIRST-YEAR GPA much better ($R_{xy} = .94$) than the best single predictor by itself

Practice Test Answer: Chapter 8 (see Fig. C.8)

PERCENT OF ABSENTEEISM IN DEPARTMENTS THIS PAST QUARTER

ENGINEERING	MANUFACTURING	SALES	ADMINISTRATION
3	6	2	4
5	8	5	8
6	10	4	6
8	7	1	7
7	9	3	2
4	10	5	3
2	12	4	1
1	5	2	6
3	12	5	8
5	8	4	5
4	7	1	4
3	6	3	
2		4	
		2	

$H_0: \mu_1 = \mu_2 = \mu_3 = \mu_4$

$H_1: \mu_1 \neq \mu_2 \neq \mu_3 \neq \mu_4$

ABSENT3

Anova: Single Factor

SUMMARY

Groups	*Count*	*Sum*	*Average*	*Variance*
ENGINEERING	13	53	4.08	4.244
MANUFACTURING	12	100	8.33	5.333
SALES	14	45	3.21	2.027
ADMINISTRATION	11	54	4.91	5.491

ANOVA

Source of Variation	*SS*	*df*	*MS*	*F*	*P-value*	*F crit*
Between Groups	189.064	3	63.021	15.189	5.3E-07	2.807
Within Groups	190.856	46	4.149			
Total	379.920	49				

MANUFACTURING vs. ENGINEERING

1/n MANUFACTURING + 1/n ENGINEERING	0.16
s.e. MANUFACTURING vs. ENGINEERING	0.82
ANOVA t-test	-5.22

Fig. C.8 Practice Test Answer to Chap. 8 Problem

Let ENGINEERING = Group 1, MANUFACTURING = Group 2, SALES = Group 3, and ADMINISTRATION = Group 4

(b) H_0: $\mu_1 = \mu_2 = \mu_3 = \mu_4$
H_1: $\mu_1 \neq \mu_2 \neq \mu_3 \neq \mu_4$

(f) $MS_b = 63.021$ and $MS_w = 4.149$

(g) $F = 15.189$

Practice Test Answer: Chapter 8 (continued)

(h) Mean of MANUFACTURING = 8.33 and Mean of ENGINEERING = 4.08

(j) critical F = 2.807

(k) Result: Since 15.189 is greater than 2.807, we reject the null hypothesis and accept the research hypothesis

(l) Conclusion: There was a significant difference in absenteeism between the four departments.

(m) H_0: $\mu_1 = \mu_2$

H_1: $\mu_1 \neq \mu_2$

(n) df = $n_{TOTAL} - k = 50 - 4 = 46$

(o) $1/12 + 1/13 = 0.08 + 0.08 = 0.16$

s.e = SQRT (4.149 * 0.16)

s.e. = SQRT (0.66)

s.e. = 0.81

(p) ANOVA t = (4.08 – 8.33)/0.81 = –5.25

(q) critical t = 1.96

(r) Result: Since the absolute value of –5.25 is greater than the critical t of 1.96, we reject the null hypothesis and accept the research hypothesis

(s) Conclusion: MANUFACTURING had a significantly higher absentee rate than ENGINEERING (8.3 % vs. 4.1 %)

Appendix D: Statistical Formulas

Mean $\overline{X} = \frac{\Sigma X}{n}$

Standard Deviation $\text{STDEV} = S = \sqrt{\frac{\Sigma(X - \overline{X})^2}{n-1}}$

Standard error of the mean $\text{s.e.} = S_{\overline{X}} = \frac{S}{\sqrt{n}}$

Confidence interval about the mean $\overline{X} \pm t\, S_{\overline{X}}$

where $S_{\overline{X}} = \frac{S}{\sqrt{n}}$

One-group t-test $t = \frac{\overline{X} - \mu}{S_{\overline{X}}}$

where $S_{\overline{X}} = \frac{S}{\sqrt{n}}$

Two-group t-test

(a) when both groups have a sample size greater than 30

$$t = \frac{\overline{X}_1 - \overline{X}_2}{S_{\overline{X}_1 - \overline{X}_2}}$$

$$\text{where } S_{\overline{X}_1 - \overline{X}_2} = \sqrt{\frac{S_1{}^2}{n_1} + \frac{S_2{}^2}{n_2}}$$

and where $df = n_1 + n_2 - 2$

(b) when one or both groups have a sample size less than 30

$$t = \frac{\overline{X}_1 - \overline{X}_2}{S_{\overline{X}_1 - \overline{X}_2}}$$

$$\text{where } S_{\overline{X}_1 - \overline{X}_2} = \sqrt{\frac{(n_1 - 1)S_1{}^2 + (n_2 - 1)S_2{}^2}{n_1 + n_2 - 2}\left(\frac{1}{n_1} + \frac{1}{n_2}\right)}$$

and where $df = n_1 + n_2 - 2$

Correlation

$$r = \frac{\frac{1}{n-1}\Sigma(X - \overline{X})(Y - \overline{Y})}{S_x\, S_y}$$

where S_x = standard deviation of X
and where S_y = standard deviation of Y

Simple linear regression

$Y = a + b\,X$
where a = y-intercept and b = slope of the line

Multiple regression equation

$Y = a + b_1X_1 + b_2X_2 + b_3X_3 +$ etc.
where a = y-intercept

One-way ANOVA F-test

$F = MS_b/MS_w$

ANOVA t-test

$$ANOVA\ t = \frac{\overline{X}_1 - \overline{X}_2}{s.e._{ANOVA}}$$

where $s.e._{ANOVA} = \sqrt{MS_w\left(\frac{1}{n_1} + \frac{1}{n_2}\right)}$
and where $df = n_{TOTAL} - k$
where $n_{TOTAL} = n_1 + n_2 + n_3 +$ etc.
and where k = the number of groups

Appendix E: t-Table

Critical t-values needed for rejection of the null hypothesis (see Fig. E.1)

Fig. E.1 Critical t-values Needed for Rejection of the Null Hypothesis

sample size n	degrees of freedom df	critical t
10	9	2.262
11	10	2.228
12	11	2.201
13	12	2.179
14	13	2.160
15	14	2.145
16	15	2.131
17	16	2.120
18	17	2.110
19	18	2.101
20	19	2.093
21	20	2.086
22	21	2.080
23	22	2.074
24	23	2.069
25	24	2.064
26	25	2.060
27	26	2.056
28	27	2.052
29	28	2.048
30	29	2.045
31	30	2.042
32	31	2.040
33	32	2.037
34	33	2.035
35	34	2.032
36	35	2.030
37	36	2.028
38	37	2.026
39	38	2.024
40	39	2.023
infinity	infinity	1.960

Index

A
Absolute value of a number, 73
Analysis of Variance
  ANOVA t-test formula, 191
  degrees of freedom, 191–192
  Excel commands, 192–195
  formula, 188
  interpreting the Summary Table, 188–189
  s.e. formula for ANOVA t-test, 191
ANOVA. *See* Analysis of Variance
ANOVA t-test. *See* Analysis of Variance
Average function. *See* Mean

C
Centering information within cells, 6–8
Chart
  adding the regression equation, 151–154
  changing the width and height, 6
  creating a chart, 129–130
  drawing the regression line onto the chart, 129–130
  moving the chart, 138
  printing the spreadsheet, 140–142
  reducing the scale, 140
  scatter chart, 131
  titles, 132
Column width (changing), 6
Confidence interval about the mean
  95% confident, 38–39, 41, 42, 82, 233
  drawing a picture, 46
  formula, 41
  lower limit, 38–39
  upper limit, 38–39
Correlation
  formula, 122
  negative correlation, 117, 119, 120, 149, 154
  positive correlation, 117–119, 154, 161
  9 steps for computing, 122–124
CORREL function. *See* Correlation
COUNT function, 9, 56
Critical t-value, 63, 192, 254

D
Data Analysis ToolPak, 142–145, 166, 183
Data/Sort commands, 28
Degrees of freedom, 91–92, 94, 95, 97, 107, 191–192, 196, 198, 200

F
Fill/Series/Columns commands
  step value/stop value commands, 5, 24
Formatting numbers
  currency format, 15–17, 65, 66, 235
  decimal format, 147

H
Home/Fill/Series commands, 5
Hypothesis testing
  decision rule, 57
  null hypothesis, 52–63, 65, 66, 69
  rating scale hypotheses, 52–55
  research hypothesis, 52–55
  stating the conclusion, 57–62

T.J. Quirk, J. Palmer-Schuyler, *Excel 2016 for Human Resource Management Statistics*, Excel for Statistics, DOI 10.1007/978-3-319-40063-1

Hypothesis testing (*cont.*)
- stating the result, 57
- 7 steps for hypothesis testing, 55–62

M

Mean
- formula, 1

Multiple correlation
- correlation matrix, 173–177
- Excel commands, 173–177

Multiple regression
- correlation matrix, 173–177
- equation, 165
- Excel commands, 173–177
- predicting Y, 165

N

Naming a range of cells, 8–9

Null hypothesis. *See* Hypothesis testing

O

One-group t-test for the mean
- absolute value of a number, 73
- formula, 71
- hypothesis testing, 71–76
- s.e. formula, 71
- 7 steps for hypothesis testing, 71–76

P

Page Layout/Scale to Fit commands, 32

Population mean, 37–40, 51, 53, 54, 71, 72, 74, 90, 97, 183, 189, 190, 192

Printing a spreadsheet
- entire worksheet, 154–156
- part of the worksheet, 154–156
- printing a worksheet to fit onto one page, 140–142

R

RAND(). *See* Random number generator

Random number generator
- duplicate frame numbers, 26–30, 35, 36
- frame numbers, 27–28
- sorting duplicate frame numbers, 28–31

Regression, 129–139, 142–154, 156, 158, 166, 237

Regression equation
- adding it to the chart, 151–154
- formula, 151
- negative correlation, 154
- predicting Y from x, 165
- slope, b, 149
- writing the regression equation using the Summary Output, 154
- y-intercept, a, 149

Regression line, 129–139, 149–154, 157, 160–162

Research hypothesis. *See* Hypothesis testing

S

Sample size
- COUNT function, 9

Saving a spreadsheet, 12–13

Scale to Fit commands. *See* Standard error of the mean

Standard deviation
- formula, 2

Standard error of the mean
- formula, 3

STDEV. *See* Standard deviation

T

t-table. *See* Appendix E

Two-group t-test
- basic table, 89
- degrees of freedom, 91–92
- drawing a picture of the means, 96
- formula, 97
- Formula #1, 97–104
- Formula #2, 105–111
- hypothesis testing, 88–97
- s.e. formula, 97, 107
- 9 steps in hypothesis testing, 88–97